IMPLEMENTING BEHAVIORAL PROGRAMS FOR SCHOOLS AND CLINICS

The Proceedings of the Third Banff International Conference on Behavior Modification

IMPLEMENTING BEHAVIORAL PROGRAMS FOR SCHOOLS AND CLINICS

The Proceedings of the Third Banff International Conference on Behavior Modification, April, 1971.

edited and introduced by

F. W. Clark
University of Calgary

D. R. Evans
University of Western Ontario

L. A. Hamerlynck
University of Calgary

Research Press Company
2612 North Mattis Ave.
Champaign, Illinois 61820

Copyright © 1972 by Research Press Company
All rights reserved. Printed in the United States of America. No part of this book may be reproduced by mimeograph or any other means without the written permission of the publisher. Excerpts may be printed in connection with published reviews in periodicals without express permission.

Copies of this book may be ordered from the publisher at the address given on the title page.
ISBN 0-87822-030-5

PREFACE

This is the third publication of the proceedings from the Banff International Conference on Behavior Modification. The conference takes place each spring in Banff, Alberta, Canada, and provides a forum for the sharing of new data and ideas in the area of behavior modification. Contributors to the conference are outstanding behavioral scientists whose work sets the pace and direction for the development of behavioral research and application.

Continuing requests for the International Conference monographs have served to encourage the annual planning of the program and publication of its proceedings. As may be expected, sustaining a major program requires the inter-dependent efforts of many people. This year we were very fortunate to receive the unqualified assistance of The University of Calgary's Division of Continuing Education in the planning and execution of the Conference program. Many skilled hours of labor were contributed by Kurt Longman, Acting Associate Director of Continuing Education; Betty Buchanan, Conference Supervisor; Donna Frasier, Conference Coordinator; and Paddy Bossert, Conference Assistant.

Continuous support from Dr. Tim Tyler, Director, School of Social Welfare; Dr. W. R. N. Blair, Chairman, Department of Psychology; Dr. Keith Pearce, Head, Division of Psychiatry; Dr. J. G. Woodsworth, Head, Department of Educational Psychology; and Dr. Mike Manley, Director, University Counselling Service, made it possible for planning committee members to spend considerable time in developing the themes and objectives of this year's effort, and in selecting, contacting, and working with the contributors of this volume.

Our fellow program committee members, who provided their planning talents over the entire year preceding the International Conference, deserve special appreciation. They are Dr. Peter McLean, Assistant Professor, Psychology; Dr. Peter Roxburgh, Associate Professor, Psychiatry; and Dr. Lee Handy, Associate Professor, University Counselling Service. The conference planning group has been pleased to play a part in the dissemination of significant research and demonstration findings.

Feedback from Dr. Ogden Lindsley, University of Kansas Medical Center, who provided a functional analysis of the behavior of conference presenters, the presenters themselves, and all those in attendance at Banff this year will aid us in developing next year's program.

Finally, the consequations provided by our wives, Lana, Dorothy, and Marilyn, will ensure that the fourth Banff Conference on Behavior Modification will be keenly anticipated.

                Frank W. Clark David R. Evans Leo A. Hamerlynck

CONTENTS

PREFACE v

INTRODUCTION ix

CONTRIBUTORS xiii

SECTION I   PREPARING CONSULTANTS FOR CLINICAL SETTINGS   1

1. The Role of Social Work Education in Innovative Human Services. Richard B. Stuart.   3

2. Training Behavioral Counselors. Carl E. Thoresen.   41

3. Teaching Operant Technology to Psychiatric Nurses, Aides, and Attendants. Garry L. Martin.   63

4. Training Behavior Change Agents: A Five-Year Perspective. Ernest G. Poser.   89

SECTION II   AGENTS OF CHANGE FOR THE CLASSROOM   101

5. Special Education and Consulting Teachers. Hugh S. McKenzie.   103

6. The Responsive Teaching Model: A First Step in Shaping School Personnel as Behavior Modification Specialists. R. Vance Hall and Rodney E. Copeland.   125

7. Direct Intervention in the Classroom: A Set of Procedures for the Aggressive Child. Gerald R. Patterson, Joseph A. Cobb, and Roberta S. Ray.   151

INTRODUCTION

This monograph is directed at eliminating the logical inconsistency tragically illustrated in classes concerned with learning theory where the principles such as approximations, reinforcement, and behavioral goals are ignored in the actual teaching process. More simply put, *lecturing* on the Law of Effect is the usual university teaching procedure. Ogden Lindsley (1967) provided the precise analysis of this usual process as being the provision of a stimulus for acquisition without concern for the consequences. Another view of the condition was made by Patterson (1969) describing the work in behavior modification as emerging from the "whoopee stage," where the Law of Effect was rediscovered, into a stage with fewer dramatic results but of greater scientific validity. We suspect that Patterson was including the problem of applying the science to the scientific activity.

The necessity of these pursuits need not be dictated by the logical inconsistency or a respect for balance of concept. Non-behavioral critics and the behaviorist members themselves are well aware of the paucity of follow-up studies demonstrating generalization across situations and time. The observations are accurate, but the interpretation by non-behaviorists that it constitutes evidence of the lack of validity for behavior modification remains an empirical question. The framing of the questions are quickly seen by reference to social learning theory — the simplest conception sufficing — behavior is taught and maintained by the consequences of the social system. The social system is not static across time and settings; consequently, the behavior established in one social environment will only persist to the extent that subsequent environments are similar in terms of stimulus events and consequences. The presentations within this text represent the initial attempts at developing the procedures for assuring the best fit of social environments for the generation and maintenance of adaptive behaviors and the extinction of deviant behaviors.

Furthermore, one may also note that while behavior change techniques applied to individuals appear to be relatively efficient in terms of time and cost, the development of programs applicable to the mass amelioration and prevention of behavior disturbances with comparable efficiency remain as a major challenge in the 1970's and beyond. One important facet of the latter challenge is the need for educational and training programs to meet ever-growing manpower needs for skilled behavior change agents, and in the need for attention to be given to the organizational settings which play a significant role in determining whether the change skills that may be developed will be maintained and strengthened over a given period of time.

These emergent problems and challenges were by no means unanticipated by social learning scientists and can be understood from the common assumptions underlying various behavioral programs. These related successive assumptions are:

1. Individuals behave in the context of a social environment and in interaction with it.

2. . Social behavior is learned by individuals. Learning, according to Hilgard (1956), ". . . is the process by which an activity originates or is changed through reacting to an encountered situation, provided that the characteristics of the change in activity cannot be explained on the basis of native response tendencies, maturation, or temporary states of the organism (e.g., fatigue, drugs, etc.)" [p. 3].

3. Social environments teach and maintain the behavior of individuals. Since individuals interact in the context of various physical and social systems, the observed behavior of the individual changes as a function of the differences in social system topography and functional contingent responsiveness. To understand individual behavior one must observe the operative social conditions prior to and after the occurrence.

4. Social learning is a process of reciprocal influence. All individual members as components of a social system are, therefore, both "teachers" and "learners." As Bandura (1969) suggests, "Psychological functioning, in fact, involves a continuous reciprocal interaction between behavior and its controlling conditions. Although actions are regulated by their consequences, the controlling environment is, in turn, often significantly altered by the behavior" [p. 46].

5. The reciprocal influencing process may be explicit or implicit, planned or unplanned. It does operate systematically. If the analysis fails to show systemity, it can be the consequence of three possibilities: inadequate analysis of interchange; inadequate conceptualization of the operative social system; or lack of responsiveness to social stimuli (as in the case of infantile autism) by one or more social system components.

6. All behavior has a social referent and is fundamentally defined as appropriate or inappropriate, desirable or undesirable, relative to a given social system. The terms desirable and undesirable act to define the boundaries of acceptability for behavior rather than a state of inherent malfunction, defect, or qualitative difference. Thus the acquisition, maintenance, and change of both desirable and undesirable behavior can be considered to follow the same functional principles of social learning.

Since the locus of behavioral change and maintenance is in the immediate social environment, one would expect that changing individual behavior requires changing the social environment. Maintaining individual behavior requires maintaining the relevant contingent responsiveness of the changed social environment.

In considering the effectiveness of a change program it may be useful to differentiate between effectiveness in *producing* change and effectiveness in *maintaining* behavioral change. To make such a distinction necessarily calls for follow-up studies to assess the maintenance question. Currently there appear to be few well-designed follow-up assessments in the behavior modification literature. The scientist-practitioner would be well advised to assume for the present that behavioral change *does not* equal maintenance of change. In fact, it is also clear that there is no permanent change possible — behavior is lawfully in constant change.

Another observation which needs to be made and which is supported by the contributors to this volume is that behavior modifiers may find it somewhat easier to apply stimulus control and reinforcement techniques to students and clients than to themselves and to other staff members. Yet it seems both possible and desirable to apply the same analysis of behavior here as well.

The contributors to this monograph illustrate an important professional role shift which we believe will become increasingly dominant over the next two decades. The shift is away from a role as direct participant in client and student intervention, and toward a role as trainer and educator of intervention teams, with primary responsibility for the change and maintenance of *staff* behavior through the application of behavioral principles.

An interesting and fruitful model of this evolving role is illustrated by the Behavior Research Project of Tucson, Arizona, developed by Tharp and Wetzel (1969). The goal of the program was to explore the feasibility of offering social and mental health services by using nontraditional community workers to implement behavior modification programs in the natural environment. The traditional model for intervention is described as dyadic, i.e., the professional or consultant specialist and the client or change target. Tharp and Wetzel assume that those individuals in the client's immediate environment who both possess and control access to the most powerful reinforcers must occupy a position intermediate to the client and the professional or consultant. The intervention model in behavior modification is thus seen as triadic: consultant, mediator, and target.

> The professional (consultant) attention is to be directed to the modification of the mediator behavior. The consultant will choose mediator behaviors as goals which will result in the desirable modification of the actions of the target; but the consultant operates upon the mediator, and he must not forget it. If he does forget, and attends directly upon the target, he will have made two serious errors. First, he will have failed to modify the maintaining stimuli for the target's misbehaviors; thus the target would revert to misbehavior upon the withdrawal of the consultant. The second error is much more visible: in all

likelihood, the erring consultant would fail to alter the behavior of the target since the mediator is the individual who controls the reinforcers most powerful for the target. [1969, p. 57]

This triadic model may be applied at any point along an endless chain in a social system. For example, if the consultant's behavior becomes the target, the mediator for his actions is likely to be his supervisor, who is likely, in turn, to have as his consultant the director of the program.

One may also notice that on a direct client intervention level, the triadic model described above becomes a means of maximizing professional usefulness while minimizing professional expertise in direct service activities. Professional expertise is demonstrated through staff training based on behavioral principles rather than demonstrated through therapy.

The distinguished contributors to this volume have elaborated this triadic model — consultants, mediators, target — in a variety of clinical and educational settings. Additionally, many of the practical problems of developing a triadic model of intervention are also discussed. The chapters to follow serve to illustrate the evaluation of applied behavior technology and the means by which such questions as the costs and benefits of intervention and maintenance of change are likely to be increasingly answered in the coming decade.

Bibliography

Bandura, A. *Principles of behavior modification.* New York: Holt, Rinehart and Winston, 1969.

Hilgard, E. R. *Theories of learning.* New York: Appleton-Century-Crofts, 1956.

Lindsley, O. Theoretical basis for behavior modification. Address to Department of Psychology, University of Oregon, Eugene, May 1967.

Patterson, G. R. Comments during the First Banff International Conference on Behavior Modification, private communication, April, 1969.

Tharp, R. G. and Wetzel, R. J. *Behavior modification in the natural environment.* New York: Academic Press, 1969.

CONTRIBUTORS

1. **Richard B. Stuart**
   School of Social Work
   University of Michigan
2. **Carl E. Thoresen**
   School of Education
   Stanford University
3. **Garry L. Martin**
   Department of Psychology
   University of Manitoba
4. **Ernest G. Poser**
   Department of Psychology
   McGill University and
   Douglas Hospital, Montreal
5. **Hugh S. McKenzie**
   Special Education Program
   University of Vermont
6. **R. Vance Hall**
   Bureau of Child Research and
   Department of Human Development and Family Life
   University of Kansas
7. **Rodney E. Copeland**
   Bureau of Child Research and
   Department of Human Development and Family Life
   University of Kansas
8. **Gerald R. Patterson**
   Oregon Research Institute and
   Department of Special Education
   University of Oregon
9. **Joseph A. Cobb**
   Oregon Research Institute and
   Department of Special Education
   University of Oregon
10. **Roberta S. Ray**
    Oregon Research Institute

Section 1
PREPARING CONSULTANTS FOR CLINICAL SETTINGS

Current training programs directed toward meeting manpower requirements of the social services are both limited in terms of the number of people being trained, inefficient in the selection of training modes, the use of monies, and available manpower, and ineffective because of an emphasis on therapy defined as intra-individual change.

Richard Stuart, the first contributor to this volume, carefully documents the observations noted above in the area of social work education. He goes on to develop a training model geared to uncertainty and change, and identifies both system foci for change and the tactical skills available for its stimulation within system levels. Training techniques discussed are directed toward decision-making, values, and operationalized skills.

In the next article, Carl Thoresen describes the demand characteristics of counseling psychology viewed as applied social learning, and relates these characteristics in detail to the Stanford Behavioral Systems Training Program which is a competency-based performance training system.

The use of behavioral principles in not only developing, but maintaining, the highly skilled performance of nurses, aids, and attendants at the Manitoba School for Retardates is described next by Garry Martin. Through careful attention to assessment of variations in the training program, he has begun to identify the training conditions crucial to the production of more effective behavior modifiers.

The three contributors above, which are directed toward preparing consultants for clinical settings, provide the reader with a wealth of information regarding the implementation of behavioral training programs. They challenge the reader to at least momentarily divest himself of preconceptions regarding education and training which are the legacy of one's own learning experiences. In the final contribution to this section, Ernest Poser challenges a training model currently embraced by clinical psychology on the basis of his experience with interns of the Behavior Therapy Teaching Unit at the Douglas Hospital, Montreal.

While the general clinical teaching program simultaneously emphasizes both sophisticated research and practice competence as the sine qua non of expertise, experience and the data gathered by Poser lead him to question whether we should not now begin to realize that two quite different programs are needed for researchers and practitioners. This willingness to challenge more traditional training practices, conceptually and empirically, characterizes all of the contributions to this section.

The Role of Social Work Education in Innovative Human Services[1]

Richard B. Stuart

THE CRISIS IN SOCIAL WELFARE SERVICES

The current state of human welfare services in the United States is one of chaos and crisis stemming from growing demands for services which have become progressively less effective. While it is commonplace to attribute such failures to an insufficiency of resources, recent history has shown that the commitment of vast resources to problematic situations often has the paradoxical effect of deepening the quagmire and impeding the prospect of change. Certainly more resources in the form of money and manpower will be needed in order to stem the tide of human misery in the United States. But these resources, when not accompanied by revolutionary changes in the technology through which they are applied, are likely to be little more than palliatives. To facilitate these necessary changes in technology, all of the human service professions will have to educate students for changing rather than static roles in society, providing them with skills which have sufficient flexibility to prove their value in programs not yet conceived.

This paper is concerned with the role which social work education can play in promoting the needed technological change. Following a documentation of the growing human services crisis, it will be shown that social work education has erred in the direction of training its graduates for participation in tradition-bound services which focus on intra-individual changes, when the need exists for situation-change-oriented techniques. The paper will then conclude with recommendations for reprogramming schools of social work with respect to methodological content, training in decision-making and values, and the development of the skills of evaluation and implementation.

The Crisis in Human Services

Social welfare activities have become a big business, as reflected in the rise of expenditures for this purpose over the past three decades. Between 1940 and 1969, for example, the gross national product (the value of all goods and services produced) of the United States rose by over 900 percent, from 99.7 to 923.3 billion dollars, while expenditures for social welfare programs (including educa-

---

[1]The author wishes to acknowledge his gratitude for the thwarted attempt at editorial assistance by Miss Lynn Nilles.

tion, social insurance, public aid, health and medical programs, housing, veterans programs and others) have risen over 1350 percent, from slightly under 9 to slightly over 121 billion dollars yearly.[2] Therefore it is obvious that social welfare programs have accounted for an increasing proportion of the national wealth, rising from 9.2 percent in 1940 to 14.1 percent in 1969 and from $63.38 per capita in 1940 to $497.14 per capita in 1967. While on one hand it is reassuring to know that the federal, state, and local governments are devoting increasing resources to promote human welfare, it is alarming to realize that the need for such expenditures has grown at the staggering rate implied in the expenditures. (See Figure 1.)

The rise in the demand for human welfare services is clearly reflected in the number of persons served. For example, during the decade between 1960 and 1970, the number of persons receiving public assistance and child welfare (noninstitutional) services rose 1475 percent. Furthermore, the rate of rise began to escalate sharply during 1970 with the following net increases in the number of recipients of these services: July, 154,000; August and September, 214,000 each; October, 235,000; and November, 282,000 (Associated Press dispatch dated March 4, 1971). At these rates, the number of persons served will increase by 3.4 million annually. If each of these persons received an average of $600 each, the increase in cost to all levels of government would be $1.4 billion annually. The changes in demands for services by mental health facilities are equally great but are complicated by a radical change in character. In 1960, there were 611,000 inpatients in mental hospitals in the United States, while 181,000 persons were offered treatment at outpatient psychiatric clinics. In 1968, there was a net reduction of 25 percent in the number of mental hospital inpatients (457,000) and a net increase of almost 400 percent in the number of outpatients (711,000). Therefore, in the same way that public assistance and child welfare programs are called upon to provide service to a population of mushrooming size, mental health facilities must cope with similar increments in the size of the population served as a result of a change to a demand for community-based rather than hospital-based service.

In much the same way that a ship built to transport five thousand persons must be qualitatively very different from a canoe built

---

[2]The sources for all data dealing with the needs and resources of human services were found in *Statistical Abstract of the United States, 1970* (Washington, D.C.: Superintendent of Documents, 1971). Data descriptive of the trends in social work education were derived from *Statistics in Social Work Education, 1961* and *1969* (New York: Council on Social Work Education, 1962 and 1970). Data reflecting changes in the psychiatric, psychological, and social work manpower were obtained directly from the American Psychiatric Association (Washington, D.C.), the American Psychological Association (Washington, D.C.) and the National Association of Social Workers (New York).

Figure 1

Trends in Gross National Product and Total and Per Capita Expenditures for Social Welfare Programs in the United States, 1930-1970

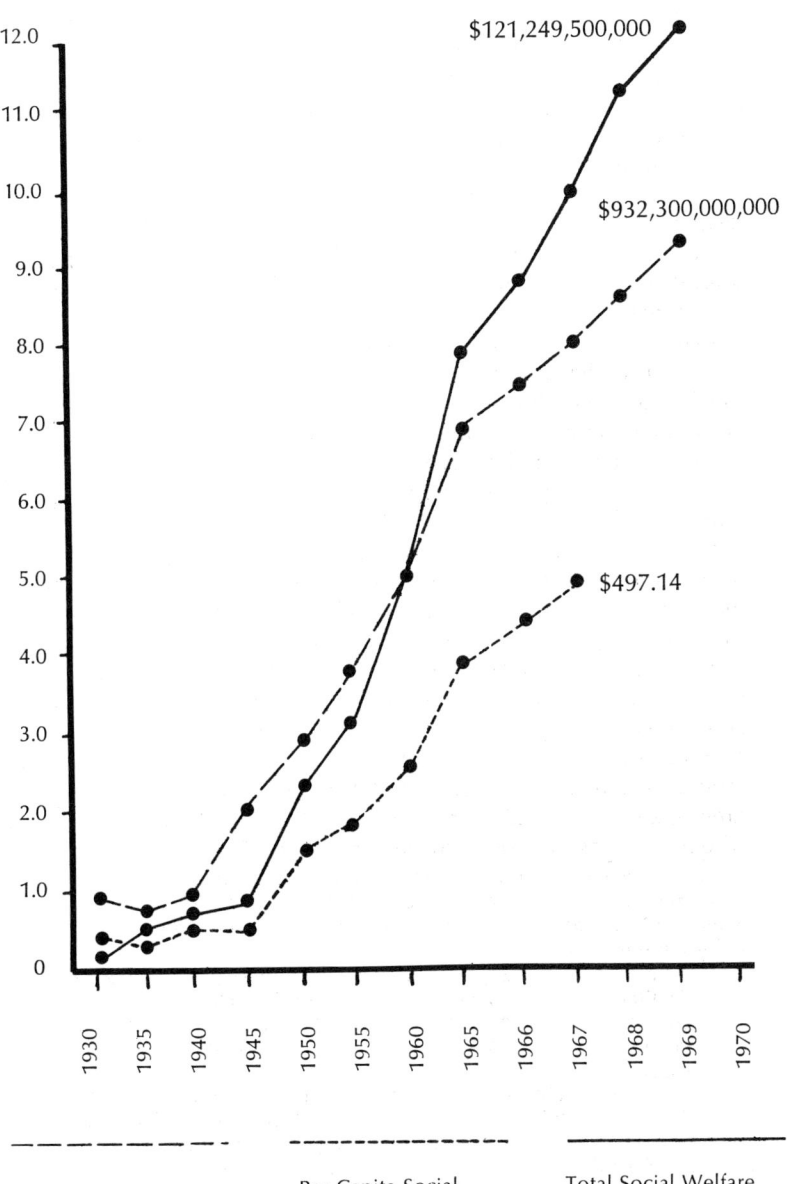

to carry five persons, so too must there be qualitative changes as programs grow geometrically in their consumption of human and material resources and in the scope of service offerings. Some of the changes must be reflected in the types of service organizations which mediate program delivery. For example, the use of neighborhood service centers in community development activities, representing a radical change from the traditional centralized agency settings to the broadened use of mental hygiene clinics, illustrates a major change in organization of human services necessitated by greater caseloads. Beyond organizational change, the size of the caseload also requires realignment of responsibilities among existing personnel. This has been reflected in the increased use of nonprofessionals (National Institute of Mental Health, 1969) and in the development of "associate" training for personnel expected to perform specific tasks (Witte, 1963). Finally, the demands of size necessitate changes in the nature of the core technology. Unfortunately the needed changes in technology have not yet appeared.

Just as the demand for social welfare activities has grown, so too has the available pool of manpower increased. In the mental health field alone, for example, the number of psychiatrists increased just under 50 percent between 1960 and 1969 (from 11,037 to 17,050), the number of psychologists increased over 50 percent during the same period (from 18,215 to 28,785) and the number of professional social workers almost doubled (from 26,612 to 50,471).[3] Therefore while it may be true that the need for manpower has outstripped the available supply, it is clear that the training institutions responsible for the supply are making great strides forward in an effort to keep abreast of need. For example, taking social work training in the United States as an index, while the national population rose by approximately 11 percent between 1960 and 1969, the number of schools of social work rose 20 percent, from 56 to 67 (with 9 other schools awaiting accreditation in 1969); the number of M.S.W. degrees granted rose 150 percent, from 2087 to 5060; and the number of doctoral degrees rose 330 percent, from 27 to 89.[4]

[3] For comparative purposes, the following figures may be useful. In 1967, 3,410,000 persons were employed in the health services (Public Health Service, 1968). The following professional groups were represented by the following numbers:

Dentists	235,700	Pharmacists	128,000
Dietitians	35,000	Psychologists	9,000
Educators	19,800	Secretaries	250,000
Physicians	305,500	Social Workers	20,200
Nurses	1,791,000		

[4] Exactly comparable figures are not yet available for Canadian institutions. However, while the Canadian national population increased from slightly under 14 million in 1950 to slightly over 20 million in 1966, the number of graduates from professional schools of social work increased from 53 to 276. This rise accelerated during the past five years as indicated by the phenomenal increase to 473 graduates in 1969 alone.

Figure 2

Rate of Growth of the Principal Mental Health Professions Compared to the Rate of Population Growth in the United States, 1920-1970

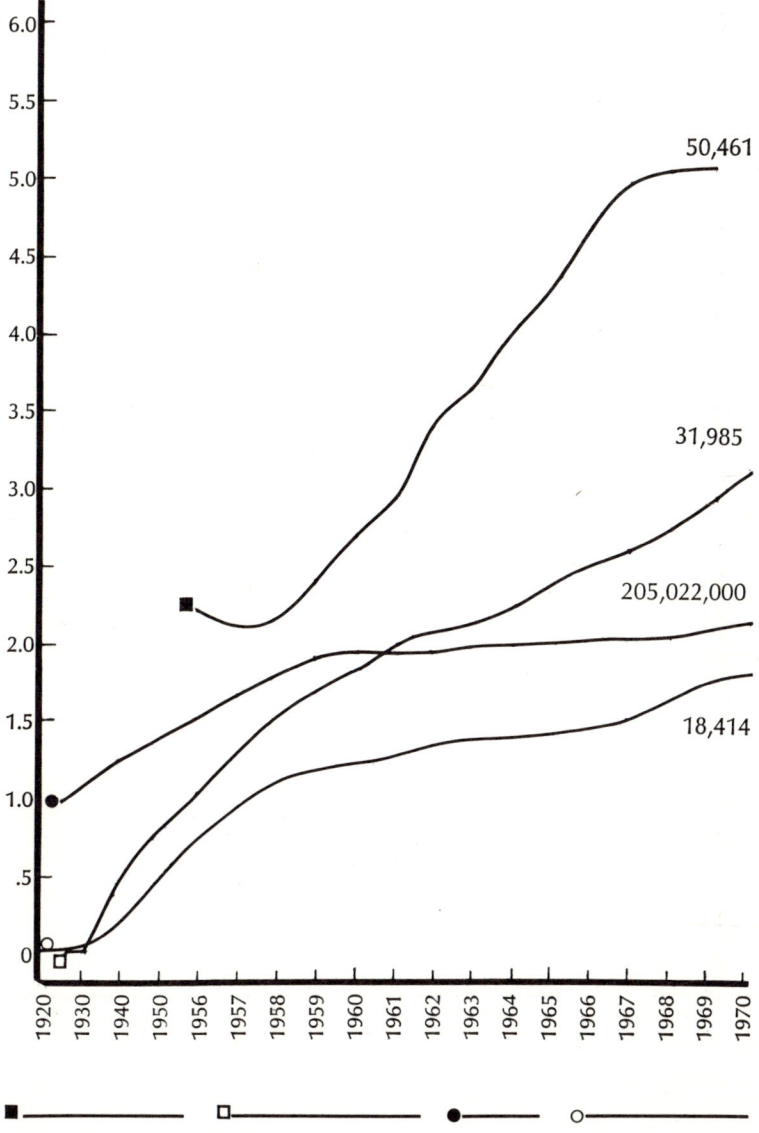

Figure 3

Rate of Growth of Social Work Education Compared to Population Growth in the United States, 1920-1970

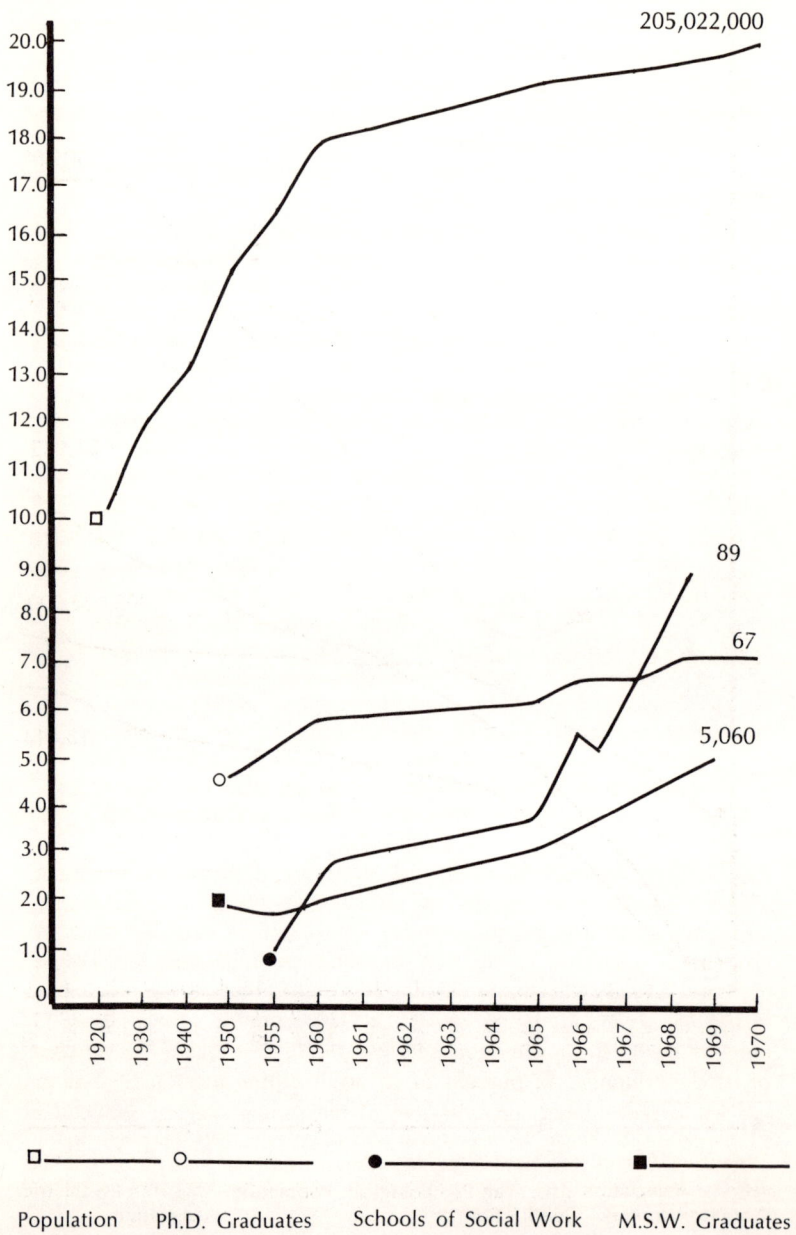

THE TECHNOLOGY GAP

In the face of rising demands for service, increasing resources in the form of manpower and money have become available. However despite these presumed increments to our problem-solving capabilities, the failure of these services is evident to even the most casual observer. It is equally apparent that the dismal failure of social welfare programs can be attributed more to the reliance upon inappropriate and technologically unsound remedies than to any lack of enthusiasm on the part of those vested with the responsibility to promote constructive changes.[5]

In the area of public assistance, for example, the 1962 Public Welfare Amendments called for services to:

> . . . all families with adults with potentials for self-support, all unmarried parents and their children with special problems, all families disrupted by desertion, all children in need of protection, all children with special health, education, or emotional problems . . . all aged and disabled individuals who require services . . . [or who are] in need of protection [and] all blind and other-disabled persons with potentials for self-support [Winston, 1965, p. 3].

To meet this broad array of problems, the only service which was specifically required was the familiar, individually focused casework process, despite the fact that the existence of poverty has been attributed to macrosocial deficiencies in health, education, and housing. For example, it has been recently noted that:

> . . . as a family's income drops, so does the condition of its housing. And as the housing conditions decline, indications of all types of illnesses rise: stillbirth, infant mortality, lack of normal advancement in school, sickness-absence rates, juvenile delinquency, school dropouts, higher accident rates, especially among children and youths, and mental and emotional disturbances among adults [Select Committee on Nutrition and Human Needs, 1971, p. 33].

This linkage between poverty and other social problems has been amply illustrated in a study of statistics gathered in Sacramento, California (Welfare Administration, 1966) which revealed that 20 percent of the city's population (residing on 8 percent of its land area and paying 12 percent of its taxes) consumed 50 percent of its health services, 51 percent of its law enforcement services and 25 percent of its fire protection services while producing 36 percent of its delinquency, 42 percent of its adult crime and 76 percent of

---

[5]For cogent attacks upon the role of the various medical societies in perpetuating the inadequacies of the health services, see the many publications of Health PAC, Inc. The Center for Responsive Law has published similar data supporting attacks upon the various governmental agencies responsible for food and drug safety.

its tuberculosis (see also Lindsay, 1969; National Institute of Mental Health, 1969). It is therefore absurd to conceive of casework as the only or even primary service supplementing administration of the financial component of public assistance programs.

In a similar vein, individual services have been advanced as a primary means of combating mental retardation, juvenile delinquency, mental disease, and malperformance in the schools. In a recent volume concerned with programming in mental retardation, Hurley (1969) observed:

> Contrary to the mode of thinking illustrated by medical research, no spectacular breakthrough can be made until the whole structure of the culture of poverty is destroyed, a structure which includes substandard housing, underemployment and unemployment, inferior education, inadequate health services, poor nutrition and discrimination. Each facet of poverty overlies the other in the etiology of pseudo-mental retardation [pp. 72-73].

Martin, Fitzpatrick, and Gould (1971) note that the fundamental question raised by the clear and present failure of the juvenile justice system in the United States (Stuart, 1969) is not one of seeking new means of dealing with the problems presented by individual deviants but one of seeking new social institutions which will eventuate in lower rates of deviance. The critical questions do not, in their view, concern which individual influence strategy is best but rather:

> Will existing agencies dealing with delinquency continue to function, to maintain, and to reinforce, the status quo—that is, will these agencies continue to remain committed to conservatism? Or will these agencies, or many of them at least, come over to the side of domestic reform in the struggle for equality and justice for the nation's poor? [p. 6].

And Mechanic (1969) has speculated that the response of the mental health agencies to the problems of human misery brought to their attention has been premised upon psychotherapy, about which he believes:

> Regardless of how one feels about traditional forms of psychotherapy, its effects are too limited and unimpressive and the expense of instituting it on a far-reaching basis is too great in terms of cost and personnel to justify it [pp. 49-50].

Finally, Sarri and Vinter (1969) conducted a carefully controlled study of the effects of social services as a means of stemming the problem of malperformance in high school and found, among other things, that (a) malperformers valued the long-term goals of success as much as well-performing children (contrary to the popular notion that they do not hold dear the ideal of success); and (b) that malperformers, showing greater deviance and fewer academic skills than their well-performing peers, were isolated from the main stream of opportunity in the school. Therefore the authors believe that:

> The school itself may maintain or even generate the very malperformance it seeks to eliminate by offering limited opportunity for educational attainment for some pupils, by judging pupils adversely because of attributes that are independent of their actions, by undermining existing motivation through unwise use of control practices, and by making it exceedingly difficult for the pupil to "find his way back" once he has been defined as a malperformer [p. 118].

Following from these observations is the obvious conclusion that it is necessary to change the opportunity structure of the school to enhance performance and that individual treatment along classical therapeutic lines is as much a palliative in educational service as it is in the areas of public assistance, mental retardation, and juvenile justice.

Each of these service areas presently shares the same basic point of departure—an assumption that at the core of the problems of human misery and deviance is to be found a deficient individual. This assumption is in keeping with the concepts of both Social Darwinism and mental illness. The Social Darwinist assumed that the deserving few enjoyed the just reward of their moral integrity while the undeserving majority suffered their poverty as a consequence of their moral and personal inferiority. In a clear demonstration of sophistry and circularity, the poor were shown to be inferior because they were poor. The mental illness assertion is quite similar in its postulate that deviant behavior is a pathognomonic sign of a disease of the mind, in turn proven by the occurrence of deviant behavior (Stuart, 1970). Commenting upon the concept of mental disease, one clinician stated: "Diseases called mental . . . are not diseases of the mind any more than febrile diseases are diseases of the temperature [Llopis, 1959, p. 11]."

Following from these similar basic assumptions is a set of technological procedures which seek to change the behavior of the individual without reference to change of the institutions which generated his behavior. As Cloward (1968) suggests, intervention derived from Social Darwinism seeks "to humanize systems without acknowledging, much less challenging, the fundamental inequalities upon which these systems are based [p. 70]." In a similar vein, Grob (1966) suggests that intervention approaches based upon the concept of mental disease result in "therapeutic nihilism [p. 357]" which precludes alternative, constructive programming. Both approaches, then, permit the appearance of intervention while at the same time precluding effective change.

THE CURRENT STATE OF SOCIAL WORK EDUCATION

What has been described as a technology gap in the preceding section can be restated as an unwarranted stress upon individually focused direct services. To some degree the perpetuation of this inadequate service model is attributable to the fact that schools of social work have done little to develop alternative approaches and that graduates of these schools, upon attaining administrative positions, continue to advocate the direct-services model. This is a consequence of two factors. First, schools of social work did originate as institutions for training volunteers working for charity service organizations in direct-service methods (Bruno, 1944; Meier, 1954; United Nations, 1958). They have probably continued a function in this tradition at least in part as a path of least resistance. Second, schools are typically units in university settings and are limited by an inevitable conservatism in universities which are dependent upon private or public sponsorship for economic support and for markets for technological, academic, and training outputs which are their products (Harbison and Myers, 1964; Millett, 1967). Because of this, universities are appropriately responsive to the values prevailing in their communities and allow these values to influence virtually every facet of instructional and behavioral control on their campuses. Therefore it is not surprising that one recent study (Contracting Corporation of America, undated) found that administrators of schools of social work based their decisions about whether to participate in Head Start training programs upon their reading of the attitude toward such participation by the leadership of the organizations providing their support. Specifically this study found:

> State schools must keep in mind the reactions of state regents and other officials. Schools in general must maintain their good standing with all their funding sources when making policy decisions and commitments or be threatened with reduced funds or no funding in the future [p. 16].

Against this background, it is possible to investigate the current status of our knowledge about schools of social work and their practice. It is a dismal reality that research seeking to identify those aspects of the teaching situation which are associated with more effective learning have consistently met with unimportant results. Whether the explanation is that the variables under study are too coarse to detect subtle differences (Coleman, 1966) or that the major variance in learning is attributable to experiences which occur outside of the teaching environment (Stephens, 1967), research has so far revealed little to guide the educator. It is therefore not surprising that the observed "uneven character of professional programs in the 57 schools of social work [p. 215]" found by Hollis and Taylor in 1951 was still found to be true two decades later in the Cooper report (Cooper and Company, 1970), or that any discussion of the development of social work education must inevitably reflect a tortuous history of polemics, for in the absence of empirical data disputes among the protagonists of opposing points of view cannot but rely upon pejoratives to resolve their disagreements.

Compared with the amount of prescription and speculation, the amount of knowledge about social work education is very small indeed! Such knowledge as exists can most fruitfully be divided among the three segments of the educational process (Dreeben, 1968; Gagne, 1970):

INPUT ⟶ PROCESS ⟶ OUTPUT.

The *input* in the social work educational process includes characteristics of the students, resources of the educational institutions, boundary conditions including the students' home environments, the broader professional community and the educational institutions of which social work schools may be a part.

Kadushin (1958) noted that the selection of social work as a career is "not a single act but rather a series of interrelated decisions [p. 17]" which represent "compromises between competing needs, interests, values, and aptitudes within the individual [p. 17]." These factors are balanced against the range of opportunities, with a recognition that the ultimate choice of a profession must be differentiated from the preference "choice being regarded as implemented preference [p. 18]." An important basis for career choice in social work has been shown by Lauffer (1968) to be social work experience (83.4 percent of 2,319 subjects studied) with additional influences such as undergraduate course content or friends and relatives in the field (cited by approximately half of those selecting social work). Beyond selection of social work as a general field, Steinman (1968) demonstrated that personal values influence choice of subspecialty (e.g., casework, community practice, or administration) with the most conservative students choosing direct-service careers.

This may be explained in part by Pins' (1963) data describing the modal social work student as upwardly mobile, more likely to be a member of groups which are underrepresented in the professions (nonwhite, female), and somewhat older than graduate students generally, perhaps because over 80 percent of the 2,771 subjects in this study had prior paid or volunteer social work experience. More recent statistics (1969) show that women outnumber men in both American and Canadian schools of social work (3,297 to 2,236 and 266 to 207 respectively) in receiving masters' degrees although men outnumber women in receiving doctoral degrees from American institutions, 58 to 33. Approximately 80 percent of the social work students are white, approximately 12 percent black, with other races accounting for the remaining 8 percent. And the largest age group for women is the under 25 group and for men the 26-30 group.

The selection of social work students may be less discriminating than is true in other fields—in 1969 10,724 candidates were accepted from a field of 19,386 applicants, and of these 6,453 enrolled. The process through which the selection of students is made is undoubtedly subject to the biases inherent in any administrative procedure, and although these biases are reduced as objective criteria replace the earlier reliance upon interview screening, the formulation of objective policies itself may merely serve to systematize bias. Decisions made by schools are also influenced by such extra-university factors as the realities of educational economics, regional availability of training programs, and an interaction between the demands of full-time study and family responsibilities which undoubtedly serve to further limit access to social work training for various groups.

With respect to the range of resources available within schools as a source of input, Hollis and Taylor (1951) noted in an early study that a school of social work would require from one quarter to one half million dollars for capital costs (in 1950 dollars) in addition to $1,000 per student (compared with $2,364 for medical students at that time) for operating costs. More recent cost data (Cooper and Company, 1970, pp. 106-118) suggest that costs per student range from $4,200 to $5,900 per year depending upon which elements are included in the cost formula, what effect regional and institution-specific economies might have, and the range of teaching alternatives offered. Assuming an average cost of $5,000 per student per year, the cost of educating the 12,094 students in American and Canadian schools of social work in 1969 rose above 60 million dollars, of which approximately 27 million was spent for salaries for the 2,037 full-time classroom and field work instructors working in 1969 (assuming an average annual salary of $13,500). Clearly these costs cannot be defrayed by tuition alone, and therefore schools of social work are unmistakably dependent upon the good offices of the federal and state governments as well as local university and agency sources.

When one thinks of the *process* of social work education, he naturally thinks of both curricula content and modes of presentation. Within curriculum, educators commonly distinguish between theory and practice content (Meyer, 1959), recognizing that some theory will take the form of basic, social-science-derived formulations, some will pertain to the activities of social workers and social welfare organizations and some will serve as a basis for practice principles (Vinter, 1967). Basic theoretical material derived from the social sciences has the possible disadvantages of being irrelevant to the tasks at hand, of introducing as novel to social work some notions which are outmoded in the original field, and of interposing parametric observations as bases for nomothetic inferences (Stuart, 1965). Therefore much care should go into the screening of social science materials utilized by social work educators. Knowledge pertaining to the operation of social workers and their organizations has proven invaluable in identifying operational artifacts which impede service delivery and therefore must be an essential ingredient in social work education. For example, Cloward and Epstein (1965), Schorr (1967), and Shea (1967) all noted the inexorable course of the disengagement of private social agencies from the needs of the poor because of factors intrinsic to agency operational procedures, while reference to problems of secondary deviance for those served (e.g., Sarri and Vinter, 1969; Segal, 1970) provides another timely caution about patterns of service. Finally, practice principles, according to Vinter (1967), (a) must specify the desired ends of action, (b) must be ethically acceptable, (c) must be based upon validated core knowledge, and (d) should lead to specific interventional alternatives under specific conditions.

Curricular content in schools of social work is commonly divided into five major categories—social theory, research, social work history, social policy, and practice (Aptekar, 1969)—with the balance between the relative amounts of each category and its organization relative to field instruction varying somewhat among institutions (Taber, 1969; Kindelsperger, 1969; Lawrence, 1969; Fellin and Vinter, 1969). Instructional procedures range from the classical use of lecture/discussion presentations and straightforward audio-visual illustrations of practice models to game and case simulations in the classroom, while discussion in direct supervision, peer and group consultation, and the observation of models are all familiar techniques in field instruction. Whether field instruction is rendered in practice agencies or in university-connected service centers (Brieland, 1969), training is generally achieved through supervised direct practice experience with individuals, families, groups, or community organizations.

It is regrettable that social work education is virtually void of any research directed toward gleaning the comparative effectiveness of varied means of instruction. Despite the facts that methodologies exist for differential decision-making concerning techniques (Kirkpatrick, 1959; Odiorne, 1961), that sophisticated procedures are available for the description of class management and pedagogical strategies (Amidon and Hunter, 1967) and that advanced technologies have been developed for teacher training (Gordon, 1968), social work education has appeared to frankly neglect precise evaluation of teaching techniques in favor of bland statements of instructor preference unsupported by experimental data (e.g., Family Service Association of America, 1966).

The process through which schools of social work arrive at curricular decisions has similarly remained a mystery, no research even in the form of participant observational studies having appeared in the literature. The major effort of schools of social work to monitor and update their curricula, the Curriculum Study of the Council on Social Work Education (Boehm, 1959), has had a certain amount of impact as seen in the shifting accreditation requirements listed by the Council. But the thirteen volumes of the study, many of which (e.g., the casework volume) were the work of single individuals working in the service of, or despite, the wishes of task force committees, do not set forth coherent and generally accepted notions of the essentials of curriculum. In the absence of a research orientation or of a cogent authority, and aided by assertions of academic freedom, schools have been free to determine their own curricula with decision-making seemingly predicated primarily upon the biases of existing faculty. It has only been since the advent of broadened student participation in curricular decision-making (Witte, 1970) that the processes through which decisions are made have become more visible and the content of the decisions more responsive to dynamic service concepts.

Finally, an area of educational process which has received no attention in the literature, but which will increasingly become an object of attention, is the control of social deviance in the schools, hitherto referred to as the "socialization of students as professionals." Recognizing that virtually every aspect of school programming, ranging from student selection through curricular and policy decisions, are means of encouraging or delimiting specific acts, certain policies and procedures have been believed to have singular influence upon the behavior control processes seen in schools. Some have recently become the objects of critical attention. One of these is the previously sanctified concept of education (particularly field instruction) as a modified form of involuntary psychotherapy (see, for example, Austin, 1952; Zetzel, 1953; and Feldman, Spotnitz and Nagelberg, 1953) in which any evidence of noncompliance was viewed as a defect of personality. Others include the use of student evaluations and references to surreptitiously "blacklist" candidates for preferred field placements or jobs and other generally unsatisfactory practices involving administrative decision-making without representation of the students. Among the forces which are leading to the revision of these policies are an increasing awareness of the relevance of civil rights to all spheres of human behavior and the assertion by students of a voice in decision-making, perhaps modeled after and vicariously reinforced by the success of similar efforts by client groups such as the Welfare Rights Organization. These changes, in turn, are associated with an erosion of such traditional controls as grades and the increasingly popular requirements that faculty decisions about students be subject to review by joint faculty-student committees and that students receive an opportunity to sit in judgment of faculty members on such critical matters as appointment, retention, and promotion.

Decisions about which process variables to expand and which to eliminate or reduce are dependent upon specification of *output* variables, for no process is intrinsically either useful or problematic. Neenan (1971) has postulated two classes of output benefits relevant to educational undertakings. The first, investment benefits, refers to the direct economic or other immediate consequences of a particular activity. For example, investment benefits for the automobile industry are measured in terms of the rate of return per investment dollar. Consumption benefits, on the other hand, are indirect economic or other consequences of an event. The decision to purchase an automobile may, for example, facilitate moving a sick member of one's family to the hospital quickly in an emergency, a psychological advantage. It also contributes, however, to the vast (200 tons in 1970) amount of hydrocarbon particulate pollution covering the 1.4 percent of the nation's land area comprising the metropolitan areas in which are to be found 14 percent of the nation's 86 million cars (Urban America, undated). Therefore while one would be better able to secure prompt medical care through the purchase of a car, he is also more likely to need this care.

Applying Neenan's variables to the evaluation of social work education, it can be seen that one measure of the investment benefits of the training is the relative contribution to general productivity made by professionally trained as opposed to untrained social workers, while one measure of the consumption benefits of social work training is the impact which this training has upon the general human condition. A jaundiced observer might suggest that professional training for social workers has the joint disadvantages of increasing the cost of social work services while at the same time diminishing their effectiveness, clearly leading to a condition in which marginal program benefits are exceeded by program costs.

At the most basic level, social work educational institutions are vested with the responsibility of turning out an unspecified number of program graduates. Were the mere fact of program completion by selected individuals a sufficient criterion, the interaction between input, process, and output variables would be clearly specifiable and would inevitably lead to a net reduction in the complexity of input and process variables. The charge of social work educators goes beyond sheer numbers, however, and requires the introduction of qualitative variables referring to the graduates' competence in service delivery, commitment to ethical values of the profession, and creativity and responsiveness to evolving practice objectives.

Regrettably, the concern expressed by Hollis and Taylor twenty years ago is still true today. They noted:
> An attempt to define the scope and functions of social work must grapple with many formidable obstacles, the most insurmountable of which is the absence of criteria that can be used to identify the professional social worker [1951, p. 46].

If the nature of social work practice is unclear, then it follows that the criteria for evaluating practice must likewise be vague. This, in turn, compounds the problem of evaluating the social work process.

It has been fashionable for some time for social work practitioners and educators to malign each other for alleged unresponsiveness to the verities of practice on one hand or theoretical innovations on the other. For example, twenty years ago Hollis and Taylor argued:
> Due to the rapid expansion and increasing complexity in social services, the lag between current social work education programs and needs of practice is perhaps greater today than it was a quarter of a century ago [1951, p. 277].

And more recently, Kenneth Clark (1965) observed:
> To my knowledge, there is at present nothing in the vast literature of social science treatises and textbooks and nothing in the practical or field training of graduate students in social science to prepare them for the realities and complexities of . . . involvement in a real, dynamic, turbulent, and at times seemingly chaotic community. And what is more, nothing anywhere in the training of social scientists, teachers, or social workers now prepares them to understand, to cope with, or to change the normal chaos of ghetto communities. These are grave lacks which must be remedied soon if these disciplines are to become relevant to the stability and survival of our society [p. xv].

The resolution of this conflict, however, depends upon resolution of the criterion problem in precisely the same fashion that evaluation in educational practice awaits practice criteria.

In the absence of refined qualitative standards to determine the adequacy of practice, demographic comparisons of professional and student populations may offer some guidelines for measuring the coincidence of education and practice. During the years between 1961 and 1970, the proportion of social workers in direct-service roles (casework, group work, and community practice) declined from 51 to 36 percent while the percentages in administration, teaching, or consultation and in research roles rose from 35 to 42.2 and from 14 to 22 respectively. During the same period, enrollment in related programs in schools of social work showed a corresponding drop from approximately 99 percent (including 9 percent who were not in field placements) to 84 percent in direct-service training. This switch in training emphasis is not uniform across schools, however, although the number of students in administration, policy, and research placements at the University of Michigan did increase from 6 (5 percent of the total enrollment) to 102 (20 percent of the total enrollment) between 1959 and 1969.

Explanations for the schools' continuing emphasis upon direct-service training than would appear to be indicated by employment patterns in the field can be found in several places. First, it is clear that teaching, supervision, and consultation typically are not roles which are likely to be offered to students, despite the fact that one recent study (Schultz, 1970) showed that 60 percent of the social workers polled occupied such positions within two years of the completion of their graduate training. Second, field agencies have continued to request large numbers of students for direct-service placements. Finally, the fact remains that placements in non-direct-service skill areas are frequently difficult if not impossible to develop, partly because students are used to provide service so that agency staff can be freed for other responsibilities, because students are needed to augment the service capacities of training agencies, and because agencies are genuinely committed to offering training in direct service.

In summary it can be said that an adequate means of specifying the role of social work education in adequate preparation of personnel for social work practice is not currently available. Cooper and Company (1970) arrived at a bleak conclusion pertaining to the prospect of assessment of social work educational output. They note:

> Although some commonly accepted school or university goals and objectives do exist, there appear to be none which effectively guide the decisions made by faculty. Inputs are unmeasured and unknown. The idea that scarce educational resources (or dollars) should not be wasted is not one which appears to play a large role in faculty deliberations [p. xii].

A curious comfort may be gained, however, from the fact that Coleman (1970) came to the same bleak conclusion with respect to education in general.

A MODEL FOR SOCIAL WORK TRAINING

In the foregoing section it was suggested that social welfare programming is changing in size and character at a rate unprecedented in the history of human services and that the process of social work education is subject to conservatizing influences more likely to maintain standardized practices than to modify them. In this section a model of social work training geared to uncertainty and change will be developed. This model is premised upon a typology of change processes identifying three levels of intervention—the pursuit of intraindividual change, change in the microsocial environment, and/or change in the macrosocial environment—with two clusters of techniques, informational or coercive control, available for use at each level. Following this model, suggestions are made for the need to train social work students in decision-making processes, the value premises which should underlie decision-making and skills for program implementation and evaluation.

A Typology of Social Work Methods

Background. Methods sequences in social work education and practice have typically referred to the selection of client populations—with caseworkers addressing individual clients or familial groups, group workers addressing multiple-client cohorts, and community practitioners addressing individuals or groups in the power structure. These distinctions, however, have been somewhat artifactual—Bisno (1971) referred to them as "gravely misleading [p. 76]"—as the ecology of service delivery has found caseworkers dealing with individuals and groups of varying composition (e.g., spouse or parent treatment groups), group workers offering extra-group service to individual group members, and community practitioners using the skills associated with each of these methods. Moreover, it is clear that the differences between ideological groups having different objectives are more significant than the differences between varying implementation skills. Therefore the following discussion is addressed to pointing out the differences between social work groups with differing philosophical positions with the assumption that the methods and techniques used by each are more similar than different.

At least since that fateful day when Porter Lee (1929) drew a line of demarcation, and probably for at least a quarter of a century earlier, social work has contended with a schism between advocates of social work as a cause and proponents of social work as a function. The conflict between the two was clearly stated by Lee in the following pictorial language:

> The emblazoned banner and the shibboleth for the cause, the program and the manual for the function; devoted sacrifice and the flaming spirit for the cause; fidelity, standards and methods for the function; an embattled host for the cause, an efficient personnel for the function [p. 14].

In modern dress, the conflict is seen by Lind (1970) as an impatience of the advocates of "power to the poor" with the gradualism of the "family adjustors" who are fearful that their clients will suffer through the realignment of priorities sought by the former group. While there are those who argue that the conflict between the two groups is needless (e.g., Pernell, 1970), the recent abrupt and total program change of the Community Service Society in New York City from a classical, old-line service agency to a community action group with *no* casework service *(New York Times,* January 21, 1971) clearly shows that the value controversy is being played out against the backdrop of a zero-sum game—a one-winner, all-spoils-to-the-victor encounter. Indeed this is as it must be, for Lind (1970) has noted that the various groups seek to gain control over the same resources.

Those advocating social work as a cause draw upon client groups as a source of their legitimacy (Miller, 1968; Briar, 1968) while those treating social work as a function look to the profession and the bureaucratized agency for legitimization. The proponents of social work as a cause draw upon sociological (and particularly systems) theory, while the more tradition-oriented group utilizes psychological theory. Writers of varying orientations have begun to question the validity (Stuart, 1970) and legitimacy of classical psychological theory as a basis for social work action. For example, the eminent British scholar Noel Timms (1964) has referred to value implications of the use of psychological theory in the following words:

> Caseworkers have asserted a faith in the potentialities of the human being to change himself and his society, whilst on the other hand, espousing a group of psychological theories which appear to place severe limitations on the capacity of the individuals to change [p. 61].

Even when psychological theory, stressing the responsibility of the individual for relief of his own distress, does not limit the expectancy of change, the failure of change to occur may be attributed to: (a) the clients' limited capabilities rather than to the failure of the treatment (Pratt, 1970); or (b) the interpolation of diagnosticians and testers between the client and therapist, insulating the latter from directly facing clinical failure (Rosenblatt and Mayer, 1970). Therefore the effect of the clinical use of psychological theory is seen as reducing the likelihood that corrective efforts will be taken to improve the technology.

Rein (1970) has reached the following conclusions in his comparison of "traditional" (function) and "radical" (cause) casework:

> A dispassionate analysis of current social policy would confirm the conclusion that social work programs have been used as a substitute for more searching policies to redistribute income, power and resources [p. 27].

He endorses Shriver's (1965) view that social work must seek to change institutions, thus repudiating Kahn's (1967) view that individual change efforts must rest at the core of community change efforts. Starting from the premise that "social work, by itself, has almost nothing to contribute to the reduction of interrelated problems of unemployment, poverty and dependence," p. 27, Rein (1970) recommends that social work:

> . . . move away from altering the environment on behalf

of a given client to altering the environment in general without reference to a specific client . . . [p. 28].

The implication of Rein's position is that the general character of the entire field of social work must change in order to arrive at an accommodation between practice and the value premises of social reform. Were such a change feasible, and there is considerable doubt whether it would be possible in view of the resistance to such a change by the entrenched service power structure, it would require the displacement of both traditional approaches and the more enlightened views of such writers as Bell (1970) and Siporin (1970) whose positions call for the retention of individually focused service in some instances, with clients given a large measure of control over the character of these services. Given the facts that a large clientele still exists for direct services and that emerging (behavioral) technologies offer a promise of effective intervention for the first time in recent history, it would seem that the complete abandonment of the individual or direct-service model is ill-advised.

Recommendations. The dichotomous choice between traditional (function-oriented) and radical (reform-oriented) services offered by Rein can perhaps be best understood if one were to consider three theoretical bases for social work activities as represented in Figure 4.

Figure 4

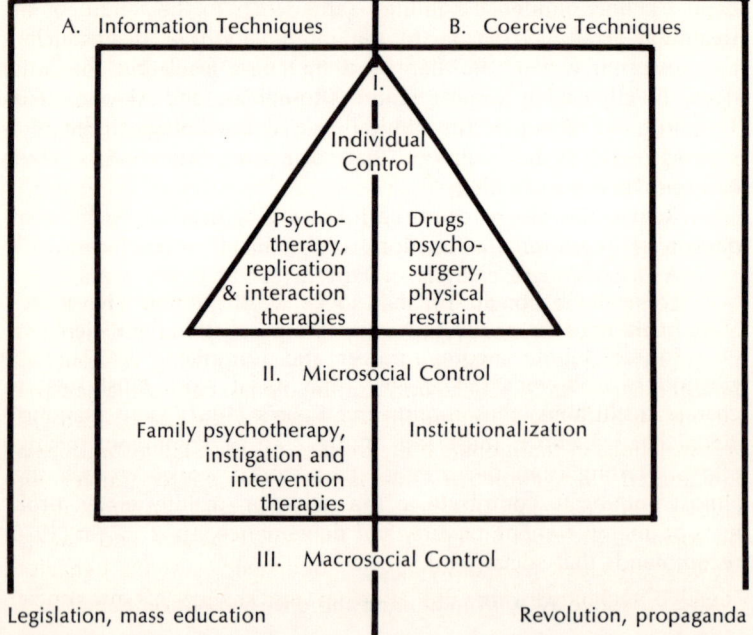

Three Levels of Efforts to Control Human Behavior

Two subsystems of influence techniques cut across the three major theoretical orientations to behavioral control. The informational subsystem is concerned with efforts to reduce uncertainty or overcome perceptual or judgmental errors in order to enhance individual or group behavior, allowing the persons subject to influence to accept or reject the implied or stated behavior change objectives. The coercive subsystem does, as the name implies, seek to limit the range of choices through restraining the individual's opportunity to make alternative responses. Informational processes have been differentiated from coercive processes by London (1969) as follows:

> The real difference between informational control and coercive control is that the former does not deliberately attack the physical structure or the organism in order to do its work, while the latter does. This is not a distinction of intent or of effect as far as the behavior in question is concerned, only one of technique [p. 28].

London further notes that informational and coercive controls are most accurately considered to be points on a continuum, with some processes (e.g., placebo effects) being midpoints.

These informational and coercive control techniques can be identified at each of the three major levels of interpersonal influence. At the individual level, informational controls are found in the use of interpretation (in personality-oriented approaches) and of deconditioning and reconditioning (in behaviorally-oriented approaches), while coercive controls are evident in the use of drugs, psychosurgery, and physical restraint. The goal of these procedures, whatever their origin, is the management of individual behavior; the guiding assumption underlying the procedures is a belief that the individual is the "symptom bearer" and can be helped best through direct manipulation of his own behavior. In this approach, then, the traditional clinical model of individual- rather than situation-focused treatment is perpetuated. Perhaps the only deviation from this model associated with the use of behaviorally-oriented techniques is an explication of the techniques used and a probable use of more operationally defined and therefore more evaluatable procedures.

At the level of microsocial change, modifications are undertaken in the face-to-face social environment of the client involving his family, teachers, employers and others supplying referents or reinforcements for his behavior. Informational controls associated with this level of intervention are illustrated by the use of feedback or instructions in traditional family therapy or those behavioral therapies termed "instigation" or "intervention" procedures (Kanfer and Saslow, 1969). In each instance, the therapist seeks to "reprogram the social environment" (Patterson, McNeal, Hawkins, and Phelps, 1967) of his client by modifying the contingencies of his behavior. Coercive techniques are also used in the service of microsocial change goals. These are illustrated by institutionalization in which the entire microsocial environment is changed and are typically ascociated with the use of restraints geared to maintaining the individual's physical presence in the change environment.

The goal of microsocial change techniques is modification of the individual's behavior, a goal held in common with approaches seeking intraindividual change. The difference lies in the fact that microsocial change agents believe these changes must be sought through environmental change, the environment being viewed as both the only source of the individual's behavior and the only set of conditions which maintain it. Within the scope of microsocial change procedures, then, fall efforts to modify the classroom environment rather than the disruptive child (Stuart, in press a), the family rather than the delinquent (Stuart, 1971) or the marital interaction rather than the overweight person (Stuart and Davis, 1972).

At the level of macrosocial change, modification in the actions of large-scale systems are sought using informational controls taking the form of legislative reform or mass education; coercive controls take the form of revolutions which seek to forcibly proscribe large groups from taking selected actions. Like the goals of the two foregoing levels, macrosocial change agents seek changes of individuals —but individuals as members of collectives.

If this typology is a true description of intervention alternatives, it is suggested that social work educators terminate their emphasis upon the promulgation of change procedures targeted to intraindividual change because these procedures have not demonstrated sufficient utility to justify their perpetuation within the rubric of social work. It is further suggested that schools teach actively the use of microsocial change techniques as a basis for interpersonal helping, social treatment, or direct service and the use of macrosocial change techniques as a basis for social welfare policy formulation and implementation. For each of these two preferred levels it is possible to generate a set of values, a framework for assessment, a means of selecting intervention techniques, and a system for the evaluation of treatment effectiveness, complete with means of feeding this information back into self-corrective processes of intervention planning (Stuart, in press c). This approach would then lead to a new level or relevance and parsimony in social work education, replacing the familiar "shotgun" curricula which seek to unselectively include in social work training virtually everything which has been known or believed about human behavior and values (e.g., Dolgoff, 1971).

Training in Decision-Making

If the content of social work education followed this prescription, the objectives would begin with training students in the skills of decision-making among alternative goals and techniques. Pumphrey (1959) phrased this objective as follows:

> Social work should be presented as a process of responsible decision-making—the making of choices between desirable values (particularly the needs of individuals immediately concerned versus the needs of other individuals) and larger and more remote groupings, and short-time versus long-time objectives [p. 119].

Whether the decision-making process is based upon formal' logic (e.g., Lehrman, 1962), innovative approaches to rhetoric (e.g., Young, Becker, and Pike, 1970) or the functional analysis of behavior (e.g., Verhave, 1966), stress should be laid upon the skills of decision-making per se rather than upon the specific content of decisions. That is, in order to allow social workers to have the skills to deal with the changing array of human problems and resources available for combating these problems, process and not form must be taught. Form teaching leaves social workers with skills for dealing with "motivated" clients but not for dealing with the vast body of involuntary clients (Billingsley, 1965), for conservative and highly structured public assistance programs but not for innovative services rendered by social agencies of a form not yet conceived (Ginsberg, 1970; Piven, 1967; Vasey, 1970), or for services requiring extended periods of service when more time-constrained techniques have been shown to be not only more economical and more effective, but also less potentially iatrogenic (Stuart, in press b).

Along with decision-making, which will permit trained social workers to deal constructively with uncertainty resulting from rapid technological change, training is also needed in the skills associated with making constructive use of conflict. Conflict is inevitable in any time of social change. As suggested earlier, the human services field must not be considered a nonzero-sum game in which resource expansion is continuous in the same sense that Eddington's hypothetical universe undergoes unceasing expansion. Instead, the available resources are limited in scope and value, and those who exercise control over them are likely to seek to extend, consolidate, or at least maintain that control while those seeking to gain control, often in the name of progress, work to extend their spheres of influence. This inevitable conflict can be wearing and can lead to the polarization of services which will suffer thereby. Conversely, conflict can also strengthen the effectiveness of programming to the extent that through discourse accommodations are produced in the conception or implementation of service activities. It is therefore essential for social work education to equip its students with the capabilities of operating within an arena of conflict as opposed to the more familiar and troublesome arena of complacency.

Training in Values

Beyond training in decision-making and the strategy of constructive conflict, social work education should also train its students in the valuational basis of the field. In the judgment of Stein (1970), the absence of this training would yield a graduate who is a "crass professional [p. 15]." Two problems are immediately apparent, however, in beginning to think about instruction in values. The first pertains to the selection of which values to teach. For some time there was generally consensual agreement on the value of "self-determination" for social work with clients, which Hollis (1964) understands to mean "the right to make his own choices . . . and direct his own life [p. 13]." More recently, however, it has been acknowledged that one cannot not influence the behavior of others (Stuart, 1970) and, further, that behavioral control is at this time in history "scientifically inevitable, socially necessary and psychologically prepared for [London, 1969, p. 11]." Therefore the effort to shield oneself in the cloak of the belief that his clients could possibly exercise unconstrained choice is as naive as it is morally irresponsible—naive because it belies the facts and irresponsible because it evades the responsibility for making objectifiable commitments by the change agent.

If client self-determination in the purest sense is impossible, it should be replaced with the requirement that the direction of behavioral influence should be clearly stated. Where the client is voluntary, he should agree explicitly to the goals and means of treatment in an explicit therapeutic contract (Stuart, in press c). Where the client is involuntarily receiving treatment—as in correctional settings or when treatment is made a requirement for eligibility for some service in public assistance or adoption—client agreement is less ethically essential but the requirement for precise statements by the therapist of his goals must be subjected to even more careful scrutiny.

Beyond the ethical requirement that the basic dimensions of the treatment must be made explicit, other ethical requirements include but are not limited to: (a) that the client be given an opportunity to participate in the selection of treatment goals and methods; (b) that the behavioral controls exercised be primarily undertaken in the client's interest; (c) that the client's privacy be respected; (d) that the client be shielded from unwarranted intrusions into his daily affairs; and (e) that the selection of intervention procedures be based upon the best available research, that they are the most parsimonious procedures, and that they are subjected to careful empirical evaluation throughout the course of treatment so that at no time is the client needlessly asked to continue a procedure which exacerbates his distress.

The selection of these or any other values as objectives of

social work training should depend upon the answer to the second problem: Which values can be effectively taught? McLeod and Meyer (1967) used post hoc, correlational data to show that certain values (security-satisfaction, group responsibility, interdependence, innovation-change, cultural determinism, individual worth, and diversity) appear to be associated with the amount of social work training for certain subgroups of students while other values (individualization, relativism-pragmatism, and personal liberty) do not show this relationship. In a more rigorously designed test of the same question, Varley (1968) demonstrated that in schools undertaking specific teaching in this area, the commitments of students to the values of service, psychodynamic-mindedness and universalism underwent erosion during training while only one value appeared to be strengthened as a result of social work training—equal rights. Taken together with Gagne's (1970) observation that little to nothing is known about the consequences of value training, let alone the effective techniques for training values, the research described here must lead to the conclusion that an answer to questions pertaining to the efficacy of social work value instruction is premature at this time.

Skill Training

The author's recommendations for skill training for direct service have been explicated elsewhere (Stuart, in press c). Essentially the skills believed necessary fall into seven categories as follows:
1. Observation skills;
2. Problem formulation skills;
3. Skill in the functional analysis of behavior;
4. Skill in interpersonal management with relevance to the processes of inducing, maintaining, and terminating client participation in treatment through persuasion (including cognitive restructuring) and techniques of interpersonal influence (including differential social reinforcement);
5. Skill in treatment assessment;
6. Skill in the analysis and change of agency and organizational variables which facilitate or impede service delivery; and
7. Business skills such as benefit/cost analysis and record keeping.

Each of these seven categories can be greatly expanded into a series of detailed procedures, and each is considered to be an inherent dimension of effective practice. Furthermore, each can be readily taught through social work instructional resources which are presently available within the faculties of all accredited training institutions.

For illustrative purposes only, the general matter of record keeping (a business skill) highlights an arena in which training changes are in order. For example, Dwyer and Urbanowski (1966) are representative of contemporary social work educators who still advocate the use of process recording—albeit somewhat structured—and the Child Welfare League of America (1959) continues to advocate the use of detailed case studies despite the fact that the reliability and usefulness of such records are very dubious.

The unreliability of process recording is an inevitable consequence of the fact that two to four typed pages cannot adequately reflect the details of a one-hour exchange which would require forty to seventy pages of typescript. But even if the reliability problem could be solved, the more pressing issue still remains—of what use are the records? Allport (1951), as a social scientist looking in upon social work practices, was astounded to find 22,000 single-spaced pages of case records generated by the Cambridge-Somerville Youth Project, records which had prima facie uselessness because of their sheer bulk. Furthermore, a study by Frings, Kratovil, and Polemis (1958) clearly established the fact that records were not used by caseworkers in planning their strategies of intervention, while other studies have shown that the expansive diagnostic data called forth in social work records are irrelevant to case planning which is characteristically based upon a few facts (Rosenblatt and Mayer, 1970; Shinn, 1968). Finally, it can be shown that the process of record keeping has a seriously deleterious effect upon the amount of service rendered, recent studies having shown that case recording occupies from 28.2 to 31.3 percent of workers' reported use of time (Briar, 1966) with no economy of time resulting from the use of more parsimonious record-keeping systems (Frings, 1957).

In light of these findings, it is clear that new uses of case data must be found to justify the use of the procedure and that new formats must be developed to enhance its continuance. A number of systems are available for case recording, ranging from shortened means of describing the use of conventional strategies which stress intervention processes (e.g., Frings, 1957; Seaberg, 1970; Seattle Atlantic Street Center, 1964) to the use of data reporting which emphasizes an interaction between intervention process and outcome (e.g., Stuart, 1971). It is strongly suggested that only the latter recording procedures, which use a brief description of specific intervention strategies in association with ongoing monitoring of the effects of these strategies, can engender in students an appropriate respect for recording as a useful means to the end of expediting treatment planning and evaluation.

Sequence of Training

Four levels of training objectives can be identified for training social work students in the decision-making, values, and skills in behavior modification. Each of these levels of objectives serves as a framework for organizing performance criteria, pedagogical technique, and instructional content as summarized in the following outline.[6]

GOAL I: Commitment to the values of social work and behavior modification

    a. Criteria: verbal statements and discrimination problem solving

    b. Technique: lecture to train students in the logic of the approach; discussion to produce commitment to the approach

    c. Content: value premises such as the beliefs that change is possible, that measurement is essential, that positive behavior should be accelerated prior to attempting to decelerate undesirable behavior and that change must be undertaken for the good of the client, responsibility of therapist (vs. client) for treatment outcome, etc.

GOAL II: Skill in application of the technologies of social work and behavior modification

    a. Criteria: correct identification of the controlling conditions of initial, intermediate, and target behaviors and formulation of effective short range behavior modification programs for self, another person, and ultimately a client

    b. Technique: demonstration to produce commitment to methods, practicum to produce skills

    c. Content: response specification (including basic observation corrected for observer effects and irrelevancies), formulation of testable hypotheses for behavior change involving reliance upon controllable antecedent and consequent events, minimal use of synthetic controls, use of small steps geared to client performance and including criteria for rejecting therapeutic hypotheses, and skills in initiating and maintaining client involvement in treatment activities including prestructure of the initial contact, development of rapport and acceptance and follow through with respect to prescribed data collection and behavior change activities.

---

[6]This schema was suggested by Dr. Tony Tripodi, whose contribution is gratefully acknowledged.

GOAL III: Develop responsive sensitivity to treatment-produced data and to the interaction process in service delivery

   a. Criteria: effective therapeutic outcome with respect to behavior change, parsimony of intervention procedures, client acceptance of treatment, and persistence of intervention through variable response patterns

   b. Technique: training students in error nullifying responses to the questions—Am I doing what I am supposed to be doing?—and—Is what I am doing helping the client sufficiently?

   c. Content: training in means of construing client produced data as answers to technique questions in addition to recognition of: the specificity of behavior to the situations in which it occurs; the balance between cognitive and behavioral change; the need for fading in and out of treatment technology; and the inevitability and importance of rule testing, etc.

GOAL IV: Value discrimination resulting from effective differential decision-making

   a. Criteria: optimum service outcome at lowest possible marginal cost

   b. Technique: elucidation of bases of decision making through specification of factual and value premises through discussion, reactions to models and direct practice experience

   c. Content: value issues including but not limited to the critical role of maintenance of therapeutic change, the need for parsimony in treatment as opposed to the seduction of technologically complicated intervention, the larger consequence of behavior change as seen in its impact upon others in the client's milieu and social values such as the opportunity limiting effects of race, social class, and related factors.

For each of these levels of objectives it is possible to generate specific "probes" useful for assessing student performance. These probes, in turn, are useful for determining the appropriate placement of students within a training program and in applied or treatment settings. The general format of the training program is summarized in Figure 5 which suggests means of allocating training objectives to the various training technologies. To implement this form of training it is necessary to meet several organizational prerequisites.

Figure 5

Objectives, Content, and Techniques for Training Social Work Behavior Modifiers

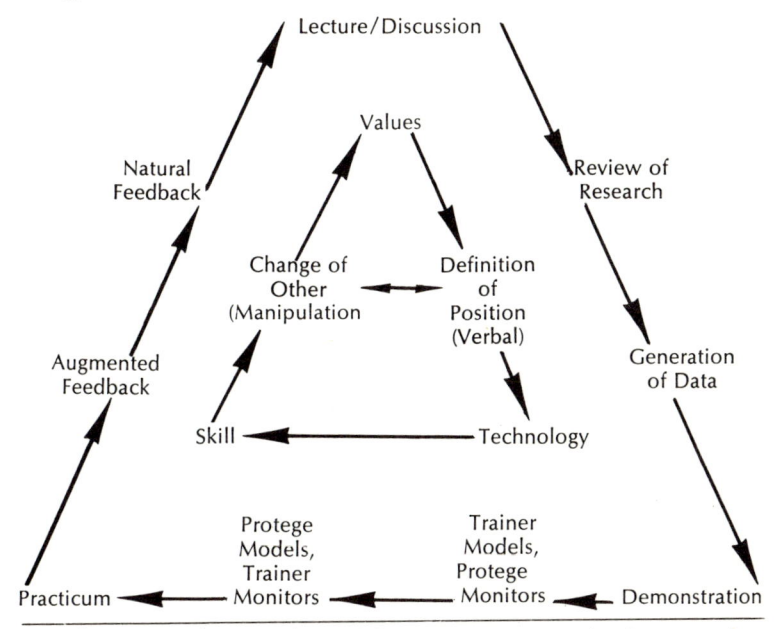

```
                    Lecture/Discussion
                           
                         Values
      Natural                          Review of
      Feedback                         Research
                   Change of    Definition
                   Other    ↔   of
                   (Manipulation)  Position
                                (Verbal)
      Augmented                        Generation
      Feedback                         of Data
                   Skill  ←  Technology

                  Protege         Trainer
                  Models,         Models,
                  Trainer         Protege
      Practicum ← Monitors  ←  Monitors ← Demonstration
```

First, decision-making in the training-treatment organization must be democratized and non-hierarchicized in order to permit maximum participation by learners in every facet of decision-making. Second, the policies and procedures of the setting should provide the best possible modeling for students. For example, data collection and recording procedures must be maximally adapted to parsimonious treatment planning and evaluation, and organizational requirements such as work hours and work load must be maximally adapted to treatment requirements. Third, all aspects of service delivery should be consequated as immediately as possible. For example, all major decisions about intervention should be formally recorded at least as statements of the present situation, hypothetical change technique and expected outcome, and clients should be provided with means of giving therapists prestructured feedback about the manner in which every therapeutic session is conducted. Finally, trainees should be accorded a degree of autonomy commensurate with their level of performance in order to provide them with the broadest possible range of opportunity for skill development. It is only when training is organized according to sequential objectives, each step with its appropriate criteria, technology, and content, and when training organizations are rationally designed that the best possible training output can be expected.

CONCLUSION

Following from the observation that the size and character of human welfare programs have been changing radically in recent years, it has been suggested that social work education is in need of comparable far-reaching changes. Social welfare programs have been expanded along the lines of treating individuals rather than the systemic malfunctions which are at the base of their problems. It has been suggested that the only realistic hope for change in the presently dismal course toward the failure of human services programs is a shift in ideology from efforts to use direct, individually focused services to the use of indirect, socially oriented intervention procedures. To facilitate this change in emphasis, social work training programs would be required to shift from their efforts to engender skills in classical individual treatment (whether derived from psychotherapeutic or behavior modification models) to the development of skills basic to changing the situational determinants of behavior on either a microsocial or a macrosocial scale. To do this, it has been suggested that the traditional casework-group work-community practice differentiation within curricula be replaced with a differentiation which stresses the levels of change goals and the relative balance of informational versus coercive control techniques, while continuing to offer training in decision-making, values, and skills in program analysis and interpersonal influence.

This paper concluded with a brief outline of the objectives and technology through which these changes can be effected, and the organizational structures through which their achievement can be consolidated. Additional changes, not discussed, must be made in the professional organization and service delivery agencies in order to translate ideological change into the enhancement of programmatic effectiveness.

REFERENCES

Allport, G. W. Foreword. In E. Powers and H. Witmer, *An Experiment in the prevention of delinquency: The Cambridge-Somerville Youth Study.* New York: Columbia University Press, 1951.

Amidon, E., and Hunter, E. Interaction analysis: Recent developments. In E. J. Amidon and J. B. Hough (Eds.), *Interaction analysis: Theory, research and application.* Reading, Mass.: Addison-Wesley, 1967.

Aptekar, H. H. Differentiating types of knowledge in the classroom and teaching centers. In *Modes of professional education: Functions of field instruction in the curriculum.* New Orleans, La.: Tulane University School of Social Work, 1969.

Austin, L. N. Basic principles of supervision. *Social Casework,* 1952, *33,* 411-419.

Bell, W. Services for people: An appraisal. *Social Work,* 1970, *15,* No. 3, 5-12.

Billingsley, A. Education for uncertainty in social welfare. In *Education for social work with "unmotivated" clients: Papers in social welfare, No. 9.* Waltham, Mass.: Brandeis University, 1965.

Bisno, H. A theoretical framework for teaching social work methods and skills, with particular reference to undergraduate social welfare education. In F. Loewenberg and R. Dolgoff (Eds.), *Teaching of practice skills in undergraduate programs in social welfare and other helping services.* New York: Council on Social Work Education, 1971.

Boehm, W. *Objectives of social work curriculum of the future: The comprehensive report of the Curriculum Study.* New York: Council on Social Work Education, 1959.

Briar, S. Family services. In H. Maas (Ed.), *Five fields of social service.* New York: National Association of Social Workers, 1966.

Briar, S. The casework predicament. *Social Work,* 1968, *13,* No. 1, 5-11.

Brieland, D. Broadening the knowledge base through a social services center. In *Modes of professional education: Functions of field learning in the curriculum.* New Orleans: Tulane University School of Social Work, 1969.

Bruno, F. J. Twenty-five years of schools of social work. *Social Service Review,* 1944, *18,* 152-164.

Child Welfare League of America. *Child Welfare League of America standards for foster family care service.* New York: Child Welfare League of America, 1959.

Clark, K. B. *Dark ghetto.* New York: Harper & Row, 1965.

Cloward, R. A. Commentary of a subversive version of the great society. In H. Stein (Ed.), *Social theory and social intervention.* Cleveland, O.: Case Western Reserve Press, 1968.

Cloward, R. and Epstein, I. Private social welfare's disengagement from the poor: The case of private family adjustment agencies. In *Proceedings of the Annual Social Day Institute: State University at Buffalo.* Buffalo, N.Y.: State University Press, 1965.

Coleman, J. S. *Equality of educational opportunity.* Washington, D.C.: Office of Education, U.S. Department of Health, Education & Welfare, 1966.

Coleman, J. S. Comments on conference. In Office of Education, *Do teachers make a difference?* Washington, D.C.: U.S. Department of Health, Education & Welfare, 1970.

Contracting Corporation of America. *Planning for the involvement of social work education in the Head Start Program.* Chicago: American Training Institute, undated.

Cooper and Company. *The cost and output of graduate social work education: An exploratory study.* Washington, D.C.: Social and rehabilitative service, U.S. Department of Health, Education & Welfare, 1970.

Dolgoff, R. Basic skills for practice in the human services: A curriculum guide. In F. Loewenberg and R. Dolgoff (Eds.), *Teaching of practice skills in undergraduate programs in social welfare and other helping services*. New York: Council on Social Work Education, 1971.

Dreeben, R. *On what is learned in school*. Reading, Mass.: Addison-Wesley, 1968.

Dwyer, M. and Urbanowski, M. Student process recording: A plea for structure. In Family Service Association of America, *Trends in field work instruction*. New York: Family Service Association of America, 1966.

Family Service Association of America. *Trends in field work instruction*. New York: Family Service Association of America, 1966.

Feldman, Y., Spotnitz, H., and Nagelberg, L. One aspect of casework training through supervision. *Social Casework*, 1953, *34*, 150-155.

Fellin, P. and Vinter, R. D. Curriculum development for contemporary social work education: University of Michigan. In *Modes of professional education: Functions of field learning in the curriculum*. New Orleans: Tulane University School of Social Work, 1969.

Frings, J. Experimental systems of recording. *Social Casework*, 1957, *38*, 55-63.

Frings, J., Kratovil, R., and Polemis, B. *An assessment of social case recording*. New York: Family Service Association of America, 1958.

Gagne, R. M. Policy implications and future research: A response. In Office of Education, *Do teachers make a difference?* Washington, D.C.: U.S. Department of Health, Education & Welfare, 1970.

Ginsberg, M. I. Changing values in social work. In K. A. Kendall (Ed.), *Social work values in an age of discontent*. New York: Council on Social Work Education, 1970.

Gordon, J. Two systems for evaluating videotaped instruction. Paper presented at the annual meeting of the American Educational Research Association, Chicago, February 10, 1968.

Grob, G. *The state and the mentally ill*. Chapel Hill: University of North Carolina Press, 1966.

Harbison, F. and Meyers, C. A. *Education, manpower and economic growth: Strategies of human resource development*. New York: McGraw-Hill, 1964.

Hollis, E. V. and Taylor, A. L. *Social work education in the United States*. New York: Columbia University Press, 1951.

Hollis, F. *Casework: A psychosocial therapy*. New York: Random House, 1964.

Hurley, R. *Poverty and mental retardation*. New York: Vintage, 1969.

Kadushin, A. Determinants of career choice and their implications for social work. *Social Work Education,* 1958, 6, No. 2, 17-22.

Kahn, A. J. From delinquency treatment to community development. In P. Lazarsfeld, W. H. Sewell, and H. L. Wilensky (Eds.), *The uses of sociology.* New York: Basic Books, 1967.

Kanfer, F. H. and Phillips, J. S. A survey of current behavior therapies and a proposal for classification. In C. M. Franks (Ed.), *Behavior therapy: Appraisal and status.* New York: McGraw-Hill, 1969.

Kindelsperger, K. W. Emerging structure and objectives of teaching centers: Kent School of Social Work. In *Modes of professional education: Functions of field learning in the curriculum.* New Orleans: Tulane University School of Social Work, 1969.

Kirkpatrick, F. H. Techniques for evaluating training programs. *Journal of the American Society of Training Directors,* 1959, 13, 3-9.

Lauffer, A. Social actionists come to school. Unpublished doctoral dissertation, Brandeis University, 1969.

Lawrence, R. G. Critique: On the Taber and K. W. Kindelsperger papers. In *Modes of professional education: Functions of field learning in the curriculum.* New Orleans: Tulane University School of Social Work, 1969.

Lee, P. Social work: Cause and function. In *Proceedings, National Conference of Social Work.* Chicago, Ill.: National Conference of Social Work, 1929.

Lehrman, L. The logic of diagnosis. In C. Kasius (Ed.), *Social casework in the fifties: Selected articles.* New York: Family Service Association of America, 1962.

Lind, R. Socialt arbete, med foranderliga uppgifter ("Social work professionals and changing social welfare functions"), *Intermediair,* August 21, 1970, Vol. 10.

Lindsay, J. *The city.* New York: Norton, 1969.

Llopis, B. The exial syndrome common to all psychoses. *Psychoanalysis and the Psychoanalytic Review,* 1959, 46, 1-32.

London, P. *Behavior control.* New York: Harper & Row, 1969.

Martin, J. M., Fitzpatrick, J. P., and Gould, R. E. Delinquency prevention and urban community development. *Delinquency Prevention Report,* 1971, 2, No. 2, 3-6.

McLeod, D. L. and Meyer, H. J. A study of the values of social workers. In E. J. Thomas (Ed.), *Behavioral science for social workers.* New York: The Free Press, 1967.

Mechanic, D. *Mental health and social policy.* Englewood Cliffs, N.J.: Prentice-Hall, 1969.

Meier, E. G. *A history of the New York School of Social Work*. New York: Columbia University Press, 1954.

Meyer, H. J. Professionalization and social work today. In A. J. Kahn (Ed.), *Issues in American social work*. New York: Columbia University Press, 1959.

Miller, H. Value dilemmas in social casework. *Social Work,* 1968, *13,* No. 1, 27-33.

Millett, J. D. The ethics of higher education. *Educational Record,* 1967, *48,* No. 1, 11-21.

National Institute of Mental Health. *The mental health of urban America*. Washington, D.C.: U.S. Department of Health, Education & Welfare, 1969.

Neenan, W. B. Benefit-cost analysis: Role of quantity analysis as an aid in government and non-government decision making. Paper presented at a conference on Cost-Benefit Analysis and Mental Retardation, University of Michigan, Ann Arbor, March 15, 1971.

Odiorne, G. *How managers make things happen*. Englewood Cliffs, N.J.: Prentice-Hall, 1961.

Patterson, G. R., McNeal, S., Hawkins, N., and Phelps, R. Reprogramming the social environment. *Journal of Child Psychology and Psychiatry,* 1967, *8,* 181-195.

Pernell, R. B. Social work values on the new frontiers, In K. A. Kendall (Ed.), *Social work values in an age of discontent*. New York: Council on Social Work Education, 1970.

Pins, A. M. *Who chooses social work, when and why?* New York: Council on Social Work Education, 1963.

Piven, F. F. Professionalism as a political skill: The case of a poverty program. In Council on Social Work Education, *Anti-poverty programs: Implications for social work education*. New York: Council on Social Work Education, 1967.

Pratt, L. Optimism-pessimism about healing the poor with health problems. *Social Work,* 1970, *15,* No. 2, 29-36.

Pumphrey, M. W. *The teaching of values and ethics in social work education*. New York: Council on Social Work Education, 1959.

Rein, M. Social work in search of a radical profession. *Social Work,* 1970, *15,* No. 2, 13-18.

Rosenblatt, A. and Mayer, J. E. Reduction of uncertainty in child placement decisions. *Social Work,* 1970, *15,* No. 4, 52-59.

Sarri, R. C. and Vinter, R. D. Group work for the control of behavior problems in secondary schools. In D. Street (Ed.), *Innovation in mass education*. New York: Wiley-Interscience, 1969.

Schorr, A. L. Poverty, politics and people: The education of social workers. In Council on Social Work Education, *Personnel in anti-poverty programs: Implications for social work education.* New York: Council on Social Work Education, 1967.

Schultz, V. M. Employment trends of recent graduates. *N.A.S.W. News,* November 1970, 26, 15-16.

Seaberg, J. R. Systematized recording: A follow-up. *Social Work,* 1970, *15,* No. 4, 32-41.

Seattle Atlantic Street Center. Seattle Atlantic Street Center recording system. Seattle, Wash.: Seattle Atlantic Street Center, 1964 (mimeo).

Segal, A. Workers' perceptions of mentally disabled clients: Effect on service delivery. *Social Work,* 1970, *15,* No. 3, 39-46.

Select Committee on Nutrition and Human Needs, United States Senate. *Housing need and federal failure in rural America.* Washington, D.C.: U.S. Government Printing Office, 1971.

Shea, M. C. Serving low-income persons: New demands on social workers. In Council on Social Work Education, *Personnel in anti-poverty programs: Implications for social work education.* New York: Council on Social Work Education, 1967.

Shinn, E. B. Is placement necessary: An experimental study of agreement among caseworkers in making foster care decisions. Unpublished doctoral dissertation, Columbia University, 1968.

Shriver, S. Poverty in the United States—What next? In *The Social Welfare Forum, 1965.* New York: Columbia University Press, 1965.

Siporin, M. Special treatment: A new-old helping method. *Social Work,* 1970, *15,* No. 3, 13-25.

Stein, H. D. Professions and universities. In H. D. Stein and A. L. Kristenson (Eds.), *The professional school and the university.* New York: Council on Social Work Education, 1970.

Steinman, R. Values in occupational choice and occupational selection: A comparative study of admissions decisions in social work education. Unpublished doctoral dissertation, Brandeis University, 1968.

Stephens, J. M. *The process of schooling.* New York: Holt, Rinehart & Winston, 1967.

Stuart, R. B. Promise and paradox in socioeconomic status conceptions. *Smith College Studies in Social Work,* 1965, *35,* 110-124.

Stuart, R. B. Critical reappraisal of selected mental health programs. In L. A. Hamerlynck, P. O. Davidson, and L. E. Acker (Eds.), *Behavior modification and ideal mental health services.* Calgary: University of Calgary Press, 1969.

Stuart, R. B. *Trick or treatment: How and when psychotherapy fails.* Champaign, Ill.; Research Press, 1970.

Stuart, R. B. Behavioral control of delinquency: Critique of existing programs and recommendations for innovative programs. In L. A. Hamerlynck, and F. Clark (Eds.), *Behavior modification for exceptional children and youth.* Calgary: University of Calgary Press, 1971.

Stuart, R. B. Behavior modification techniques for the education technologist. In R. C. Sarri (Ed.), *Proceedings of the National Workshop on School Social Workers,* in press. (a)

Stuart, R. B. Evaluative research in casework and group work. In *Encyclopedia of social work.* New York: National Association of Social Workers, in press. (b)

Stuart, R. B. *Promoting behavior change through social work.* Itasca, Ill.: Peacock Press, in press. (c)

Stuart, R. B. and Davis, B. *Slim chance in a fat world: Behavioral control of obesity.* Champaign, Ill.: Research Press, 1972.

Taber, M. A knowledge base for social work: Three positions. In *Modes of professional education: Functions of field learning in the curriculum.* New Orleans: Tulane University School of Social Work, 1969.

Timms, N. *Social casework, principles and practices.* London, England: Routledge & Kegan Paul, 1964.

United Nations. *Training for social work: Third international survey.* New York: Department of Economic and Social Affairs, United Nations, 1958.

Urban America. *Chart book.* Washington, D.C.: Urban America, Inc., undated.

Varley, B. K. Social work values: Changes in value commitments of students from admission to MSW graduation. *Journal of Education for Social Work,* 1968, *4,* 67-76.

Vasey, W. Social welfare as a human right. In K. A. Kendall (Ed.), *Social work values in an age of discontent.* New York: Council on Social Work Education, 1970.

Verhave, T. Introduction. In T. Verhave (Ed.), *The experimental analysis of behavior.* New York: Appleton-Century-Crofts, 1966.

Vinter, R. D. Problems and processes in developing social work practice principles. In E. J. Thomas (Ed.), *Behavioral science for social workers.* New York: The Free Press, 1967.

Welfare Administration. *Cities in crisis: The challenge of change.* Washington, D.C.: U.S. Department of Health, Education & Welfare, 1966.

Winston, E. New dimensions in public welfare: Implications for social work education. In A. M. Pins and W. J. Cohen (Eds.), *Social work education and social welfare manpower: Present realities and future imperatives.* New York: Council on Social Work Education, 1965.

Witte, E. F. Training social work associates. In *Education for social work: Proceedings, Eleventh Annual Program Meeting, Council on Social Work Education.* New York: Council on Social Work Education, 1963.

Witte, E. F. Student wisdom and values: The positive force of disaffection. In K. A. Kendall (Ed.), *Social work values in an age of discontent.* New York: Council on Social Work Education, 1970.

Young, R. E., Becker, A. L., and Pike, K. L. *Rhetoric: Discovery and change.* New York: Harcourt, Brace & World, 1970.

Zetzel, E. R. The dynamic basis of supervision. *Social Casework,* 1953, *34,* No. 4, 143-149.

Training Behavioral Counselors
Carl E. Thoresen

Let's listen in on part of a conversation going on between Jack, a counselor trainee, and Sue an interested friend.

Jack: Yeah, I can understand your confusion about counseling, psychotherapy, and psychiatry. I've felt that way too.

Sue: It's really so damn vague. I've read some of the articles you gave me . . . glanced at that theories book. You know what really stands out to me as someone who isn't in the field?

Jack: What?

Sue: Well, everybody's got their own labels and special language. It sounds like they're all trying to keep it a big mystery, you know, like "Don't let the natives know what it's really all about." Am I being too naive, Jack?

Jack: Not at all. I'm fed up with the word games. It makes a lot more sense, to me anyway, to look at counseling, therapy, the whole bag, as action you take to help people.

Sue: Action?

Jack: Yeah. You change what they've been doing. See, it's more than just sitting around talking to a person. You've got to do more than the "feeling talk" stuff.

Sue: Strikes me you could look at it as teaching and learning. I know that doesn't fit at all with the stuff I read. But, why not?

Jack: That's what I meant when I said taking actions to help people change.

Sue: I know I don't understand all the complex stuff, you know, about how some people get so fouled up. But, well, if you can think of counseling as teaching someone to act in better ways . . . well, why all the hocus pocus, the big abstractions and jazzy words?

Jack: I guess it's because we still don't understand very much about people, so we come up with complex words and theories to try to explain things.

Sue: You mean hide things.

Jack: Right, cover up what we don't know . . . I do know from the little counseling I've done so far that you can't just go in and do your same thing with every person. That's where most of the theories really miss it. They're unreal.

Sue: All right. So what you need to do is handle every situation as unique. People are different, right?

Jack: Well, yeah. I think it's almost like being almost a scientist. You know, really checking things out, observing and describing the person's scene before you try jumping in with some favorite technique. . .

We'll leave Jack here to carry on with Sue. Let's note, however, highlights of what was said. First of all, the field of counseling has been characterized by an excess of rhetoric and obtuseness. Skill in using abstract labels and professional jargon have often been substituted for demonstrated competence in actually helping clients. Second, there's considerable validity to Sue's idea of counseling as "teaching and learning." Third, counseling is doing things — taking action — to help others act differently. Each client presents a unique arrangement of experiences — not totally unique but differing enough from others to merit the scientific approach mentioned.

In this paper I will first present some basic characteristics of a behavioral approach to counseling. Then I will discuss briefly some concepts from a systems perspective to introduce the Behavioral Systems Training Program currently in operation at Stanford University.

COUNSELING AS APPLIED SOCIAL LEARNING

Counseling viewed from a social learning perspective involves working with a client in a multiplicity of ways, especially as regards the client's daily life environment. For it is where the client "lives" that serves as the major determinant of what the client feels, thinks, and does, i.e., how the client behaves. Counseling viewed as such involves far more than a certain type of stylized verbal interaction in an office setting. Counseling is not, as one high school student characterized it, ". . . that room where you go to be talked at."

From a social learning perspective, counseling has several basic characteristics. Let's examine briefly some of these characteristics (see Krumboltz and Thoresen, 1969; Kanfer and Phillips, 1970; Yates, 1970, for a more thorough discussion; see Bandura, 1969, for a thorough analysis of basic principles of human behavior).

Empirical Orientation

The behavioral approach, in effect, characterizes the counselor as an active interventionist who makes his decisions on the basis of data. While it is not always possible to gather the most accurate and reliable data, the behavioral counselor consistently seeks to observe, to describe, to record and to analyze data about client actions. This focus on observable data as the means to make decisions about such things as what kind of treatment to use, when to alter an intervention, and how to decide how effective counseling is, distinguishes a behavioral approach from many traditional types of counseling and therapy. The counselor as an applied behavioral scientist is concerned with understanding, predicting, and controlling human behavior (Thoresen, 1969). Why? So that the counselor can use this knowledge to help clients change. He seeks to build upon the basic hypotheses and generalizations of the behavioral sciences, especially experimental psychology, in creating and using counseling techniques that produce relevant changes in client behavior. The counselor is concerned with understanding the "total experience" of each client and using this understanding.[1] Can, for example, the counselor understand the intense fears and anxieties of a particular client in such a way that this understanding enables the counselor to help control such behavior in predictable ways? With such understanding the counselor can help the client bring about desired changes in his daily life.

If counseling involves the systematic alteration of client behavior in the desired direction, then the counselor accepts the responsibility to utilize the most effective and efficient means of bringing about change. The empirical focus highlights the *accountability* of the counselor. In every step from initially helping the client communicate his concerns to the termination of counseling, the counselor is guided by relevant data — data in terms of changes in the actions of the client. Errors and false starts are inevitable. But the counselor with this eye to gathering data from the outset has an ongoing continuous basis of knowing how things are going. He "knows" about the errors, the hunches about treatment that fail to work from the data. Further, the counselor has data — in terms of change in client behavior — to show that his counseling had desired effects. The client's behavior changed. (Of course, such evidence doesn't "prove" in a precise way that counseling caused the change. Replication of treatment across clients and situations is needed to establish causality.) The counselor is no longer cast in the role of some omniscient helper who somehow intuitively deeply understands and knows just what to do. Instead the counselor engages the client actively in a mutual searching for how they might work together to discover more clearly what the problem is and how a particular type of intervention may be most helpful — both in effectiveness and efficiency. From the beginning contact the counselor explains his role to the client as an empirically oriented helper, as someone who is willing to work cooperatively with the client in discovering and verifying what can be done to bring about desired change.

---

[1]The behavioral counselor discussed here and later in this paper shares much with the humanistic psychologist-therapist in emphasizing the unique internal as well as external experiences and concerns of each person. See Buhler (1971) for a discussion of basic humanistic concepts.

Tailoring Techniques

But what counseling technique is the most effective to use? It follows logically from the empirical focus that there is *no one best technique* for use with all clients and problems. The challenge for the behavioral counselor is to combine conceptual and theoretical rationales from the behavioral sciences with his own experience and with an empirical view to discover and assess which technique or sequence of techniques will work best with this particular client (Krumboltz and Thoresen, 1969).

Behavioral counseling seeks to tailor techniques to the individual client. Several clients, for example, all generally experiencing problems of social inadequacy having to do with opposite sex relations may each be best helped by using any number of techniques. For example, a form of symbolic systematic desensitization may be an important first step in working with an extremely shy, withdrawn 15-year-old girl where the thought or image of interacting with boys is extremely anxiety provoking. Another girl of comparable age and experience, however, may be more effectively helped in a group situation that emphasizes the use of modeling and behavior rehearsal exercises having to do with learning new social behaviors. In Figure 1 a conceptual model of behavioral counseling is presented in terms of a flow chart. Each function from Discover Problem to Terminate Counseling involves several operations that the counselor engages in with a particular client. The pathways labeled (F) indicate feedback to other main functions as a way of conveying the dynamic rather than static or linear nature of the process. For example, it is very common in attempting to establish behaviorally stated objectives with the client (3.0) that more information is presented to cause a recycling back (feedback) to reconsidering what the problem is (1.0) and gathering more baseline data (2.0). Considerable time may be spent in cycling through the first three major functions *before* a particular counseling technique is selected.

The model of behavioral counseling presented in Figure 1 highlights an often ignored, but perhaps the most important and demanding, activitiy of the counselor — that of establishing behavioral objectives cooperatively with the client. Behavioral objectives become the "targets for treatment" by clearly specifying the goals of counseling in specific client response terms. The behavioral objective tells us just what the client will be *doing* for counseling to be considered successful. Both the counselor and the client are greatly assisted in knowing just where they are going by using behavioral objectives. And knowing where you are trying to go can help you in deciding what to do to get there.

Figure 1

Behavioral Counseling Model

```
┌─────────────┐
│ Discover    │←──────────────────────────────────┐
│ Problem(s)  │                                   │
│   1.0       │         ↑F              ↑F        │
└──────┬──────┘                                   │
       ↓                                          │
   ┌─────────────┐                                │
   │ Gather Data │                                │
   │ (Baseline)  │                                │
   │    2.0      │                                │
   └──────┬──────┘                                │
          ↓                                       │
      ┌──────────────────────────┐                │
      │ Establish Behavioral     │←───────────────┤
      │ Objective(s)-Outcome(s)  │                │
      │ Cooperatively            │                │
      │           3.0            │                │
      └──────────┬───────────────┘                │
                 ↓              ↑F                │
          ┌──────────────────┐                    │
          │ Select Counseling│                    │
          │ Technique(s)     │                    │
          │         4.0      │                    │
          └────────┬─────────┘                    │
                   ↓                              │
              ┌──────────────────────┐            │
              │ Evaluate Change(s) in│            │
              │ Relevant Behavior(s) │            │
              │            5.0       │            │
              └──────────┬───────────┘            │
                         ↓                        │
                    ┌──────────────────────┐      │
                    │ Terminate Counseling │──────┘
                    │            6.0       │
                    └──────────────────────┘
```

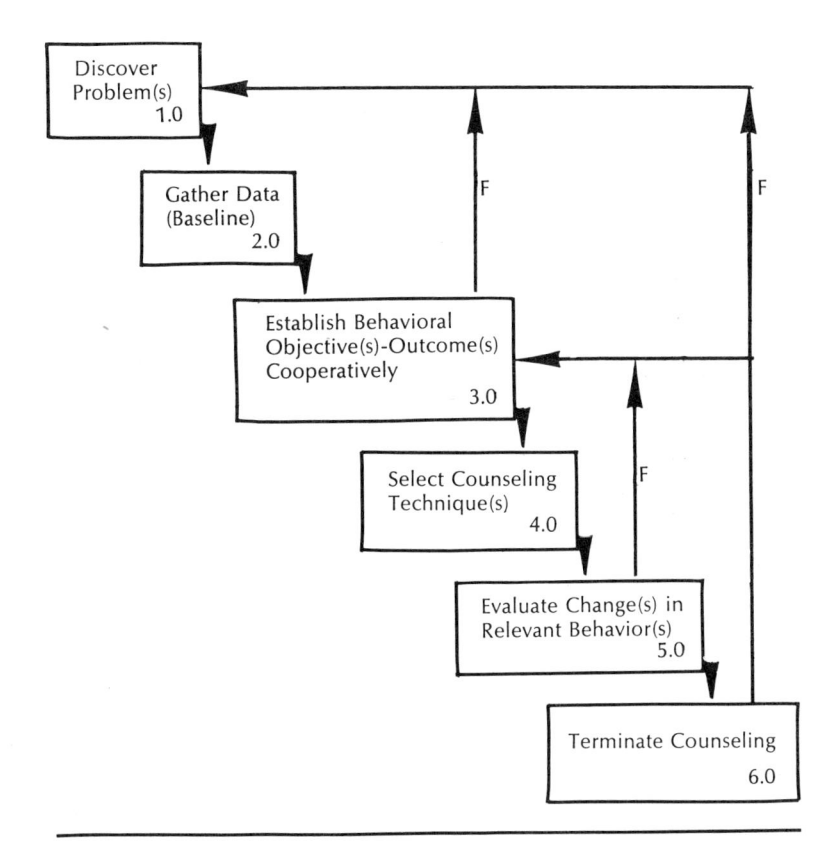

Figure 2 presents the basic criteria for an adequately stated behavioral objective with some examples. A behavioral objective may be used as a final outcome towards which counseling is focused or it may be used as a very immediate sub-goal towards which the counselor and client are working. For example, a final behavioral objective in a marital case may have to do with increasing the reported personal satisfaction of sexual intercourse to a specific level that both husband and wife experience (an average of at least 5 on a 7 point rating scale) for a period of two months. However, a very immediate behavioral objective in the same marital case could be that Gretchen will practice physical relaxation exercises each evening after dinner for at least 30 minutes in the bedroom alone during the next week.

Figure 2

Identifying Criteria of Behavioral Objectives

The basic criteria for an adequate behavioral objective include:

1. A behavioral objective specifies the response to be performed to an extent that it may be reliably recorded by some observer (although the observer may be the client).

2. A behavioral objective specifies a criterion level in terms of how much (how long, how many times, how hard, etc.) of the behavior is required to meet the objective.

3. A behavioral objective specifies under what conditions (circumstances) the behavior is to occur.

Indicate by each statement below how many of the criteria are met.

_____ 1. John will put the pants that he wore that day in his dresser drawer every night before he goes to bed.

_____ 2. The teacher agrees to look at David's math homework during the first study period each day and will hand it back to him with it marked before the study period ends.

_____ 3. Lawrence states, "I will go to dinner without the medallion three times next week."

_____ 4. John will do five math homework problems correctly between 8:00 and 8:30 each school night, in his room with the radio off, for four weeks.

_____ 5. In the next psychology discussion session, the client will volunteer comments.

_____ 6. The student will arrive on time at his first class in the morning.

_____ 7. Ian will study math in a quiet study room for thirty minutes each day for the next week.

_____ 8. Larry will respond to his wife three times in a more positive way (smiling, interested, friendly, attending to her).

_____ 9. The teacher will give a check mark to Jane every time she behaves.

_____ 10. The client will approach a caged, harmless snake during the next counseling session in the presence of the counselor.

_____ 11. The client will apply .2 milliamps for .5 seconds from the shock box when he has abnormal thoughts.

_____ 12. Jim will concentrate for thirty minutes while he does his physics homework in his room, at his desk, with the radio off, and light coming over his left shoulder.

_____ 13. The student will listen to the teacher five times during social studies class.

_____ 14. Gretchen and Chuck will each independently report at least three "extremely satisfying" intercourse experiences per week for a period of two months.

_____ 15. Kay will initiate at least two conversations per day for the next week with male students with whom she has not talked before.

_____ 16. Carl will report five positive self-thoughts or more per day by the end of April.

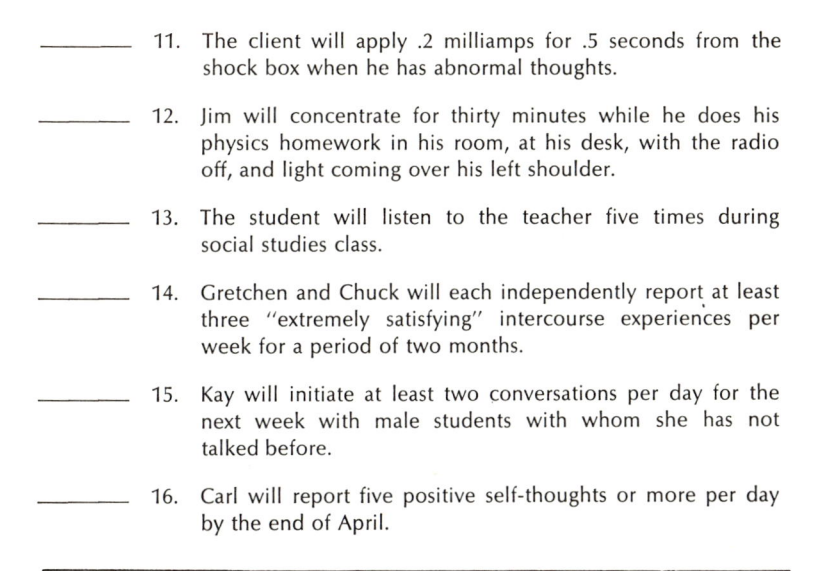

It is helpful to make a distinction between a behavioral objective and a behavioral outcome. A behavioral objective states an action that the client is to engage in to a certain minimum criterion level and within a specific situation or under certain conditions. A behavioral outcome, however, may be a change not directly involving the observable actions of the individual, such as a loss of at least 15 pounds by June or the earning of at least B average for the semester.

Establishing behavioral objectives and outcomes plays an important role in tailoring counseling techniques to the particular client situation. Without specifically stated objectives expressed in terms of desired client behaviors the task of individualizing counseling to the particular client becomes very confused. Ambiguity about the specific goals of counseling has long served in traditional therapies to perpetuate use of the same type of counseling for all clients and problems. Indeed, clients who failed to benefit in traditional approaches have usually been labeled "unready" for counseling. The idea of tailoring counseling to the individual client, of course, places considerably more responsibility and demands on the counselor for it is the counselor who tries to "fit the client," rather than expecting all clients to fit one type of counseling (of course, no counselor can at present successfully help *all* types of clients and specific problems). Stated somewhat differently, each client becomes an $N=1$ experimental study or an empirical case study (Thoresen, 1970; Yates, 1970). It is as if the counselor is conducting an individual field experiment using each client as his own control by means of gathering baseline data. Intervention in the form of a counseling procedure(s) then administered with data being gathered during the intervention as well as afterwards. The "before, during, and after" gathering of data of client behaviors is guided by using behaviorally stated objectives. In this way the counselor can either confirm or reject his working hypothesis that the selected treatment is producing the desired change. (For an extended discussion see Chassan, 1966; Thoresen, 1970; and Yates, 1970, pp. 380-385).

The "Here and Now" Environment

A third basic characteristic of a behavioral approach to counseling and therapy is the concern with the client's immediate physical and social environment. What the client is experiencing in his everyday physical and social environments is considered the most important determinant of what the client does. Conducting a behavioral analysis of the client's environment is a major task for the behavioral counselor. A modification of the concept of a three-term contingency theory (discriminative stimuli, responses, and reinforcing stimuli) from operant theory is generally employed. This is called the "ABC's." Inquiries are made into the various antecedent (A) of the target behavior (B) or responses as well as into the possible consequences (C). This kind of examination identifies what events in the client's everyday life may be eliciting the problem behavior (or in some way contributing to it) as well as what actions may be maintaining the problem behavior. For example, an adolescent client's experience of stress and tension may be specific to a certain physical environmental setting, such as a particular classroom or at home when father is around. Further, certain responses of the client may be immediately followed by those of another person such that the client's behavior is maintained by the action of this other person. A sympathetic, consoling mother, for example, who provides attention to her anxious adolescent or a teacher who singles out a student who is highly aroused and tense may be inadvertently strengthening the problem behavior.

Some type of ABC analysis is crucial for the counselor in trying to understand and operationalize just what the client's problem is (Discovering the Problem). Further, this type of analysis also helps clarify the target behavior along with its antecedents and consequences (Gathering Baseline Data). In contrast to some traditional approaches, the primary focus in behavioral counseling is on the "here and now" and what is happening in the daily life environment of the client. (Other approaches such as Gestalt and neo-Alderian also acknowledge the importance of the "here and now.")

Behavior — Internal and External

A fourth basic characteristic of a behavioral approach centers around the concept of behavior itself. The term behavior serves as a general descriptive concept that refers to a broad spectrum of human actions. A general working model of behavior, referred to by Kanfer and Phillips (1970) as the Behavioral Equation, sees behavior B as a function of:

- S — Stimuli (stimulus situations)
- O — Physiological states of individuals
- R — Responses (overt and covert)
- K — Contingency relationships
- C — Consequences

This "equation" emphasizes two important points: (1) a response is influenced by preceding and subsequent events, and (2) behavior is both internal and external.

Figure 3 represents a graphic presentation that emphasizes that antecedents of a particular response can be both *external* and observable to others as well as *internal* and covert, i.e., observable only to the individual himself. Further, Figure 3 indicates that consequences can be both overt and covert. Examples of covert or internal responses include thoughts, images, and physiological responses. Examples of covert responses are a very arousing mental picture (image) or a negative self-thought ("I'm ugly") or a marked elevation in heart rate.

Behavior, then, is viewed as including both internal and external responses based on the homogeneity assumption, i.e., that overt and covert responses obey identical laws of behavior (Skinner, 1963; Cautela, 1970; Mahoney, 1970; Thoresen, 1971; Mahoney, Thoresen, and Danaher, 1971). The behavioral counselor may work with a client in focusing on altering overt and/or covert responses. The decision, in part, is determined by the particular behavioral objectives and the results of the behavioral analysis that the counselor and client mutually carry on.

Behavior is not used in the rigid and somewhat traditional sense of referring only to those responses directly observable by others. Much of the vacuous debate between so-called behaviorists and humanists has centered around this supposed distinction, with the humanistically oriented berating the behaviorist for totally ignoring and denying internal phenomena. A behavioral counselor, however, is concerned with helping the client bring about all types of meaningful change. For a particular client meaningful change may involve reducing negative thoughts about himeslf and increasing positive self-thoughts. Mahoney (in press) has recently demonstrated the dramatic effects (immediate and long-term) on internal as well as external responses with a diagnosed schizophrenic client by focusing directly on covert responses. In a study currently underway with elementary school teachers, Hannum (1971) is directly altering negative and positive self-thoughts with behavioral techniques as a way of increasing individual self-esteem.

Figure 3

Antecedent Behaviors and Consequences:
Overt and Covert

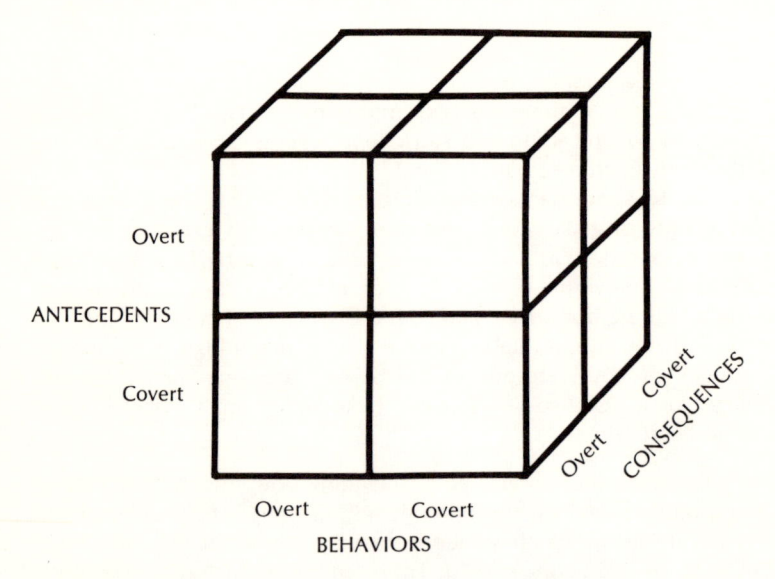

[Figure: A 3D cube diagram with axes labeled ANTECEDENTS (Overt, Covert) on the vertical side, BEHAVIORS (Overt, Covert) on the horizontal, and CONSEQUENCES (Overt, Covert) on the depth axis.]

1. An antecedent or consequent response may be positive or aversive.

2. Covert behavior may be subdivided into thoughts, images, and physiological responses.

3. Overt behavior may be viewed as verbal or non-verbal-motoric responses.

It is not yet known whether direct intervention focused on covert responses or overt responses (or both) is the more effective and efficient strategy, given a particular problem. It does seem reasonable, therefore, to pursue covert modification techniques along with overt procedures. Conceptualizing a behavioral approach from this broader overt-covert perspective should help open the door much wider towards helping individuals deal with the total experience of everyday life (Thoresen, 1971).

THE "SYSTEMS APPROACH"

The "systems approach" has evolved primarily since World War II from several areas such as general systems theory, system engineering, information theory, cybernetics, and operations research. Paradoxically a systems approach involves an elegantly simple notion and some complex procedures. The simple notion is obvious from our own experiences. Everything we do is tied in some way to many other things. Life is interactive and dynamic, not simple and unconnected. Recall how that sore thumb suddenly seems involved in everything you do. Similarly the actions of a grossly incompetent teacher can precipitate an incredible number of problems affecting the entire school. There are invariably several "chain reactions" to any one problem situation. A systems approach, therefore, acknowledges life's complexities and makes use of a variety of problem finding and problem solving techniques (Thoresen, 1969b).

What is a System?

A system is a structure which functions or operates as a whole by virtue of the interdependence of its parts (Rappaport, 1968). Two key ideas stand out in this concept of system. First, the relationships between parts of components, and secondly, the organization of these components into the whole. There are essentially two kinds of systems, natural or man-made. Examples of natural systems abound in our physical environment. The solar system stands out as a staggering example. The earth itself is a fantastically complex system, made dramatic by the ecological imbalances created by man. The short and long term systematic effects of DDT, detergents, off-shore oil drilling, are but three specific examples of how natural systems are altered by man's systems.

Man-made systems refers to those structures or organizations of components that are created by man rather than found in natural states. The current ecological crisis ranging from such things as chemical pollutants to overpopulation is in large part a confrontation between natural and man-made systems.

Open or Closed?

A system may be viewed as an open or a closed system. A system is closed if there is no input or output of energy in any of its forms, such as information, heat, sound, and movement. Many chemical reactions, for example, are closed systems, such as a highly controlled chemical reaction in a test tube. By contrast an open system is simply one in which there is an exchange of energies between components of the system and its environment. There is input and there is output. A counselor education program, therefore, is a man-made open system.

Common to most definitions of man-made systems are four characteristics: (1) objectives of the system explicitly and specifically stated in observable terms; (2) relations of parts, or components; (3) mechanisms for information flow throughout; and (4) combinations of man (manware) and machines (hardware). A systems approach involves the use of analysis and synthesis in dealing with what can be termed organized complexity. Typically involved in a systems approach is the use of simulation and conceptual models such as a flow chart (e.g., Figure 1 in this paper).

The combining of an applied social learning perspective with systems techniques is termed a behavioral systems approach (Thoresen, 1969b; Thoresen, in press). This approach is characterized as follows:

1. Behavioral objectives are stated in terms of observable trainee performances.
2. Social learning principles and hypotheses are the basis of specific counseling techniques.
3. Empirical and experimental methods are used to produce data to make training decisions about what to change, how much, and for how long.
4. Analysis and synthesis methods are used in examining existing systems and in devising new systems.
5. Cybernetic concepts and procedures such as control and feedback are employed.
6. Contemporary physical and social environments ("here and now") which control client and trainee behavior are analyzed.

STANFORD BEHAVIORAL SYSTEMS TRAINING PROGRAM

Currently at Stanford University a behavioral systems training program is under development. Consistent with basic systems theory the program is under continual modification based on the data provided by trainee performance. Figure 4 presents the major subsystems of the current training program. These subsystems became operational in September, 1970. During the first three months each trainee participated in every subsystem except the Preventive Systems and Research areas. Each trainee worked on specific tasks in each subsystem area at their own rate. Some trainees, for example, worked primarily in Foundations subsystems during the first six weeks, later shifting their efforts to the Behavior Change Methodology area. Others, however, did just the opposite, while still others worked on tasks in all of the subsystems.

A basic characteristic of the Stanford program is its competency or performance basis. Rather than assigning letter grades competitively among trainees, evaluation is instead based on each trainee providing evidence that he has successfully accomplished a specified performance. Rather than a letter grading system, there is a "pass or try-it-again" procedure. Some trainees can successfully accomplish a task the first time by meeting the criterion level while others may need more practice and different kinds of preliminary experiences.

Figure 4

Behavioral Systems Training Program

The system is divided into eight subsystems. Examples of performance areas are listed for each major subsystem.

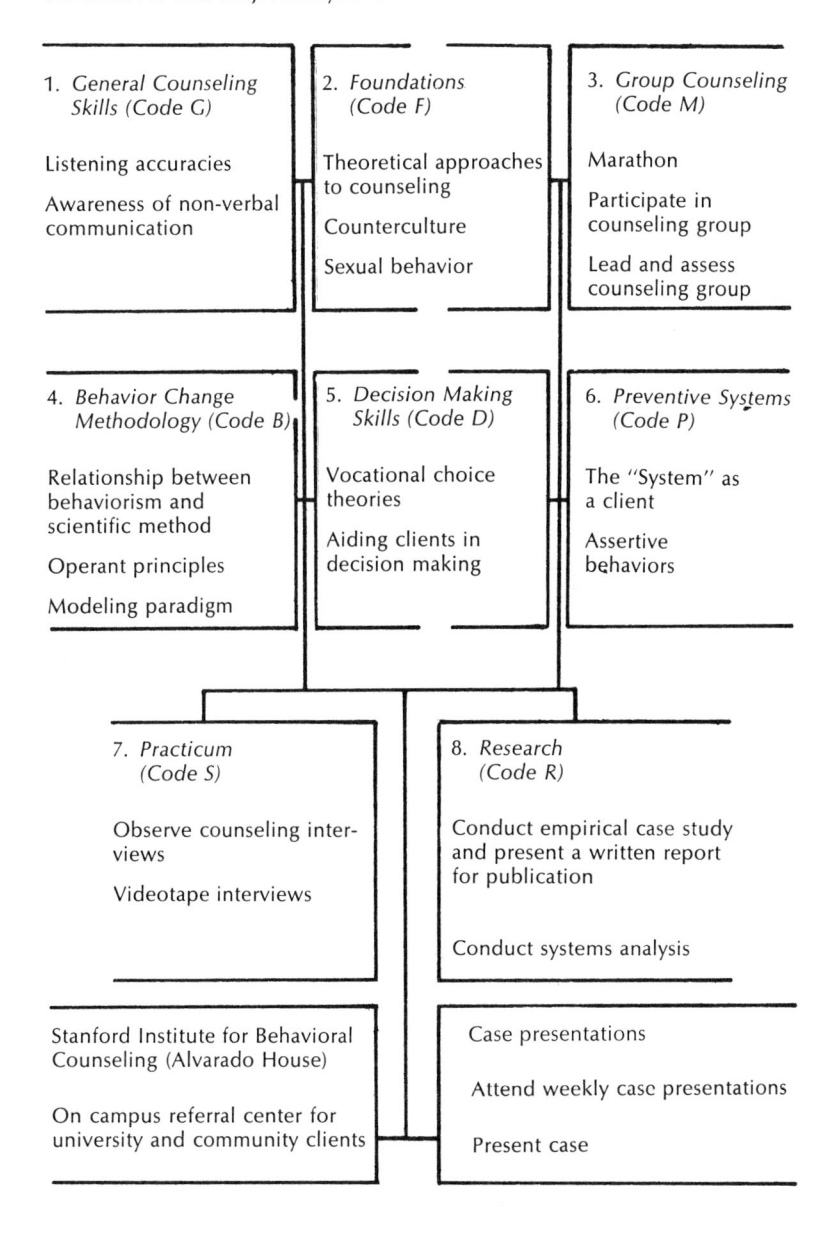

1. General Counseling Skills (Code G)

Listening accuracies

Awareness of non-verbal communication

2. Foundations (Code F)

Theoretical approaches to counseling

Counterculture

Sexual behavior

3. Group Counseling (Code M)

Marathon

Participate in counseling group

Lead and assess counseling group

4. Behavior Change Methodology (Code B)

Relationship between behaviorism and scientific method

Operant principles

Modeling paradigm

5. Decision Making Skills (Code D)

Vocational choice theories

Aiding clients in decision making

6. Preventive Systems (Code P)

The "System" as a client

Assertive behaviors

7. Practicum (Code S)

Observe counseling interviews

Videotape interviews

8. Research (Code R)

Conduct empirical case study and present a written report for publication

Conduct systems analysis

Stanford Institute for Behavioral Counseling (Alvarado House)

On campus referral center for university and community clients

Case presentations

Attend weekly case presentations

Present case

Figure 5

Stanford Behavioral System Training Program Subsystem:

Counseling in Groups
(Code M)

Describe in writing one particular problem situation in your field setting that you would like to work with, explaining how the use of counseling in a small group would be an appropriate method of intervention. Consult with supervisor.	Completed _____ (date) _____ (Monitor)	Instructor: Thoresen Approved
Explain orally to counselors, parents and/or teachers the "whats, hows, and whys" of counseling in group (max. 10 min.). Present audio tape.	Completed _____ (date) _____ (Monitor)	
Present orally the basic features of counseling groups to some potential group members, e.g., classroom group. Answer any of their questions. Present audio tape.	Completed _____ (date) _____ (Monitor)	
Conduct pre-group interview with prospective group member covering (1) responsibilities of each group member and leader, (2) metagoals, (3) individual behavioral objectives—outcomes, (4) time, place, agenda for first meeting. Present audio tape. Consult with supervisor (listen to tape).	Completed _____ (date) _____ (Monitor)	
Describe in writing the following concerning the group you plan to lead: (1) Metagoal(s) for this group. (2) Two examples or more of individual behavioral objectives. (3) Possible counseling techniques you plan to use. (4) Possible evaluation—assessment procedures you plan to use. (max. 5 pages)	Completed _____ (date) _____ (Monitor)	

Each trainee at the beginning of the program is provided with a list of performances in each of the subsystem areas. For example, Figure 5 presents the first five tasks in the group counseling subsystem. Note that each task is followed by a place for the task monitor to sign and for an approval signature. In this particular sequence the monitors were two doctoral students who assisted the instructor. In addition, a supervisory "check" was built in by having the trainee's practicum supervisor listen to tapes, read and discuss trainee writeups, and consult with the trainee on particular tasks. When the trainee had successfully performed the task the approval signature was added. In this particular subsystem the trainee was asked to complete the tasks in order of presentation, doing the first task before the second. However, in other subsystems the trainee may "skip around," selecting a particular series of tasks (e.g., systematic desensitization) and completing them at his own rate.

Figure 6 is selected from among a long series of tasks in the behavior change methodology subsystem. Note that the trainee in item 52 is asked to discuss, rather than write, the counter-conditioning and desensitization approach. But why talk about it rather than write? An analysis of what terminal behaviors a counselor would typically engage in revealed that seldom would he be asked to write about the counter-conditioning procedure. However, he may be expected to make an oral presentation or discuss counter-conditioning with a group, such as a group of parents or administrators or counseling colleagues.

Much of what goes on in typical clinical and counseling training programs has very little to do with what a counselor will be doing on the job after training. Writing term papers and taking lecture notes has little to do with the on-the-job terminal behaviors of a working counselor or therapist. A guiding principle of a behavioral systems orientation is to move as quickly as possible during training from low fidelity to high fidelity simulations of the on-the-job terminal performance. Most training experiences, therefore, emphasize use of the "modeling, guided practice, immediate feedback, and positive reinforcement" routine, i.e., show the trainee the performance, help him practice, provide corrective information on his performance and reward him for successful approximations. Figure 7 is a page taken from a training unit on systematic desensitization. Here the trainee is given a model of how to control his voice and what exercises to use in muscle relaxation. The trainee's recorded effort is reviewed by himself. In the laboratory shortly after this other trainees and a supervisor will listen to his tape.

SOME PROBLEMS AT PRESENT

Anytime one changes part of the "system" — in this case a graduate school counselor training program—a host of problems are created Three problem areas will now be described.
1. *Insufficient Feedback:* One of the important features of a systems approach, as discussed earlier, is the use of feedback mechanisms. Recall that feedback by definition is information that flows from one component into another component, changing the latter. A major problem to date has been in creating and main-

Figure 6

Stanford Behavioral System Training Program
Subsystem: Behavior Change Methodology

50. A. Submit 2 behavior control programs in any two of the following areas:
    1. Behavior acceleration with M, S, or SC.
    2. Behavior deceleration with M, S, or SC.
    3. Self-control program with log and either S or SC.
    M — Modeling
    S — Shaping
    SC — Stimulus Control
   B. Programs must be successful

    Completed
    ───────
    (date)
    ───────
    (Monitor)

52. A. Can verbalize:
    1. Understanding and conditions of application of counter-conditioning paradigm and desensitization.
    2. Critical evaluation of research methodology outcome of desensitization.
    3. Cite research studies to support 1 and 2.
    4. Complete probe on 1 and 2.
    5. Compare to OC techniques.
    Resources:
    1. Bandura — Chap. 7; Wolpe — gen.
    2. Franks — Chapters 2 & 3, 6, 7.
    3. Open + Yates
    4.
    5. Franks — Chapters 1-11.

    Completed
    ───────
    (date)
    ───────
    (Monitor)

53. A. Verbalize paradigm and implementing of relaxation exercises.
    B. Submit a tape substantiating mastery of the technique.
    Resources:
    A. Wolpe — Chapter 8,
       Rosenberg — various tapes at SIBC

    Completed
    ───────
    (date)
    ───────
    (Monitor)

54. A. Construct a desensitization hierarchy for a spontaneously specified problem.
    Resources:
    Open

    Completed
    ───────
    (date)
    ───────
    (Monitor)

taining effective feedback mechanisms in the training system. Feedback procedures can be viewed from a small to very large perspective. For example, feedback can be a very specific flow of information used in teaching a specific skill, such as eye

Figure 7

Behavioral System Training Program
Stanford University

Subsystem: Behavior Change Methodology
Systematic Desensitization

Homework for Unit One

Your homework for this unit consists of two parts.

Part I is designed to help you become more familiar with relaxation training. You will need to do three things.

1. Listen to the tape by A. Lazarus on deep muscle relaxation. Analyze the content and listen to his voice quality.

2. Listen to the same tape and let yourself go. Enjoy the experience of deep muscle relaxation.

3. On the blank part (last part) of this same side, record your own voice. Attempt to make it as soothing and relaxing as possible. Go through part of the deep muscle relaxation instructions. You should repeat this until you are satisfied with the results.

Part II is designed to give you practice in hierarchy construction.

On side two of the tape there is an interview from which you can construct an anxiety hierarchy. After listening to the interview and constructing your hierarchy you should play the remainder of the tape and compare your hierarchy with the hierarchy constructed by the counselor who made the tape. If you have difficulty, you may go back and replay parts of the interview, but do not play the remainder until you have your own hierarchy completed.

---

contact during interviews. Or feedback can be viewed as the flow of different kinds of information from former trainees (and their supervisors) who are working full-time.

To date there has not been a sufficient variety of feedback mechanisms throughout the training system. The keeping of daily behavioral logs by trainees was one procedure tried this past year. A senior staff member monitored the logs on a weekly basis. However, it proved difficult to use the data to make changes since there was such variability in the reported experiences of each trainee.

Field coordinators, who were full-time counselors or psychologists from the various field settings where trainees were placed, were expected to provide data on trainee performance. However, their information was typically not concrete enough to use it in changing the training system.

What may be termed "data transmission" has proved to be a major obstacle. How can information about different performance of a trainee be transmitted in a form appropriate for use as feedback? Information was used as feedback on trainee performance *within* a particular training sequence. For example, trainees listened and rated excerpts of counseling interviews. Trainees with high error rates were recycled through the tape listening experiences.

In the group counseling subsystem a preliminary exercise in establishing behavioral objectives within a group setting provided data that over seventy-five percent of the trainees incorrectly established behavioral objectives. This data is being used to revise the behavioral objectives subsystem for the coming year. However, the data was provided too late to change the behavioral objectives subsystem, since trainees had already completed it before starting the group counseling sequence.

2. *Synthesizing Subsystems:* The problem of insufficient feedback relates closely to problems of integration between subsystems. The natural tendency, given the social learning history of students (and faculty!), is to act as if each subsystem area was a separate course. This past year revealed the "demand" of trainees to reshape the training system to fit more comfortably their learning history. Trainees would typically respond to a staff member as if he were teaching one of the courses. The fact that certain times and places were set for particular training experiences (e.g., basic counseling skills) inadvertently encouraged trainees to view them more as discrete courses. Staff behavior also reinforced this view in such ways as having certain senior staff monitor a particular competency area.

Currently, the monitoring and system sequence is under major revision. The major effort is to identify particular tasks *across* all subsystem areas that relate in terms of performance. Learning how to establish behavioral objectives with clients provides an example. Rather than separating this task and dealing with it independently in subsystem areas (e.g., group counseling, preventive systems, decision making), the skills of establishing behavioral objectives in all areas will be learned concurrently. Another modification to foster synthesis will involve having the senior staff monitor in all subsystem areas.

The most significant change will involve the practicum and Stanford Institute for Behavioral Counseling (SIBC). Data gathered this year clearly demonstrated major problems for trainees in using the SIBC and field practicum setting. The generalization or transfer of a training problem was considerable in that trainees did not have sufficient control of the practicum environment to use counseling skills. The "hours spent" conception of field work, dictated by tradition and credential requirements, was inconsistent with a performance, competence-based experience. Currently a problem centered performance-based practicum is under development.[2] A team will be employed that consists of 6 to 8 trainees and staff members who are "expert" on a general problem area, e.g., classroom management, marital-family counseling, drug abuse. New trainees will assume minor responsibilities, spending considerable time, at first, observing the performance of more skilled trainees and staff. Later, the beginning trainee will work as a co-counselor and finally, depending on performance, will assume major responsibilities for a particular problem situation.

SIBC, the on-campus referral center, and the practicum will be integrated in that all teams will be based at SIBC. The intervention team will move into a problem environment after a request for assistance has been received. For example, a local high school concerned about drug problems would request help. A team would then work together as a unit in conducting the necessary assessments in order to determine what type of intervention might be most effective and efficient.

The task of synthesizing and integrating all of the training components of the total system are great. However, it is quite possible to solve synthesis problems if one is open to a training system that is always temporary and tentative, and open to changing the system based on trainee performance data.

3. *Inadequate Modeling and Reinforcement:* The effectiveness of providing immediate, positive consequences contingent on certain actions of learner has been well documented. Less well recognized is the power of using social modeling to teach new behaviors, especially complex behaviors, as well as to eliminate fears and anxieties (disinhibit behavior). The combination of using social modeling and positive consequences contingently, i.e., showing the learner, letting him rehearse what was observed, and positively reinforcing his successive approximations of the modeled performance is an extremely powerful learning strategy (Bandura, 1969).

Unfortunately, not enough use has been made in the Stanford system of the modeling-reinforcement strategy. An analysis of trainee behavior this year suggests that trainees may have spent relatively too much time reading traditional text-

---

[2]Additional information on this practicum approach is available upon request from the author.

books and writing and not enough time observing modeled performances and practicing. The strong and compelling tradition of reading and writing behavior as *the* mode of learning is difficult to change. (This is especially true for university professors!) The question here has to do with mode of instruction as well as content. While it may be argued that learning about theoretical concepts and explanations requires reading, the necessary understanding may be acquired by observing others talk about these concepts. Further, programmed text formats (e.g., Holland and Skinner text on *The Analysis of Behavior*) may also provide for more pinpointed, efficient reading.

Questions can be raised about the relevance of having trainees respond in writing to many tasks. Some writing skills, of course, are essential for any professional person. But the issue here has to do with how much writing behavior is required of the trainee and whether writing is the most effective and efficient mode of response. Trainees are very comfortable and accustomed to writing — as are their professors. Preliminary data from this year points to an excessive use of writing.

Currently, work is underway to examine how more use can be made of modeling and reinforced practice. Trainees this year reported the need for an increase in the systematic use of contingent positive consequences. The system in their words was "too damn lean" in positive reinforcement. Consideration is now being given to the use of a behavioral contract procedure wherein the trainee indicates the desired consequation from a "menu" of available events and things. In this way trainee reinforcement can be individually tailored.

TO CONCLUDE

The behavioral counselor is, in effect, an applied scientist who attempts to tailor his actions to the particular situation and circumstances of the client. The focus on being empirical, on behavior principles, and looking especially to the "here and now" environment provides the counselor with a powerful strategy for helping individuals. Behavior is viewed as including covert or internal responses as well as external responses. The counselor's prime responsibility is to help the client change his behavior in desired directions. Counselor competence is conceived and assessed by change in what clients do.

The Stanford Behavioral Systems Training Program represents one way of training behavioral counselors. The basic principles of systems theory and techniques have been combined with behavioral concepts to create a competency-based, performance training system. Characteristic of any systems based program, the Stanford system is under continuous development. Several problems have been identified in the current system such as problems of feedback, integration of subsystems, and insufficient modeling and reinforcement procedures.

REFERENCES

Bandura, A. *Principles of behavior modification.* New York: Holt, Rinehart and Winston, 1969.

Buhler, C. Basic theoretical concepts of humanistic psychology. *American Psychologist,* 1971, 26, 378-386.

Cautela, J. Covert reinforcement. *Behavior Therapy,* 1970, 1, 33-50.

Chassan, J. D. *Research in psychiatry and clinical psychology.* New York: Appleton-Century-Crofts, 1966.

Hannum, J. Improving a teacher's self-concept: A behavioral approach. Stanford University, unpublished manuscript, 1971.

Kanfer, F. H. and Phillips, J. S. *Learning foundations of behavior therapy.* New York: Wiley, 1970.

Krumboltz, J. D. and Thoresen, C. E. *Behavioral counseling: Cases and techniques.* New York: Holt, Rinehart and Winston, 1969.

Mahoney, M. J. Toward an experimental analysis of coverant control *Behavior Therapy,* 1970, 1, 510-521.

Mahoney, M. J. The self-management of covert behaviors: A case study. *Behavior Therapy,* in press.

Mahoney, M. J., Thoresen, C. E., and Danaher, G. B. Covert behavior modification: An experimental analogue. Stanford University, unpublished manuscript, 1971.

Rappaport, A. The promise and pitfalls of information theory. In W. Buckley (Ed.), *Modern systems research for the behavioral scientist.* Chicago: Aldine, 1968. Pp. 137-142.

Skinner, B. F. Behaviorism at fifty. *Science,* 1963, 140, 951-958.

Thoresen, C. E. The counselor as an applied behavioral scientists. *Personnel and Guidance Journal,* 1969, 42, 841-848 (a).

Thoresen, C. E. The systems approach and counselor education: Basic features and implications. *Counselor Education and Supervision,* 1969, 9, 3-17 (b).

Thoresen, C. E. The case for the empirical case approach in counseling. Paper presented at meeting of American Educational Research Association. Minneapolis, 1970.

Thoresen, C. E. Behavioral humanism: A direction for counseling research. Paper presented at American Educational Research Association. New York, 1971.

Thoresen, C. E. Behavioral systems approach to counselor education. In A. Buckheimer (Ed.), *Counselor education models for the seventies.* New York: The City University of New York, in press.

Yates, A. *Behavior therapy.* New York: Wiley, 1970.

Teaching Operant Conditioning to Psychiatric Nurses, Aids, and Attendants[1]

Garry L. Martin

INTRODUCTION

During the past five years operant conditioning programs have produced dramatic improvements in the behavior of the retarded, especially at the severe and profound levels. Interest in this area is growing rapidly and numerous institutions are adopting this approach (compare Watson, 1967, to Gardner and Watson, 1969).

Three years ago the author was asked by G. H. Lowther, the very progressive Medical Superintendent at the Manitoba School for Retardates,[2] to initiate an operant program with a group of thirty severely retarded girls. The success of that program led Dr. Lowther to strongly endorse operant conditioning as the appropriate methodology for training the severely and profoundly retarded (Lowther, 1970, 1971). Consequently the institution is currently being programmed so that the (approximately) seven hundred severe and profound retardates in residence will be trained on operant programs. The purpose of the present paper is to describe some of our attempts (successful and unsuccessful) at training psychiatric nurses, nurse aids, and nurse attendants to function as behavior modifiers within the context of the operant training programs that are being developed and extended.

The initial project with the thirty severely retarded girls began in July, 1968, when the girls were moved to Cedar Cottage, a new self-contained cottage unit designed for thirty residents. Four psychiatric nurses and six nurse aids were assigned to the cottage to cover the shifts from seven-thirty in the morning to eleven-thirty at night. In addition, three undergraduate psychology majors who had worked on a behavior modification program with autistic children during the previous year (Martin, England, Kaprowy, Kilgour, and Pilek, 1968; Martin and Pear, 1970) were assigned to work with the nurses and aids in the cottage to help set up the operant program.

By the end of September of that first summer, the students returned to the university; the regular staff became quite proficient behavior modifiers; the children showed remarkable change in a

---

[1]Preparation of this paper was supported in part by Canadian Medical Research Council Grant No. MA 3636.

[2]The Manitoba School for Retardates is the residential school for retardates in the Province of Manitoba, Canada.

variety of ways; and the Medical Superintendent stated publicly that the children had made more progress in three months than they had during their entire previous time in the institution. It appeared that the success of the summer program was the big selling point of operant conditioning at the Manitoba Training School. The administration is currently committed to training all the staff in behavior modification procedures. Thus far, ninety-five of the nurses and nurse aids have been exposed to some form of a training program. The staff has been taught in groups of seven to twenty at a time, and has been exposed to several variations in training conditions. Consequently, we are now in a position to make at least some tentative suggestions as to what produces good behavior modifiers and what doesn't. In addition, since the Cedar project has been in operation now for almost three years, we have examined some of the variables that are responsible for maintaining staff performance over a long term. Others have previously recognized the significance of concern for maintaining performance of staff who deal with the retarded (Keith and Wallace, 1970; Panyan, Boozer, and Morris, 1970; Roberts and Perry, 1970). That is, it's one thing to train staff to be good behavior modifiers with respect to one or two short-term projects; it's quite another thing to set up conditions to maintain good performance when the staff is required to monitor and modify many behaviors of all the residents on a ward throughout the working shift of the particular staff members involved for months at a time.

Consequently, the remainder of this paper is devoted to a discussion of: (1) the staff training programs for behavior modifiers at the Manitoba School; (2) problems and programs regarding the maintenance of desirable staff performance as behavior modifiers with severe retardates over a long term; (3) some future proposals for solving the staff behavior maintenance problem (and revolutionizing the civil service).

STAFF TRAINING IN OPERANT CONDITIONING AT THE MANITOBA SCHOOL

Staff training at the Manitoba School began in the summer of 1968, with the staff of Cedar Cottage. The training program for both staff and residents there has proved exceptionally successful. Following the initial summer program in which the Cedar staff was trained, several additional training programs for staff on other wards were initiated; some of these were successful, and some of these were not successful. The various steps of the training programs are outlined in Appendix I.

Staff Training Program at Cedar Cottage

The Cedar staff was exposed to steps 1, 2, 3, 5, and 6 as outlined in Appendix I. The first step occupied the first two or three days after the opening of the cottage. The remaining steps (2, 3, 5, and 6) were carried on simultaneously during the first five weeks of the program. It should be kept in mind that specific training procedures were written up prior to the start of the program, and, although modified as the program progressed, these written procedures enabled the staff to carry on their regular duties as well as participate in the training program. The only time-off allowed was that necessary to attend the lectures and discussions.

Teaching staff to specify behavior precisely, and to record and graph behavior. The staff was first given instructions in identifying and specifying behaviors (such as a child's eating behavior in the dining room) of residents precisely, and recording those behaviors so that inter-observer agreement could be achieved. Sometimes the behavior that occurred was simply rated. For example, to the instructions "Put on your sweater," a child might respond within a given time limit with no physical or verbal prompts or physical guidance (rating of 1), with verbal prompts only (rating of 2), with verbal prompts and some physical prompts (rating of 3), or with verbal prompts, physical prompts, and physical guidance (rating of 4). Each staff member would, in turn, define specific behaviors or specify how the behaviors would be rated. That staff and the author would then attempt to count or rate the behavior and compare counts. Appropriate feedback followed on a minimum of 5 or 6 definitional attempts.

Teaching staff basic concepts through lectures, discussions, and reading assignments, with study questions and examinations. The staff was supplied with a specially prepared paper describing the fundamentals of operant conditioning as applied to training the mentally retarded (Martin, 1968). The paper outlined some of the major concepts, such as positive reinforcement, negative reinforcement, escape conditioning, avoidance conditioning, shaping, chaining, fading, and provided examples for each concept taken from observations around the institution. Two additional papers were also provided, which described some of the moral and ethical issues involved in the application of operant techniques (Ball, 1968; Vogler and Martin, 1969). In addition, the staff was given a set of study questions designed to guide their reading of the three papers (see Appendix II). These questions were also used to assess the written repertoire of the staff, and to assess whether they could apply the concepts to situations commonly observed around the ward. Some lectures and discussions were also held to clarify various aspects of the reading material and/or the study questions. The study questions were divided into five different exams covering five different sections of the reading materials, and each exam sampled the appropriate set of questions. Each staff member was required to take each exam (and if necessary, to retake an alternate form of the exam), until he passed each exam with at least a seventy percent correct performance.

In addition, handouts were provided which described a variety of plausible situations, responses of residents, typical consequences of those responses, and the long term effects of the situation-response-consequence contingencies (see Appendix III).

Demonstrating proper procedures to staff. The staff was given demonstrations as to how to interact with the children in a variety of ward situations, and how to carry out individual training sessions in the development of various self-care skills. For example, the staff was instructed that an optimal reinforcer for resident behavior consisted of the staff member smiling, presenting enthusiastic verbal praise, physically contacting the child (such as hugging or patting the child), and presenting some tangible reinforcing event such as a token that could later be redeemed, or a piece of candy. The desirable and undesirable ways of administering reinforcement were then demonstrated in a variety of situations.

Structuring the environment.[3] Specific programs were designed for each of the tasks to be worked on, such as grooming, dressing, dining room procedures, and procedures regarding the time-out room (Martin, Kehoe, Bird, Jensen, and Darbyshire, in press; Treffry, Martin, Samels, and Watson, 1970). Where appropriate, the rules and data sheets were posted in their proper locations (a sample of the rules posted in the dining room can be seen in Appendix IV).

Additional structuring of the environment for the staff included the introduction of various stimulus lights which signaled that certain desired behaviors should occur. For example, at coffee times, the children were required to sit quietly on the sofas and chairs around the TV room while the staff sat around a table in the middle of the room and drank their coffee. It was suggested to the staff that if they ignored undesirable behavior (such as hand-waving) and simultaneously punished other undesirable behaviors (such as wandering around the TV room and making excessive noise) by placing the children in the time-out room, and in addition, if the staff left the coffee table and socially reinforced the children who were quiet, it would not take long to condition the children to sit quietly during the coffee breaks. The difficulty was that it was somewhat aversive to the staff to leave their table and administer either social reinforcement to the residents for sitting quietly or time-out punishment for being exceptionally noisy or unruly. Therefore a distinctive green light was introduced in the TV room, with a timer attached to it, and on several coffee breaks, it was announced to the staff that we would try to develop the green light as a distinctive cue to the children for sitting quietly. In addition, it was hoped that the green light would become a distinctive cue to the staff for administering proper reinforcement contingencies. At the start of a coffee break a nurse would announce "Okay kids, the light is on; sit down and be

---

[3]Step 4 as listed in Appendix I was not applied to training the Cedar staff and this step will be discussed later.

quiet." Whenever the light was on, the residents who sat quietly were reinforced by the staff with praise, tokens, and/or candy. However, if the residents moved about or were noisy, they were immediately removed to the time-out room for a period of ten minutes of isolation. In addition, the author intermittently attended coffee breaks and supplied reinforcement and encouragement to staff members who responded appropriately with respect to the children when the green light was on. As a consequence, after several weeks of this procedure, the green light became a distinctive cue for appropriate behavior for both the children and the staff, and came to exert strong stimulus control over the children's behavior. The strength of the control of the stimulus light over the children's behavior was unknowingly tested by a staff member one night during the evening meal. On this occasion, the residents were particularly noisy. Becoming frustrated with the situation, one of the nurses decided to bring in the green light from the TV room. When the light was turned on, not only did the residents immediately become quiet in the dining room, but also the six residents who were being trained to serve the other children immediately sat down and refused to serve the remainder of the meal until the light was turned off.

In this way it is possible and desirable to make minor changes in the environmental setting in order to provide distinctive cues to control both the residents' behavior and the staff's behavior. It is essential, however, that appropriate consequences for desirable staff behavior in the presence of the distinctive cues be properly programmed.

A final example of presenting distinctive cues to staff can be seen in the behavioral assessment form shown in Appendix V. We have recently become concerned with applying a behavior rating scale to assess the performance of individual staff members after various amounts of training. The form in Appendix V was developed for just that purpose and the results of its use are described in a separate paper (Lowther, Martin, McDonald, 1971.)[4] With respect to presenting cues to the staff the form also serves as an excellent guide as to what is expected. The form is made available to the staff prior to sessions, and the staff is asked to perform appropriately with respect to the various categories outlined on the form. Each category is in turn explained in some detail in an additional handout.

Requiring staff to emit desired behaviors and supplying appropriate feedback. The staff was given both positive and negative feedback with respect to their performance in individual sessions and on the ward. For example, if a staff member socially reinforced a self-destructive child for sitting quietly rather than for slapping herself, then that staff member would receive comments from the author and/or from

---

[4]A similar approach to behavioral assessment of staff was recently described by Gardner, Brust, and Watson (1970).

the university students. If staff responded inappropriately, they would receive negative comments, and, if necessary, an additional demonstration. In our experience this type of feedback was necessary for both individual training sessions in which a nurse worked with a single child, as well as on ward situations. Some of the staff often performed well in one situation, but not well in another.

At the end of three months, the staff had progressed to the point where the four psychiatric nurses and the six nurse aids carried on individual training sessions in the morning and in the afternoon during spare hours; they conducted dressing sessions, grooming sessions, dining room procedures, and bathing procedures following prescribed programs at appropriate times throughout the day; they took data where appropriate and where instructed to do so, and they reported individual behavior problems and discussed them in behavioral language during weekly staff meetings so that some form of behavioral solution could be presented; they gave tours to visitors and described the procedures in reasonable behavioral language, and they communicated effectively with the university students with respect to basic operant conditioning procedures and techniques (Martin, 1970; Martin and Hughes, 1970).

Unsuccessful Approaches to Staff Training

Following the initial success of the Cedar project, the author, at the request of the Medical Superintendent, established two different inservice training programs. Both programs involved something less than the training sequence for the Cedar staff, and neither program was very successful in terms of influencing staff to utilize operant techniques.

For the first program, two different groups of psychiatric nurses were exposed to steps 1 and 2 as described in Appendix I. These nurses were from seven different wards. On two occasions, approximately one week and one month following the completion of step 2, the nurses were assessed regarding their application of the operant procedures discussed in steps 1 and 2. Each staff member was assessed in terms of four mutually exclusive categories:

1. Staff participated in a ward program in which at least 10% of the residents were given individual training sessions using operant procedures, session data were recorded as described in step 1, and ward rules were posted for at least one room on the ward.
2. Staff applied operant procedures to treat at least one behavior problem of a resident, persisted in the application until the problem was solved or for at least five days, and kept daily data on the problem behavior.
3. Staff reported using operant procedures but did not keep data.

4. Staff did not attempt to apply operant procedures on the ward.

For the second program, four different groups of nurses were exposed to steps 1, 2, 3, and 4 of Appendix I. Step 3 required the trainees to observe the procedures at Cedar Cottage for a two-day period. Step 4 required the nurses to do at least one behavior modification project on their own. That is, they were required to take one subject and to modify that subject's behavior in some small way. This involved taking a baseline on some behavior, such as the subject's shoelacing behavior, describing a program to develop that behavior, and then conducting a minimum of ten sessions in an effort to change the behavior in a desired way. At least three of those sessions were supervised by the author, one of the Cedar staff, or by somebody who was skilled in the application of operant conditioning techniques. One week and one month following the completion of steps 1, 2, 3, and 4, the nurses were assessed regarding their application of operant techniques as described above. The results of these programs can be seen in Table I.

Neither program was particularly successful. That is not to say that our efforts at training were entirely wasted. One of the problems in developing operant programs at an institution is that of overcoming resistance of staff who have been dealing with the severely retarded in a set way over a given period of time. If nothing else, the above three attempts at teaching operant conditioning led to an apparent change in attitude of many of the staff (as assessed by questionnaire data). Many were more receptive to what the Cedar staff were doing, and were willing to accept the behavior modification approach at Cedar as a bona fide and legitimate approach to the training of the severely retarded. However, as far as changing their own behavior back on their own ward was concerned, that behavior was changed little or not at all.

Additional Successful Training Programs

During the past year, two additional programs have been successfully established and maintained. One program involved a group of seven staff and twenty-six severely retarded teenage boys. The second program involved six staff and fifteen severely and profoundly retarded teenage girls. The staff on both programs were trained according to steps 1, 2, 3, 5, and 6 as described in Appendix I. However, it is noteworthy that on both programs, the individuals involved in training the staff members on steps 3, 5, and 6 were psychiatric nurses who had undergone previous training at Cedar Cottage. The author was involved in steps 1 and 2, and provided only minimal consultation thereafter.

Table I

Summary of training of psychiatric nurses, aids, and attendants and their subsequent application of operant conditioning procedures at the Manitoba School.

No. of Staff Receiving Training	Training Steps Completed	No. of staff who applied operant conditioning to a ward program
32	1, 2	0
32	1,2,3,4	11
31	1,2,3,5,6	31

No. of staff who applied operant conditioning to individual behavior problems and took data	No. of staff who reportedly applied operant conditioning to individual behavior problems but did not take data	No. of staff who did not attempt to apply operant conditioning
1	6	25
1	3	17
0	0	0

A Minimal Training Program

On the basis of our experiences thus far, we propose that a minimal training program should include steps 1, 2, 3, 5, and 6 as outlined in Appendix I and as described above. With respect to step 2, teaching basic concepts and theory, we suggest that proficiency of the language be developed through the use of study questions and examinations; however, films, tapes, and perhaps a variety of other ways of presenting information could be utilized.

Although staff could be trained to manage behavior precisely without becoming fluent in the phraseology, it seems advantageous to have at least the psychiatric nurses fluent in the terminology that's germane to the procedures for several reasons: (a) it appears to contribute to precise communication concerning residents and presumably increases the probability of reading new literature such as that found in the *Journal of Applied Behavior Analysis;* (b) it's valuable in giving tours to informed as well as uninformed audiences, and in answering questions as to the rationale for certain procedures; (c) intuitively, it seems that knowledge of the basic principles helps in developing new procedures based on the principles. For example, the staff is taught to discuss the basic features of the backward chaining procedure, and its use in teaching bedmaking and dressing with certain clothing items. Following this training it was observed that the staff developed their own procedures using the chaining technique to teach children to brush their teeth and to eat with a spoon. Finally, certain reinforcers (such as attending the Banff Conference) can be dispensed contingent upon adequate background preparation.

In summary then, to appropriately train staff for a ward of twenty to thirty residents, it has been necessary to have at least one individual who has at least three-quarters of his working time assigned to training new staff members at various stages, setting up training programs, assigning individual sessions with respect to residents and staff, and structuring the ward environment to produce optimal behavior from both staff and residents. This individual is typically involved in training the staff for a three to five week period. The staff being trained is exposed to a minimum of ten hours of lectures, many demonstrations and examples, and a minimum of three to five weeks of full participation in an operant program. These conditions have enabled us to train psychiatric nurses and nurse aids to reliably initiate and/or perform in an operant program, at least in training the severely retarded. It appears that lectures and discussions and examinations alone, even when coupled with an assignment involving the completion of one behavior modification project, is not enough to generate persistent desirable behavior in people being trained in behavior modification. This suggestion undoubtedly has implications for the typical sort of "inservice training" involving a few lectures, and sometimes a film or two. In short, it is our experience that it is necessary to expend extensive time and energy conditioning the staff to condition the residents.

MAINTAINING STAFF BEHAVIOR IN AN OPERANT PROGRAM OVER A LONG PERIOD OF TIME

The conditions responsible for inducing staff members to participate in training programs are usually quite different from the conditions that are in effect after the training program has been completed. Concerning staff participation in the initial training programs, and during initial stages of ward programs, it seems that at least the following variables were operative at the Manitoba School. First, the Medical Superintendent of the institution publicly applauded operant techniques and asked for interested volunteers to learn about operant conditioning. Second, the training programs usually involved visiting Cedar Cottage, a brand new ward, to observe the procedures there, and this was usually reinforcing for many of the staff. Third, nurse aids working at a nurse aid I level, were informed that they could advance to a nurse aid II by passing the exams and by participating successfully in the operant program for six months. This meant a slight increase in their wages. Fourth, there were usually pleasant social contingencies in effect for those participating in initial aspects of training programs, such as pleasant interaction with the university students, time off work to attend lectures, and the occasional free beer from the author. Fifth, the residents usually showed much improvement during the first three or four months of a new program, and this was reinforcing for many of the staff.

After several months of a new program, however, conditions change, and the enthusiasm of the staff typically tapers off. This can be attributed to several factors. First, with the severely retarded, after their high-frequency undesirable behaviors have been decreased and the behaviors currently in their repertoire have been increased, the problem is one of developing extensive self-care skills such as dressing, grooming, work skills, and so forth, and these are developed much more slowly. Therefore, one of the staff reinforcers, namely, the improvement of the children, is not nearly so great. Second, when one attempts to conduct a program with thirty residents, it's impossible to graph all behaviors of all residents that you would like to change. It, therefore, becomes necessary to develop some system of testing the children periodically, such as weekly or monthly, in order to assess behavioral change. However, this again removes one of the staff reinforcers, namely, the observation of the daily feedback of the changes in the child's graph. Third, some of the staff members are simply not reinforced by gross changes in the residents' behavior, let alone small changes (this point has been made by Patterson, 1969, with respect to training parents). Fourth, as the novelty of the new program wears off, and in the absence of specific contingencies to the contrary, competing staff activities often begin to interfere with the discussion of interest in the program itself. Fifth, it usually requires much more work and effort to try to maintain a program than to simply perform various tasks for the children. That is, it's much easier and much quicker for a nurse to dress a group of severely retarded children than for that nurse to sit and reinforce successive approximations to self-dressing. Finally, the staff must continually monitor their own behavior throughout the ward to make sure that when they attend to a child at any time, the attention is contingent upon desirable behavior. During staff training an observer, such as the author, is usually present to reinforce trainees for appropriately monitoring their own behavior. However, when this reinforcement is no longer coming, the self-monitoring behaviors are likely to deteriorate.

Other writers have recognized that the performance of trainers of the severely retarded might require special reinforcers. Panyan, et al. (1970) were able to effectively maintain trainer behavior through weekly feedback sheets to publicly draw attention to the performance of attendants. We have recently extended this approach at Cedar Cottage.

First, we designed the shifts so that all staff were present on Wednesdays, and we specified a particular period of time that could be used for the Wednesday meetings. At the Wednesday meetings: (a) each staff member is given specific assignments with respect to reporting the results of the use of the time-out room for the previous week; (b) individual assignments are given for reporting progress in grooming and dressing sessions; (c) some time is devoted to discussing individual ward problems, and procedures are outlined to deal with particular recurring behavior problems that appear on the ward that don't seem to be affected by the time-out room. Examples of such recurring problems: one resident was consistently and cleverly stealing food from the dining room; another resident was consistently self-destructive (see Martin and Treffry, 1970). The Wednesday meetings provide the author with the opportunity to show a great deal of enthusiasm for any and all staff members with respect to their performance during the week. It also provides an opportunity to dispense additional reinforcers, such as announcements of staff parties, special favors, or reports of favorable comments from visitors. Although the Wednesday meetings were valuable in many respects, they did not satisfactorily maintain staff performance during the week. As examples, the sessions would not always start on time and the coffee breaks frequently lasted too long. Although the psychiatric nurse in charge of the cottage was instructed to make an attempt to start sessions on time and to finish sessions on time, the psychiatric nurse is also influenced by the other staff, and by the contingencies controlling the other staff. When sessions were completed, the children progressed, albeit slowly. The problem was, therefore, one of maintaining the rather tedious behavior of persisting in resident training by staff. After checking the actual number of sessions that were possible, and the percentage of potential sessions that were completed over a two-month period, we instituted the assignment sheet shown in Appendix VI. This sheet was designed to function as follows. Each morning the psychiatric nurse in charge, at the morning coffee break, would complete the assignment sheet so that the topic of conversation at coffee break would be the assignment sheet for the day. Each staff member was given specific assignments, and if sessions were not completed the reasons were indicated. Although using aversive control to some extent, this provided an opportunity for the author to check on sessions that were not completed, and also to dispense a good deal of approval at the Wednesday meetings for assignments that were completed. As can be seen

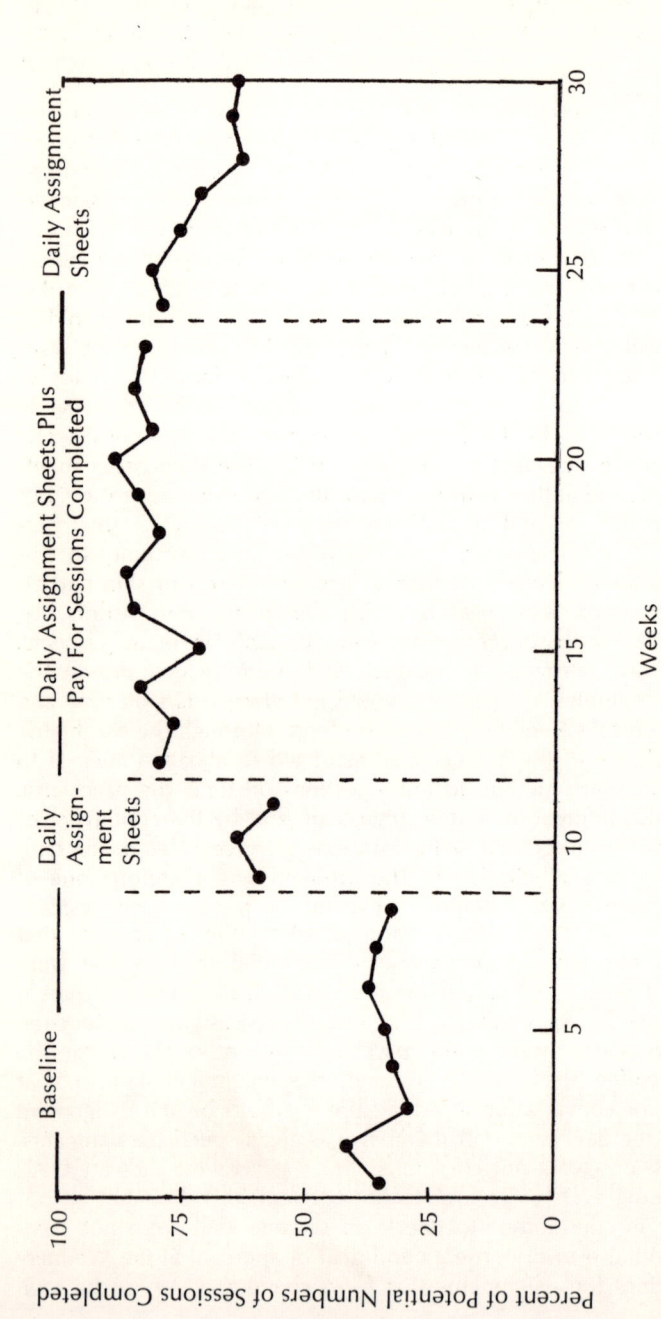

Figure 1. Percent of potential number of training sessions completed by Cedar Cottage staff during several conditions. Each entry represents the average percentage of potential number of sessions completed per week with training time allotted on six days of each week.

in Figure 1, the assignment sheet alone improved the average percentage of sessions completed from day to day. After observing the influence of the assignment sheet for a three-week period, the following additional group contingency was introduced. On days that 100% of the sessions were completed, five dollars were placed in a staff party fund; on days that greater than 75% of the sessions were completed, two dollars were placed in the fund; on days when less than 45% of the sessions were completed, two dollars were taken out of the fund. This program was initiated on October 7, 1970, and lasted until January 7, 1971, when the author ran out of money. The staff used the money for a New Year's Bash.

Running out of money necessarily enforced a reversal to previous conditions, the results of which can be seen in Figure 1. Over January and February, the results decreased to their "pre-money" level. During February, several new, group-training programs were initiated on alternate days with individual sessions. The daily session assignments are still completed on days when individual sessions are still in effect. The recent results of the reversal can be seen in Figure 1.

Although the individual session assignments and the money contingencies have not been in effect for an extensive period of time, we are encouraged by their influence thus far.

FUTURE CONSIDERATIONS

We are presently considering and planning two additional solutions to the problem of maintaining staff performance. One solution involves effective programming of schedules of reinforcement. That is, consider a suggestion proposed by Skinner in his recent book, *Contingencies of reinforcement: A theoretical analysis*:

> Consider a room full of people playing Bingo. The players sit quietly for many hours. They listen with great care as numbers and letters are called out. They arrange markers on cards rapidly and accurately, and they respond instantly when a particular pattern has been completed. What would industry not give for workers who behaved in that way. And what would workers not give for work that absorbed them so completely.

Recently, we began to take this suggestion seriously, and we asked the staff members which of three alternatives they would prefer: either (1) continuing on the group money contingency previously described, and earning a maximum of $50.00 per month towards the staff party fund (ten staff are involved); or (2) being individually paid for sessions completed, and earning a possible maximum $5.00 each per month; or (3) having the opportunity to win one $50.00 bill each month in a Bingo game. All ten staff, without exception, chose the Bingo game, although the rules of the game were not clearly spelled out to them. Although we have not yet worked out all the details of the proposal, we anticipate that our initial "Bingo game" will proceed in this way. At the beginning of each month, all staff members will be issued a Bingo card, with all of the squares of the Bingo card covered by tape. Each time a staff member meets various conditions during the daily work schedule, then that staff member will be allowed to remove the tape from one of the squares of the Bingo card. When the staff member has all the tape removed from the Bingo card, she can then draw a number from an urn of Bingo numbers each time that she meets the specified conditions during the working day. At the end of the month, a set number of additional numbers will be drawn. If nobody wins the game then everybody starts over and the jackpot is increased to $100.00. It will be to each staff member's individual advantage to have the tape off all the squares, and to have earned several of the numbers toward completing the covering of her Bingo card by the end of the month. All games will be a complete blackout (all numbers must be covered on the Bingo card).

With respect to criteria for earning tape removals and numbers, the conditions will be structured such that it's highly unlikely that any one individual will earn the $50.00 prior to the end of the month. However, it will also be structured such that staff members can make good gains towards completing their blackout game as the end of the month draws near. Conditions for earning tape removals and numbers will consist of completing the assigned sessions during the day, performing appropriately during five random checks made by the psychiatric nurse with respect to ward procedures during the day (one tape removal or draw per check), and finally, improvement in child performance. Again, our Bingo game is not yet in effect, but we recently outlined it roughly to the staff members who will be involved, and all have voiced extreme enthusiasm for at least the general idea. Several staff asked if they would be allowed to earn additional numbers for skipping coffee breaks, coming early, or staying late after work to do additional sessions.

It seems that it would be extremely desirable if, over and above the civil service pay scale, staff would consistently apply behavior modification procedures and be able to earn bonuses under the same sorts of schedules that produce persistent Bingo playing, persistent green stamp saving, or persistent slot-machine playing in Las Vegas. Certain intermittent schedules of reinforcement are at the heart of these contingencies that maintain persistent gambling behaviors. Not only do they maintain persistent behavior, but the people "like it." One of the main concerns of such a system is to ensure that the system is not abused, and that the system is in operation over and above the usual pay scales. If our proposed Bingo game at Cedar Cottage has the effects that we anticipate, we visualize a revolution in civil service, with the unions demanding not only hourly and monthly wages, but also their Bingo games.

Our second proposal concerns an analysis of the contingencies that typically influence supervisors in a civil service institution. At the Manitoba School, a psychiatric nurse is in charge of each ward, unit supervisors are in charge of several psychiatric nurses and their wards, assistant directors are responsible to the director of psychiatric nursing, who in turn is responsible to the Medical Superintendent. It seems that interaction down this chain of command most often follows the pattern of showing concern for problems and difficulties, rather than showing enthusiasm and reinforcement for smooth operations and innovations. For example, one often observes a unit supervisor enter a ward and ask if there are any problems. If the charge nurse has no problems, the supervisor leaves. If the charge nurse has problems, the unit supervisor remains, and attempts to solve the problem. If the problem is of a minor sort, such as related to staff scheduling, then the problem is typically solved without much aversiveness involved. However, if the problem is of a major sort that is likely to involve those above in the chain of command, then the unit supervisor may be somewhat aversive with respect to the charge nurse since involving those above reflects badly on the supervisor. Thus, charge nurses are reinforced for presenting minor problems to their unit supervisor, since that is when their unit supervisor talks to them. Unit supervisors are reinforced for discussing minor problems with their assistant directors, and so on up the line. Undoubtedly, this is an oversimplification of the contingencies involved. Yet it seems that, in our experience at least, such conditions are in effect a good portion of the time. Charge nurses are simply not given appropriate consideration and recognition from above for doing a good job of initiating and maintaining a program. It's therefore not worth their while to be innovative. Rather, the contingencies influence them to stay out of trouble and produce lots of minor problems that generate interesting discussions with unit supervisors.

In order to solve this problem, we are currently engaged in making a detailed listing of desirable behaviors and specific duties of charge nurses and unit supervisors. This will lead to a manual of specific behaviors and detailed job specifications for each position. Our second step will then be to analyze the reinforcement contingencies that can be brought to bear, such that some positive reinforcement is dispensed for completing the jobs and emitting the desirable behaviors rather than for unproductive forms of behavior. Perhaps "Bingo games" might also be appropriate at some of the higher administrative levels as well.

REFERENCES

Ball, T. S. The re-establishment of social behavior. *Hospital and Community Psychiatry*, 1968, 230-233.

Gardner, J. M., Brust, D. J., and Watson, L. S. A scale to measure skill in applying behavior modification techniques to the mentally retarded. *American Journal of Mental Deficiency*, 1970, 74, 633-636.

Gardner, J. M. and Watson, L. S. Behavior modification with the mentally retarded: An annotated bibliography. *Mental Retardation Abstracts*, 1969, 6, 181-193.

Keith, K. D. and Wallace, A. R. Inservice training in behavior modification techniques. Paper presented at the Region VIII Conference of the American Association on Mental Deficiency, Winnipeg, Manitoba, 1970.

Lowther, G. H. Science and sentimentality. *The Manitoba School (MS) Journal*. 1970, 2, 4-5.

Lowther, G. H. Behavior modification procedures in the management of severe and profound mental retardation. Paper presented at the 2nd Western Regional Meeting of the Canadian Psychiatric Association, Vancouver, B.C., February, 1971.

Lowther, R., Martin, G. L., and McDonald, L. A behavioral checklist for assessing behavioral modification skills in an operant training program with severely and profoundly retarded. Paper presented at the Canadian Psychological Association Meeting, St. John's, Newfoundland, June, 1971.

Martin, G. L. The fundamentals of operant conditioning as applied to the training of the retarded. Unpublished paper, 1968.

Martin G. L. Operant conditioning treatment of autistic and mentally retarded children at the Manitoba Training School. In Pressey, A. W. and Zubek, J. P. (Eds.), *Readings in general psychology, Canadian contributions*. Toronto: McClelland and Stewart, 1970.

Martin, G. L., England, G., Kaprowy, E., Kilgour, K., and Pilek, V. Operant conditioning of kindergarten-class behavior in autistic children. *Behavior Research and Therapy*, 1968, 6, 281-294.

Martin, G. L. and Hughes, G. R. Operant conditioning at the Manitoba Training School for Retardates: The Cedar Cottage Project. Paper presented at National Conference of the Canadian Association for the Mentally Retarded, Vancouver, B.C., October, 1970.

Martin, G. L., Kehoe, B., Bird, E., Jensen, V., and Darbyshire, M. Operant conditioning of dressing behavior of severely retarded girls. *Mental Retardation*, in press.

Martin, G. L., McDonald S., and Omichinski, M. An operant analysis of response interactions during meals with severely retarded girls. *American Journal of Mental Deficiency*, in press.

Martin, G. L. and Pear, J. J., Short term participation by 130 undergraduates as operant conditioners in an ongoing project with autistic children. *Psychological Record*, 1970, 20, 327-336.

Martin, G. L. and Treffry, D., Treating self-destruction and developing self-care with a severely retarded girl: A case study. *Psychological Aspects of Disability,* 1970, *17,* No. 3, 125-131.

Panyan, M., Boozer, H., and Morris, N. Feedback to attendants as a reinforcer for applying operant techniques. *Journal of Applied Behavior Analysis,* 1970, *3,* 1-4.

Patterson, G. R. A community mental health program for children. In Hamerlynck, L. A., Davidson, P. O., and Acker, L. E. (Eds.), *Behavior modification and ideal mental health services.* Calgary: University of Calgary Press, 1969.

Roberts, C. L. and Perry, R. M. A total token economy. *Mental Retardation,* 1970, *8,* 15-18.

Skinner, B. F. *Contingencies of reinforcement: A theoretical analysis.* New York: Appleton-Century-Crofts, 1970.

Treffry, D., Martin, G. L., Samels, J., and Watson, C. Operant conditioning of grooming behavior of severely retarded girls. *Mental Retardation,* 1970, *8,* 29-33.

Vogler, R. E. and Martin, G. L. In defense of operant conditioning programs in mental institutions. *Psychological Record,* 1969, *19,* 59-64.

Watson, L. S., Application of operant conditioning techniques to institutionalized severely and profoundly retarded children. *Mental Retardation Abstracts,* 1967, *4,* 1-18.

APPENDIX I

Steps of training programs to teach psychiatric nurses and nurse aids to apply operant techniques during individual and group sessions and daily ward routines with severely and moderately retarded residents at the Manitoba School for Retardates. Different groups of nurses were exposed to different combinations of steps and the steps were usually carried out concurrently for any one group.

Training Time	Steps
3-5 hours spread over 2-3 days	1. Teach staff to specify behavior precisely and to record and graph behavior.
10 hours spread over 2-5 weeks	2. Teach staff basic concepts through lectures, discussions, and reading assignments with study questions, and use exams based on study questions to bring written performance to a minimal level.
3-5 hours	3. Demonstrate proper procedures to staff for individual sessions and general ward situations.
5 hours spread over 1 week	4. Require staff to modify at least one behavior of a resident, and provide feedback to the staff.
	5. Arrange events (cue lights, posted rules, etc.) on the ward to increase probability of appropriate staff behavior.
3-5 weeks working on a regular shift	6. Require staff to emit appropriate behaviors in individual training sessions with a resident, *and* during a variety of ward situations. Provide feedback to staff, i.e., condition staff to condition the residents.

APPENDIX II

Sample study questions designed to produce fluency with basic concepts:*

1. For the purposes of a training program, what is operant behavior?
2. What is a baseline? Give an example.
3. What is a reversal? Give an example.
4. What are token reinforcers?
5. How would you go about token training a child?
6. Why is being paid by the hour not a fixed interval schedule?
7. Describe two desirable and two undesirable behaviors of residents on your ward that you have been reinforcing intermittently.
8. Describe how nurses might inadvertently shape severe temper tantrums in residents.
9. Describe three situations in which you used escape conditioning to influence a resident's behavior.
10. Describe three situations where a resident influenced your behavior through escape conditioning.
11. How might a resident's behavior reinforce you for doing the wrong thing in a training situation?
12. Describe 5 S^D's that you presented to residents today. Clearly identify the S^D, the response(s), and the reinforcer(s) for each example.
13. How might you use fading to teach a child to eat with a spoon?
14. What is meant by the term *stimulus control*? Give examples.
15. Is operant conditioning like mechanistic animal training?

---

*The questions are samples from 70 questions based on material described in Ball (1968), Martin (1968), and Vogler and Martin (1969).

APPENDIX III

Sample items taken from a handout for trainees which describes plausible conditioning situations.

Situation	Response	Consequences	Long term effects
Grooming time in the bathroom; one staff member and four residents present.	Jeanne, one of the girls in the bathroom, runs out the door.	Nurse runs after her and says, "Jeanne, come back here," takes her by the arm and leads her back to the bathroom.	Jeanne is likely to run out of the bathroom more often when that nurse is around, because of all the attention she received for running out.
Residents are eating one of their meals in the dining room.	Jeanette holds up her empty glass and utters, "Mmm, mmm, mmm."	Agnes, the waitress, takes the glass and fills it with milk, and takes it to Jeanette.	Jeanette is more likely to make that same noise and hold up her glass at future meals.
Lori (a resident) and one of the nurses are in the office. Lori has been "bugging" the nurse, and the nurse has just said, "Lori, get out of here and close the door."	Lori, while still standing in the office asks, "Do you like me?"	Nurse says, "Yes, I like you; now get out of the office," following which Lori asks a few questions which the nurse answers. Finally Lori leaves.	Lori is more likely to be persistent and say, "Do you like me?" when she is told to do something, because she has just been reinforced by staff attention for persistence.
Grooming time in the bathroom.	A resident has just completed all grooming steps without help from staff.	Staff member says, "Good for you, (name)" and hands the resident a token reinforcer.	Resident is more likely to emit the desirable grooming behavior in the future, because of the attention given for her behavior.
Resident sees a staff with a bag of candies.	Resident begins to scream, "Candy, candy."	To terminate the screaming, the staff gives the screaming resident a candy.	Staff member is more likely to "give in" to the screaming resident in the future, and the resident is more likely to scream when seeing a candy bag.

APPENDIX IV

Posted procedures in the dining room at Cedar Cottage:

1. Before servers are allowed into the dining room to set tables, they must be checked to make sure they have washed their faces and hands, and are appropriately dressed (buttons fastened, shoes laced, etc.).
2. Re: Donna Gayle and Marley Ann — they should not be led by the hand into the dining room. If they do not come by themselves, when called once, they will miss their meal.
3. Liberal social approval should be presented following various desirable mealtime behaviors.
4. Time-out punishment should be given for the following:*
   a. slopping
   b. eating with fingers
   c. any excessive noise
   d. stealing food

   The procedure for applying time-out is as follows:
   a. Give a sharp "no" and pull resident's chair away from the table for a period of fifteen seconds.
   b. Repeat the procedure for three instances of undesirable behavior; if the behavior persists, remove resident from dining area for the remainder of the meal.
5. The "meals missed" chart should be marked in on every meal, regarding children who have missed their meal.

---

*The effect of time-out punishment for undesirable mealtime behaviors was reported in a separate paper by Martin, McDonald, and Omichinski, in press.

APPENDIX V

Behavioral assessment form for evaluating a nurse's performance during individual training sessions with a resident.

Type of Session _____ Session Time _____   Key √ Correct Response
Name of Trainer (T) _____ Session Date _____   X Incorrect Response
Name of Resident (R) _____ Observer _____   O Does Not Apply

A. Session Preparation: The Nurse: | Comments
  1. Has knowledge of S's original baseline
  2. Has knowledge of immediate goal of session
  3. Reviews data and procedure from previous session
  4. Prepares all material for the session before getting S
  5. Gets acquainted with S before training
  6. Tests for reinforcer effectiveness before training (reinforcer sampling)
  7. Selects an effective reinforcer

B. After Session is Completed, the Nurse: | Comments
  1. Returns S to proper location
  2. Cleans session room and replaces materials properly
  3. Summarizes or graphs S's progress during the session
  4. Returns S's file to proper place
  5. Tells nurse if data sheets or supplies are needed
  6. Tells at least one other staff member of S's progress (showing them a graph if possible)

					Comments

C. Prompting and Fading Controlling Stimuli, the Nurse:
   1. Uses child's name before a command
   2. Uses correct verbal command
   3. Uses verbal prompts correctly
   4. Fades verbal prompts correctly
   5. Uses physical prompts correctly
   6. Fades physical prompts correctly
   7. Uses physical guidance correctly
   8. Fades physical guidance correctly
   9. Allows edible reinforcer to be consumed before next trial

D. Manipulating Consequences, the Nurse:
   1. Reinforces correct response immediately
   2. Gives verbal reinforcement enthusiastically
   3. Gives physical reinforcement enthusiastically
   4. Gives verbal reinforcement with material or edible reinforcement
   5. Correctly withholds reinforcement following wrong responses
   6. Correctly withholds prompts following inattentive or other "bad" behavior
   7. Correctly applies time-out or other punishing consequences

E. Shaping or Chaining, the Nurse:
   1. Is familiar with correct sequence before session begins
   2. Demonstrates the desired behavior where appropriate
   3. Starts with the correct step
   4. Proceeds to next step when subject is ready
   5. Uses proper sequence of steps
   6. Returns to previously successful step if necessary

APPENDIX VI

Daily Session Assignments for Psychiatric Nurses and Nurse Aids

(1-9:30)

Day: _Wednesday_   Date: _Dec 8, 1971_

Staff on: _Balch_   _Spence_
          Sharp
          Jackson   _Cooper_

Time	Trainer	Observer	Subject	Task	Sess. Time	Reason if no Session
9:30-10:00	Sharp, Jackson, Spence		Brenda, Jeanne, Terri	Stacking, Swallowing, Drawing	17, 25, 25	
10:00-10:30	Sharp, Jackson, Cooper		Karly, Martine, Lisa	Imitation, Grooming, Matching	10, 27, 15	
10:30-11:00	Balch, Jackson, Spence		Donna, Marion, Lori	Dressing, Stacking, Shadowing	10, 17, 15	

86

11:00-1:00	GROOMING AND LUNCH			
1:00-1:20	sharp jackson grune cooper			
1:20-1:40	sharp jackson spence cooper	Valerie Edwina Marian Bridgette	Planting Grooming Weaving Invitation	15 15 17 17
1:40-2:00	Ruth jackson spence cooper	Marilyn Caroline Mary Gale	Invitation Verbal Sorting Operating	15 Resident to Dr. 15 15
		Janice Gay Toni Sue	Shopping Shopping Bedmaking Decorating	15 Charts 15 15
2:00-2:20	ALL STAFF AND RESIDENT EXERCISE PERIOD			
2:20-2:40	Betty jackson spence cooper	Robert Paula Kathy Brenda	Bedmaking Invitation Weaving Decorating	— Tour 17 17 17
2:40-3:00	sharp jackson spence cooper	Agnes Ann Rita Marian	Bedmaking Grooming Decorating Invitation	18 Tour 17 15

Total Possible No. of Sessions 29
Total Actual No. of Sessions 25

Total Possible Session Time 8 hrs. 10 mins.
Total Actual Session Time 7 hrs. 19 mins.

87

Training Behavior Change Agents: A Five-Year Perspective

Ernest G. Poser

The use of learning principles to effect therapeutic behavior change is now in its second decade. Though its theoretical foundations have a much longer history, the integration of behavior modification techniques into contemporary clinical training turns out to be a slow and erratic process. Seventeen years after the term "behavior therapy" was coined, and more than twelve years since the first book on its clinical application appeared, the number of graduate schools offering specialized training in this area is still very limited. Similarly, the number of field settings in which potential change agents can acquire expertise in behavior technology by applying conditioning methods to human subjects is, at this stage, totally inadequate.

One reason for this unhappy state of affairs is that clinical psychology, as traditionally conceived, finds itself committed to a precarious compromise between research and clinical service. Typically, budding clinicians are trained primarily as researchers even though many aim to devote their professional future to service careers. Consequently there is often only a tenuous bond between the content of clinical training and the professional functions post-doctoral clinicians are expected to perform.

To some extent this situation represents the inevitable outcome of the scientist-professional strategy adopted by most graduate schools of psychology ever since the Boulder Conference in 1949. This model rested on the assumption that only a professional who is also a scientist could distinguish the wheat from the chaff when it came to evaluating the evidence underlying new theories and methods in clinical psychology. Twenty years ago such a stance might have been justified but is it still appropriate in this era of accreditation, licensing, and ABEPP style examinations, all intended to assure that professionals meet at least minimal standards of scientific competence?

Two misconceptions seem to maintain the scientist-professional aim of clinical training. One is the view that *consumers* of scientific data have to be given similar training to that provided for *producers* of such data. This notion neglects the fact that it is one thing to train students to read research literature intelligently and to apply its data wisely, yet quite another to train them in the identification and exploration of researchable problems, statistical data analysis, and the writing of papers for publication in scientific journals. Surely the former type of training is all that is required for those professional psychologists destined to become behavior change agents.

The other point frequently cited in defense of the scientist-professional model is that the body of well established psychological knowledge applicable to the solution of social problems is too meager to support an effective technology of human behavior at this time. Those who hold that view seem to expect that at some future time there will emerge such a body of knowledge sufficient to warrant a purely professional training program. When behavioral science will reach that point, or whether it will ever reach it is, of course, difficult to predict. What seems more certain is that the science and the profession of psychology will be better served if we were to train graduate clinical students *either* with a service *or* a research orientation, but not both. When this comes about, and there are indications that it might, some graduate psychology departments will offer training in experimental psychopathology and professional schools will provide training in applied psychology (Cummings, 1969). There is no need for this distinction to impede communication between researchers and practitioners. In fact, there is reason to believe that such communication may be enhanced when clinical practitioners and clinical researchers feel secure in one of these areas of expertise rather than insecure in both.

Other reasons also have impeded the development of a close professional link between applied behavior modification and clinical psychology as traditionally conceived. It must be recognized that the orientation basic to the exploration, teaching, and practice of behavior modification is fundamentally at variance with current principles taught in most clinical training programs. This is evident both at the theoretical and technological level. It is, for instance, difficult to reconcile the clinicians' emphasis on endogenous causes of psychopathology with the behavior modifiers' insistence that deviant behavior is largely maintained by environmental stimuli. Likewise the behavior therapist's preoccupation with baseline assessment-and-change stands in sharp contrast to the clinician's concern with nosology and process variables in psychotherapy.

Even more fundamental is the rift between adherents of the two schools when it comes to their self-concept as professionals. Nowhere has this emerged more clearly than in Albee's (1970) perceptive analysis of differences between clinicians and researchers along the dimension of "public" versus "private" knowledge. In his presidential address to the American Psychological Association, he made the point that while researchers prize public examination of their work and the controversy this often engenders, professionals shun such public inquisitions, shroud their techniques in mystery and protect themselves and their fellow professionals against criticism by "outsiders." Yet on this "public" versus "private" continuum practitioners of behavior therapy tend to align themselves with researchers, i.e., they favor public scrutiny of their techniques and participation by the patient in the process of therapy and its evaluation. Hence they strive to perfect methods of behavior modification amenable to automation, to administration by technicians or, ideally, to self-administration by patients. Such a trend is clearly inconsistent with the traditional clinician's preference for guarding the therapeutic mystique which some regard as an active ingredient of therapeutic change.

Luckily behavior modification, as a relative newcomer to the professional scene, need not share the difficulties encountered by clinical psychology. Due to its close ties with experimental psychology, its methodological dissimilarity to psychiatry, and its potential for community-wide application through use of non-professional assistants, behavior therapy is uniquely placed to make a fresh start in the application of behavioral science to social learning and its deviations. Whether it will take this opportunity or content itself with being just another variant of clinical psychology may well determine its destiny for years to come.

So far little information has become available on the relative merits of different training models for behavior change agents. Hence it is the purpose of this paper to evaluate one such model adopted during the last five years in the Behavior Therapy Teaching Unit at Douglas Hospital in Montreal. From the start this program was intended to provide specialized training for behavior change agents, not as a practicum to be superimposed on traditional training in clinical psychology. Hence, our trainees were not selected from among clinical psychologists only, but included also psychiatric residents, graduate nurses, nursing assistants, and other mental health professionals.

The setting is a twelve-bed, in-patient, facility located in a psychiatric teaching hospital. It differs from all other services in that institution in that admissions to the Unit, behavioral treatment services, and discharge planning are the responsibility of psychologists. Because it is primarily a teaching unit, patients are selected with a view to presenting at any one time as wide a spectrum as possible of those behavior deviations known to respond to one or more of the learning therapies. The most frequent categories of referral include anxiety states and phobic disorders, addictions, sexual deviations, and obsessive reactions. Some psychotic patients with systematized delusions are treated occasionally but most psychotics are referred to an operant unit in another part of the hospital where token economy systems are used.

The structure and content of this training program has been described elsewhere (Poser, 1967; Poser and Ashem, 1968; Poser, 1969). Here only an outline of the course will be given with special reference to those aspects which distinguish it most clearly from traditional clinical training programs.

In our Unit two levels of practical training are offered. One of these focuses on the technology of behavior modification and is intended for co-therapist technicians in institutional settings. The second level of training is for mental health professionals wishing to practice behavior modification or to teach it. At this second level the practical work is supplemented by case study seminars and the discussion of theoretical issues relevant to new methods of behavior modification. At both levels of training students are "apprenticed" to one, or several, more experienced therapists whom they understudy in their day-to-day activities.

Diagnostic psychological testing is not part of the curriculum. Trainees are, however, encouraged to use quantitative assessment methods wherever possible. The stress is on prognostic rather than diagnostic techniques. Hence, self-rating scales, tests of autonomic and verbal conditioning, as well as behavior check lists and performance assessments are used rather than intelligence tests or projective techniques. New methods for the quantification of behavior are under investigation, notably the use of radio telemetry to monitor autonomic responses of patients undergoing stressful life situations.

Completion of the training program carries no academic credit, but the hospital issues a certificate of attendance to those who wish it.

The training sequence as described has now been in operation for five years and has provided training at level I or II for over fifty trainees from four different mental health professions, i.e., psychology, psychiatry, psychiatric nursing, and social work. The overriding impression I have gained from that experience is that previous training in clinical psychology is by no means an essential prerequisite for the achievement of competence in applied behavior modification. In fact those who came to us with a solid foundation in experimental psychology and learning on the whole progressed faster than those who had been given extensive clinical training, perhaps because the latter had more to unlearn. It also became apparent that early exposure to patients greatly accelerates the trainees' mastery of theoretical concepts and their application. Their learning experience is further enriched by the multi-disciplinary background of their fellow trainees. Many have commented that unfavorable interprofessional attitudes they acquired in the course of their university training underwent radical change once they had an opportunity to work toward a common goal with members of allied disciplines. Lastly, it emerged that the most productive contributors to behavior therapy research are themselves often quite unmotivated to become effective agents of behavior change.

In an effort to evaluate the program from the recipient's point of view, a questionnaire was sent to all previous trainees who could be located. Eighteen psychologists, eight nurses, and five psychiatric residents returned the questionnaire. This represents 62% of the total number sent out. Because the number of social workers was too small to be representative only the findings for the other three groups will be reported. A copy of the questionnaire appears in Appendix I.

In terms of educational accomplishment, seven of the eighteen psychologists were at the post-doctoral level and the remainder were graduate students at or above the master's level or its equivalent. Of the eight nurses two were RNs and the remainder psychiatric nursing assistants. The five medically trained respondents were, with one exception, in the first or second year of psychiatric residency training. One had attained her specialist certification.

The psychologists' stay in the Unit averaged nine months (range 2-36 months), that of the nurses averaged 24 months (range 8-60 months), and all psychiatric residents spent six months, half-time in the Unit.

Five psychologist trainees had had similar training before coming to our Unit and two have had some additional training since. None of the nursing or psychiatric staff had any formal training in behavior therapy before or after their traineeship at Douglas Hospital.

More than half the psychologists, 50% of the nurses, and three out of five of the psychiatric residents ranked clinical service as being of greater interest to them than either research or teaching. A greater proportion of nurses than psychologists listed research as their major interest!

In the past psychologists engaged in therapy were frequently responsible to psychiatrists for that aspect of their work. This seems not to be the case in the present group of psychologists, nearly all of whom are now in positions where they are responsible to psychologists. However, only three reported that they are in full-time practice of behavior therapy, two are not working in that area at all and the remainder spend about half their time at work related to behavior modification. Even so it is surprising that not one of the respondents is currently responsible to a psychiatrist in matters of his clinical work.

Among psychiatric trainees the amount of time spent in behavior therapy, on completion of training, is only 10% on the average. This is not surprising since their stay in the Unit is not primarily intended as a training experience. Though many avail themselves of such training while they are with us, their primary function is to look after the physical welfare of patients. Often time does not permit them to attend the training sessions or to have much supervised practice in applying behavior modification techniques.

Five out of the eight nurses are engaged in behavior modification full-time, but most of these are doing so in our own Unit.

The overwhelming majority of all respondents felt that their behavior therapy training had prepared them adequately for their present duties — but four psychologists, one nurse, and two psychiatrists did not. In the case of nurses and psychiatrists, the most common complaint was that they had insufficient opportunity to try different methods, whereas the psychologists expressed a need for closer supervision. The number of negative responses to the question concerning adequacy of training may well have been spuriously low since no attempt was made to guard the anonymity of respondents. Hence, a question of this kind might well have been answered in the direction of "social desirability."

Most respondents in all three professional groups saw the chief strength of the program to reside in the opportunity to apply a wide range of clinical techniques to a diversity of patients. Learning to accept responsibility for patients was another point frequently cited in favor of the program. Some found it challenging to cope with the many difficulties that arise when theory is translated into practice and many lauded the enthusiasm of the teaching staff.

To discover which incentives caused trainees to seek behavior therapy training, a list of 16 objectives was compiled. Respondents were asked to rate each item on a 3-point scale. A high score indicates that the item was of great importance to the respondent at the time of his training.

RESULTS

Intercorrelation of the 16 items revealed 13 of them to be correlated at the .01 level of significance. Two item clusters emerged. The first consists of items 3, 4, 10, and 11, all of which seem to concern the achievement of competence in the helping relationship. The second cluster made up of items 7, 9, 11, and 12 appears to be more closely related to the respondents' need for self-enhancement through the exertion of social influence. Both categories are rated higher by nurses than by either of the other professions. Psychiatrists give lower ratings than psychologists to items concerned with the achievement of competence, but the reverse is true on the second cluster.

A Chi-square test run for each of the 16 items separately revealed no signficant differences between professional groups. Only items 2 and 11 approached significance. The former, as one might expect, was rated highest by psychologists, whereas item 11 was more important to psychiatrists.

That item 6 "accumulating evidence against dynamic theories" should get zero rating from all psychiatrists was to be predicted. But that it should also receive very low ratings from the other two groups encourages the conclusion that opposition to earlier schools of thought is no longer an important source of motivation for students of behavior therapy.

DISCUSSION

Evaluation of our program as reflected in this questionnaire survey is necessarily incomplete and based on a very small sample. Even so it does suggest that similarities between trainees from different professional backgrounds are more conspicuous than their differences. The survey also lends support to the point made at the outset of this paper that those seeking competence in applied behavior therapy, on the whole, show little interest in doing research.

The data further suggests that a six month, part-time learning period is not sufficient to meet the needs of psychiatric residents who wish to use these methods in other settings where they may be the only practitioners of behavior modification.

As noted above, the advantages of an interdisciplinary training program for behavior therapists outweigh the disadvantages. But there are drawbacks. They arise mainly from existing status hierarchies implicit in the traditional role assigned to mental health professionals. This is most noticeable in the nurses' interaction with other workers. Once it is established that the nursing staff can be effective members of a behavioral treatment team — as our experience clearly shows — some change of time-honored routines in their training will be necessary. One of these is the system of rotating shifts which is quite inconsistent with the systematic delivery of behavioral treatment services by nursing personnel. Again existing disparities between psychologists and psychiatrists when it comes to matters of clinical experience versus sophistication in theories of learning needs to be considered in curriculum planning. But these are minor adjustments well worth making in the service of greater interdisciplinary collaboration.

Training programs similar to the one described above are seen as a viable alternative to contemporary training facilities in university departments of clinical psychology. The latter may provide optimal settings for research training in experimental psychopathology, but they are not likely to develop facilities for practicum training of future professionals. University operated psychological clinics are rarely the answer because by nature of their funding and location they tend to be primarily research oriented, divorced from other disciplines, limited to out-patient care and thereby destined to attract a fairly homogeneous patient population with relatively minor impairments. It is difficult to see how internships in such settings can provide students with a role model adequate to the needs of future clinicians.

As university departments continue the trend of introducing courses in behavior modification at the undergraduate level it will be easier in the future to recruit candidates for the role of behavior therapy technician. This is a highly valuable group of workers, particularly in institutional settings. A system whereby a number of such technicians work in close consultation with experienced, professionally trained behavior therapists would seem to offer one of the most parsimonious solutions to the present manpower problem.

Little has been said in this paper about behavior modification research training because it really presents no major problem. The course structure in most graduate psychology programs can and does answer the needs of researchers in this field by virtue of its close association with experimental psychology. One would hope that some courses such as advanced statistics, physiological psychology, learning, and psychopathology would be taken jointly by future professionals and researchers. Likewise some practicum experience should be made available to researchers. The main departure from current university practice will be the substitution of more intensive practicum training for what is now the dissertation requirement.

What is being proposed here goes well beyond the view recently expressed by Kanfer (1970) that:

> The behavior therapy model of the clinical psychologist differers from the Boulder model primarily in its advocacy of intimate integration of clinical and research wisdom into one role and one set of activities. The Boulder model called for competence in both but treated them as two separate, though concurrent, functions.

To this one might retort that if students trained in the Boulder tradition failed to achieve competence in "two separate though concurrent functions" what hope is there for behavior therapists to succeed in the far more complex task of integrating clinical and research wisdom? Is it not more realistic to try to select the best practitioners and the best researchers and to recognize that two such pearls rarely inhabit the same shell?

The model being advocated is essentially that already implemented at the University of Illinois (Peterson, 1968). It is urged that behavior modifiers espouse this model even if that means a separation of behavior therapy from the mainstream of contemporary clinical psychology. In some respects, such a separation already exists. There is little point in accentuating it needlessly but the time seems ripe for trying new ways of aligning the means we use with the ends we seek.

REFERENCES

Albee, G. W. The uncertain future of clinical psychology. *American Psychologist*, 1970, *25*, No. 12, 1071-1080.

Cummings, N. A. Towards new schools of professional psychology. Special Bulletin of the National Council of Graduate Education in Psychology, 1969, *3*, No. 1, 1-4.

Kanfer, F. H. and Phillips, J. S. *Learning foundations of behavior therapy.* New York: Wiley, 1970. P. 642.

Peterson, D. R. The Doctor of Psychology Program at the University of Illinois, *American Psychologist*, 1968, *23*, No. 7, 511-516.

Poser, E. G. Training behavior therapists. *Behaviour Research and Therapy*, 1967, *5*, 37-41.

Poser, E. G. and Ashem, B. Establishing a behavior therapy teaching unit. *Newsletter of the Association for Advancement of Behavior Therapy*, 1968, *3*, 5-7.

Poser, E. G. The teaching of behavior modification in an interdisciplinary setting. In R. D. Rubin and C. M. Franks (Eds.), *Advances in behavior therapy*. New York: Academic Press, 1969.

APPENDIX I

To All Past and Present Trainees in the Douglas Hospital, Behaviour Therapy Unit

For the benefit of future trainees in Behaviour Therapy we are conducting this evaluation of our training program. Your replies will be very seriously considered when we come to revise the program.

Name: Age:
Highest level of education completed:
Year of completion:

How long did you spend in the Douglas Hospital Behaviour Therapy Unit: (give approximate date)
Did you have similar training before?
If yes, please state place and duration:
Have you had further formal training in Behaviour Therapy since leaving Douglas Hospital?
If yes, please state where and for how long.

Assigning a value of 1 to "least interested" and a value of 3 to "most interested," please rank order your present interest in the following applications of behavior therapy:
a. clinical service _____ b. research _____ c. teaching _____

Where are you working at present?
To whom are you directly responsible in your work and what is the person's professional affiliation?
What percentage of your working hours is currently spent on behavior therapy or related activities?
Did your training in Behaviour Therapy at Douglas Hospital prepare you adequately for your present duties?
             Yes _____   No _____
What were the chief weaknesses of the training program?
What were the chief strengths of the program?

Objectives Sought by Behaviour Therapy Trainees

Below are listed some common reasons why indivdiuals seek training in behavior therapy. Please state how important each of these was to you at the time of your training by writing a number between zero and two in the box to the right of each item. The following scale signifies the meaning of these numbers.

0 = Irrelevant or unimportant to me
1 = Of some importance to me but not crucial
2 = Of paramount importance to me

If you can think of other rewards, motives, or reasons which in your opinion might lead people to seek behavior therapy training please list them at the end and also rate them on the 3-point scale.

1. Acquiring new professional skills ☐
2. Relating psychological theory to clinical application ☐
3. Contributing to the relief of suffering ☐
4. Attaining a diploma ☐
5. Opportunity for professional interaction with members of allied disciplines ☐
6. Accumulating evidence against dynamic theories ☐
7. Proving to yourself that you can change the behavior of others ☐
8. Qualifying yourself for a higher income ☐
9. Aspiring to greater professional independence from other mental health workers ☐
10. To learn from those patients you were unable to help ☐
11. Establishing a helping relationship with others ☐
12. The personal satisfaction of achieving mastery in a clinical skill ☐
13. Teaching other professionals ☐
14. Giving or writing scientific papers ☐
15. Working as a "systems" consultant to schools, hospitals, prisons, or industry ☐
16. Earning social approval from your superiors ☐

Section 2
AGENTS OF CHANGE FOR THE CLASSROOM

In classroom settings, the teacher's main function is to influence two types of student performance: the acquisition and maintenance of concepts and operations, and the acquisition and maintenance of on-task social and non-social behaviors such as attending, writing, and asking questions which are directly related to academic achievement. By implication, a third function related to teaching would be the prevention, deceleration, shift in stimulus control, or elimination of student behavior incompatible with learning objectives of the classroom.

Currently, however, it appears that the topics discussed by teachers most frequently, and for the longest periods of time, concern frustrations over classroom control and the topography of students' deviant behavior as opposed to the other major teaching functions described above. Effective teaching and learning must address itself to the means by which both teachers and students learn more effective classroom skills.

Current literature in school psychology indicates an increasing dissatisfaction and disenchantment with the traditional clinical, individual approach to deviant behaviors in the classroom. The most often mentioned alternative to the traditional model is the use of a behavior modification approach. However, it becomes rapidly obvious that there will never be sufficient school psychologists to perform this function, even if they do work with whole classes of children. It is, therefore, important that the behavior modifier be the teacher—not just special teachers, but all teachers. Again it becomes apparent that we must develop a behavioral technology first to train teachers, and secondly, to maintain their behavior modification practices at a very high rate. The first two papers of this section by Hugh McKenzie and R. Vance Hall describe programs which they have developed to train teachers as behavior modifiers, and to maintain their behavioral repertoire. It is evident that the school psychologist and related personnel of the future can have a vastly different job than at present: (1) to instruct teachers in behavioral principles; (2) to maintain teachers in their use of behavioral principles; (3) to act as a resource person for the solution of more complex behavior modification tasks faced by the teacher; and (4) to act as an inservice instructor to teachers such that their repertoire of behavioral principles may be updated as new discoveries are made in both basic and applied research.

To summarize and illustrate the above points, the final chapter by Gerald Patterson, Joseph Cobb, and Roberta Ray is offered. They demonstrate a basic outline for classroom social learning technology with validation data to reinforce the efforts of other scientist/practitioners.

Perhaps the sooner the cycle of activity described above is initiated, teachers will more rapidly be in a position to employ behavioral principles to the benefit of all their pupils, and not just the few deserving "special education."

SPECIAL EDUCATION AND CONSULTING TEACHERS[1]

Hugh S. McKenzie[2]

There are several strategies for delivering services to handicapped children which are now in practice in the United States. Handicapped learners may live in *institutions* which provide total care. The children receive special education as part of the institution's services.

A second approach is that of the *special class*. Children are removed from their "normal" peers. The special class may be contained in a regular school building or it may be separate from regular schools. The children typically live at home when placed in special classes.

A third approach may be called that of the *resource teacher*. A child who has learning difficulties is removed on a temporary, part-time basis from his classroom to receive diagnostic teaching from a resource teacher. The resource teacher diagnoses the child's difficulties and writes an educational prescription that the child's classroom teacher will then perform.

A fourth approach, and one that has been developing in Vermont over the last several years, is that of a *consulting teacher*. The consulting teacher assists regular classroom teachers to carry out diagnoses and to develop an intervention approach to facilitate a given child's educational development. The teacher implements both diagnosis and intervention procedures. Through this implementation with the assistance of the consulting teacher, the regular teacher receives inservice training in special education.

---

[1]The program described is funded in part by a Title VI-B, ESEA grant from the United States Office of Education to the Vermont State Department of Education, and grants from the Bureau for the Education of the Handicapped and the Bureau of Educational Personnel Development, United States Office of Education to the Special Education Program, University of Vermont. However, the opinions expressed herein do not necessarily reflect policy or endorsement of the United States Office of Education.

[2]The author wishes to thank faculty and students of the University of Vermont's Special Education Program and Jean Garvin, Director, Division of Special Education and Pupil Personnel Services, Vermont State Department of Education, for their substantial contributions to the development of the consulting teacher approach to special education and, thus, to this paper.

WHY A CONSULTING TEACHER APPROACH WAS DEVELOPED IN VERMONT

Four years ago, the state of Vermont had in operation three of the four delivery systems briefly described above: handicapped children were served in residential institutions, in special classes, and a few by resource teachers. Through these three approaches approximately 2,000 children were receiving special education. An estimated additional 8,000 children were judged to require special education. To provide special education to these 8,000 children who were of elementary school age, the consulting teacher approach was developed in Vermont. Considerations which led to this development are presented below.

Disruption, Busing, and Costs

The elementary age children who required special education services were, in general, attending elementary schools in Vermont. These schools are generally composed of small numbers of pupils (typically 200 or less) and are widely separated from one another. Thus, to remove these children from their regular classes to place them in special classes would require that regional special classes be formed to serve several elementary schools. It was doubtful that each elementary school would have enough children to form its own categorical special classes; that is, a class for the retarded, one for the emotionally disturbed, and one for the learning disabled. Thus, elementary schools would have to join with other schools to form regional special classes. This would require that children be bused from their homes. It was apparent that in many cases this busing would be extensive: children would be spending several hours a day in riding the bus.

It was also apparent that the formation of such regional special classes would be disruptive to the ongoing educational programs. Children would have to be identified and removed from their classes and all of this explained to the children and their parents.

Cost estimates (McKenzie, 1969) indicated that the formation of regional special classes would involve costs for construction of special classes, training of teachers, busing, and yearly operation much higher than those required by serving these children through a consulting teacher approach. By providing special education services to these children in their regular classrooms, skills of their current teachers, and existing buildings and materials would be available for their education.

Thus, to avoid disrupting an ongoing system and creating an aversive situation for children and parents of children requiring special services, to avoid having children spend several hours a day riding a bus, and to gain the apparent substantial savings to Vermont taxpayers, the consulting teacher approach was selected. (These considerations generally hold for a resource teacher approach, as a resource teacher requires a separate classroom which children attend.)

Increasing the Skills and Responsibilities of Regular Classroom Teachers

The addition of special class teachers, resource teachers, speech therapists, and remedial reading teachers to schools has led to a valuable increase in both the quantity and quality of services available to school children. Although assuredly unintentional, one unfortunate by-product of adding these specialists has been a tendency to remove responsibility from regular classroom teachers. The hiring of such specialists can indicate that classroom teachers are no longer responsible for ameliorating speech and reading deficits and for managing the education of children with various learning difficulties. This has had a tendency to reduce the incentive for regular class teachers to increase their own skills in these special areas.

As the specialists mentioned above work directly with the children and not through classroom teachers, it is not possible for classroom teachers to gain skills as an integral part of special services to children. An additional disadvantage is that these specialists remove the child from his classroom to provide him services, resulting in a tendency for teachers to conclude that the removal of difficult children from their classes is the only way to provide these children with adequate instruction.

Additional Arguments for a Consulting Teacher Approach

These arguments are not presented to denigrate other delivery systems for providing special education to handicapped children. (Here it should be noted that the other three delivery systems are all currently being employed in Vermont and will be continued to be employed as long as they prove functional.) These arguments are presented because they tend to increase the appeal of managing and educating handicapped children in regular classrooms wherever this is possible. Increasing the appeal of such an approach to special education also increases the appeal of developing a consulting teacher approach.

Providing special education services in regular classes would obviate the necessity of labeling children. Extensive psychological and educational evaluation which is conducted outside the classroom by professionals other than teachers could be decreased. It could be argued that such evaluation is necessary only to label the child—e.g., as *retarded*—for special class placement. Sometimes it is questionable whether or not such evaluation will discover anything more about the child with learning problems than that which has been observed by the child's teacher in the daily learning situation. In fact, if teachers (and/or parents) did not observe a degree of inappropriate and deficit behaviors in the child, it is improbable that the child would be referred for testing. This testing has the additional disadvantage of measuring behavior outside the learning situation and sampling a small cross section of behavior at a single and isolated point in time. Apparently, if labels were no longer needed, time and resources invested in individualized testing could be reduced, freeing skilled professionals to engage in more effective educational activity.

Labels are nonfunctional in regard to developing an educational program for a child. If a child has been labeled *emotionally disturbed,* this tells neither teacher nor parent what needs to be done to help the child progress socially and academically. A label may stigmatize a child and serve to isolate and alienate him from his peers. Further isolation of the handicapped learner occurs in the special class placement itself. Often handicapped learners must be bused to special classrooms which are far from their home neighborhood. Dunn (1968) has reviewed litigation and court action which has argued that labeling and special class placement involve discrimination and segregation. In one case the court disallowed labeling and special class placement of a group of children as a form of segregation.

Bateman (1967) has argued that when certain handicapped learners are placed in regular classrooms their peers show a greater appreciation of positive characteristics of handicapped learners and a greater understanding of their disabilities. Regular class placement of handicapped learners has the further advantage of offering normal and superior peer models. The present author has observed several instances where children who were disruptive in regular classrooms were grouped together in a special class and their disruptive behaviors increased rather than decreased. One factor leading to such an increase may well be that the peer models of the special class present inappropriate behavior to be imitated.

Research evidence reviewed by Darrah (1967) and Dunn (1968) indicates that at least some handicapped learners placed in regular classrooms progress as well as comparable children placed in special classrooms in spite of the fact that regular classroom teachers typically do not have training in the education of handicapped children.

Summary

A consulting teacher approach to providing special education to unserved children was favored over the extension of other kinds of existing delivery systems for the following reasons:
1. Retention of children in regular classes and consequent avoidance of disruption to the schools.

2. Avoiding extensive busing of children to regional special classes (or resource teacher classes).
3. Resultant savings of financial resources.
4. Avoidance of the stigma of labels and elimination of extensive standardized testing.
5. Avoidance of discrimination and segregation.
6. Opportunities for normal children to appreciate and understand handicapped children as well as for the handicapped children to have normal peer models.
7. Resultant training of regular teachers in special education skills.

A BEHAVIORAL MODEL OF EDUCATION

As Hanley's (1970) review indicates, applied behavior analysts have been successful in modifying a wide range of behaviors of educational significance. Implicit in each of the applications reviewed is a similar model of education. The conceptualization, training, and evaluation of training of consulting teachers are all based on such a model.

The Model

Goals which are to result from the educational process are delineated in terms of *instructional objectives*. Ultimately, such objectives are to be defined in terms of Mager's (1962) criteria: an objective must specify in terms which are observable by at least two people the conditions under which a given goal behavior will occur, an objective definition of the goal behavior, and the criteria which the behavior must meet.

With instructional objectives specified, the next task is to measure where each student is in relationship to the objectives. Such measurement determines the *entry level* of each student. If a student is found to already possess the behaviors of the instructional objective in his repertoire, teaching is not necessary.

For the child who has not achieved all instructional objectives, *teaching/learning procedures* are instigated to move the student from his entry level to the instructional objectives. Under the behavioral model, these procedures involve primarily that of reinforcement (Skinner, 1968). *Reinforcement procedures* involve arranging consequences for behaviors which lead to an increase in the frequency of these behaviors. Other teaching/learning procedures under the behavioral model are scheduling, shaping, and errorless discrimination. *Scheduling* involves the relationship of consequences to behaviors. That is, in establishing a behavior that has occurred infrequently, it is most effective to arrange for the consequence to occur contingently upon the behavior every time the behavior occurs. Once a behavior has increased to the desired level, then the consequences can be arranged to occur only occasionally. In the *shaping procedure,* behavioral sub-goals are first achieved until the goal behavior is reached. This may involve, for example, requiring that the student complete only two long division problems correctly, and then requiring four, then six, and so on. It may also involve establishing what are called *enabling objectives* for some ultimate instructional objective. That is, a child may learn to add, subtract, and multiply, which are enabling objectives for the child's learning long division.

Errorless discrimination involves procedures used to establish particular stimuli as occasions upon which behavior, if it occurs, will be reinforced. The procedures involve prompting adding cues, and gradual elimination of added cues (Terrance, 1963).

The behavioral progress of the child from entry level to instructional objectives is regularly and reliably measured. Such *measures* are compared with the entry level measures of the student, and this comparison enables an *evaluation* of the effectiveness of the teaching/learning procedures. Procedures are judged effective if the child is making adequate progress toward the instructional objectives. If he is not, then teaching/learning procedures are modified.

The Teacher's Role in the Model

The teacher is responsible for the student making satisfactory progress from his entry level toward the instructional objectives. The teacher makes frequent measures of student behaviors relevant to instructional objectives and applies the teaching/learning procedures of reinforcement, scheduling, shaping, and errorless discrimination. The teacher evaluates his use of procedures based on regular measures. He compares these measures with entry level measures of each student to insure that satisfactory progress is being made. If progress is not being made, the teacher changes the procedures being employed, or adds new procedures.

Teaching behavior is associated with applications of the teaching/learning procedures which brought about measured progress of students toward instructional objectives. Such progress should serve as consequential stimuli controlling teachers' behaviors. In the ideal situation, school administrators and society would provide rewards for the teacher contingent upon students' progress. Thus, students' progress could be considered as token reinforcers backed up by such reinforcers as promotion, salary increments, and recognition of the teacher by the community.

The Role of the Consulting Teacher in the Model

When a student is not making satisfactory progress toward objectives even though the student's teacher is employing his full repertoire in trying to achieve such progress, the teacher could turn to a consulting teacher for help in arranging for more effective teaching/learning procedures. This help would come in the form of instruction regarding the principles of the behavior model of education and applications of these principles. Thus, the consulting teacher, under this model, is an expert in applied behavior analysis and in helping teachers learn to apply the principles of behavior analysis.

Handicapped Learners

The behavioral model of education presented above does not specify which children are considered handicapped learners. Instructional objectives could apply equally to all children, regardless of where they fell on entry level skills and regardless of their rate of progress toward the objectives under the existing teaching/learning procedures. Standard definitions of handicapped learners involve the computation of averages. The handicapped learner is said to be the child who deviates from the average in one or more ways. For example, employing a traditional special education label, a retarded child is less than average in his rate of acquiring behaviors which lead toward instructional objectives. Under this model, one would be most apt to talk of *average environments* rather than *average children* (Lindsley, 1965). A given child might not be progressing at a satisfactory rate in the average teaching/learning environment that a given classroom offers. This formulation leads to change of the teaching/learning environment: changes in children's behaviors depend upon changes in the teaching/learning environment. However, as a major goal of special education in Vermont was to train regular teachers through services to referred children with the greatest need for special help, a decision rule for consulting teacher acceptance of teacher referrals was required. The rule currently employed by consulting teachers is outlined as follows:

1. Teacher identification of a student whose behaviors are not evidencing satisfactory progress toward instructional objectives.
2. Measurements of referred behaviors indicating need for improvement (i.e., behavioral changes).
3. Identified student behaviors being relevant to educational growth. For example, a consulting teacher would help a teacher arrange for the referred child to more frequently sit in his assigned seat only if the teacher also agreed to work with the consulting teacher to increase the student's spelling accuracy.

The above attempt to define handicapped children as related

to consulting teacher services leaves several questions unanswered. What levels of baseline measures are low enough to justify the services of a consulting teacher? When a child has been referred because of deficits in a particular academic behavior, should the consulting teacher insist on obtaining baseline measures for other behaviors, both academic and social? Attempts to resolve such questions are currently in progress.

TRAINING CONSULTING TEACHERS

The first program to train consulting teachers has been described by McKenzie, Egner, Knight, Perelman, Schneider, and Garvin (1970). This program was revised and strengthened during the 1969-70 school year. Fox (1970) carried out an analysis of the tasks performed by consulting teachers. Over 300 tasks were delineated and ordered into four general categories: individualizing instruction, analysis of behavior, research, and consulting/training.

Modules

The four task categories were translated into modules of instruction for the training of consulting teachers. Although not yet meeting the criteria for instructional objectives (Mager, 1962), the modules do serve as ultimate reference points in the training of consulting teachers and are described below:

1. *Individualizing Instruction:* The student will help teachers develop individualized sequences of instruction in the major areas of the elementary curriculum, with priority given to language and arithmetic behaviors. Sequences must include measurement of entry level skills, derivation and specification of instructional objectives, selection of relevant learning materials, and measurement of pupil progress. Sequences of instruction must be implemented with selected pupils and must include reliable data indicating successful completion of the sequences. A written evaluation of one instructional sequence must be presented to and approved by faculty.
2. *Analysis of Behavior:* The student will demonstrate his knowledge of the terminology and principles of the analysis of behavior by helping teachers and parents modify the behaviors of handicapped learners in the classroom setting as demonstrated by reliable measures of learners' behaviors. These applications of analysis of behavior will focus on:
    a. reinforcement
    b. scheduling
    c. shaping
    d. errorless discrimination.

3. *Research:* The student will *evaluate* research relevant to the education of handicapped learners according to the following criteria: applied, behavioral, analytic, technological, conceptual, effective, and generality (Baer, Wolf, and Risley, 1968).

   The student will *adapt* research meeting the above evaluative criteria to permit application of the research procedures to handicapped learners.

   Through consultees, the student will *apply* adapted research to handicapped learners with regular measures of learner's behaviors which reflect the effectiveness of the adaptation.

4. *Consulting/Training:* The student will consult with teachers, parents, and administrators to help them serve 32 handicapped learners as demonstrated by measured behavioral changes in these learners.

   The student will prepare and conduct a workshop on individualizing instruction and analysis of classroom behavior. School administrators, teachers, paraprofessionals, parents, and college undergraduates and graduate students may be participants in the workshop.

   The student will prepare practica involving applications of individualizing instruction and analysis of classroom behavior acceptable to the University's Special Education Program as 12 graduate credit hours toward an inservice Master of Education Program to prepare master teachers with special education skills.

   The student will make formal and informal presentations describing the training of consulting teachers, the role of the consulting teacher in the school, data from service projects performed by the student and consultees, and other related topics when called upon to do so. Presentations may be given for various special interest groups, school personnel, and other professionals.

The individualizing instruction and analysis of behavior modules describe skills that lead to an application of the behavioral model of education. Achievement of the research module enables the student to gain and apply new knowledge of individualizing instruction and the analysis of behavior. The adaptation of research which has met the Baer, Wolf, and Risley (1968) criteria is aimed at having the classroom teacher with whom the consulting teacher is working apply researched procedures. For example, in the elegant Hall, Lund, and Jackson study (1968), teacher attention was demonstrated to have reliable effects on the study behaviors of elementary school children. In order for a teacher to carry out procedures of this research, research measures employed would have to be adapted for teacher use. In the study, observers took the measures which were based on 10-second intervals. Such measurements would be difficult for a teacher to undertake. Adaptation of these measurement procedures has been made to allow teachers to sample at periodic intervals—for example every three minutes—the study behaviors of their students and obtain reliable measures of study behavior (McKenzie, 1970).

To achieve the modular objectives, over 200 specific instructional units have been developed. Figure 1 is an outline of one of the units in the individualizing instruction module.

Figure 1. A Sample Instructional Unit Used to Train Consulting Teachers.

University of Vermont   Special Education Program

Individualizing Instruction Module

Classroom Observation Unit
Unit Objectives:
The student will perform reliable (90% and above agreement or co-functional correspondence with an independent observer) classroom observations using the following three methods:
A.   Frequency recording
B.   Continuous recording
C.   Sample recording

Suggested Readings:

Suggested Activities:

Suggested Practicum Experiences:

As can be seen in Figure 1, each unit specifies an instructional objective as well as suggested activities, readings, and practica experiences which will help achieve the objective. These are suggested as the student may be able to produce evidence that he has already met the objective.

Entry level tests for the modules are not given to students. However, students who have many or all of the skills of the modules very rapidly complete units. For example, in the unit in Figure 1, if a given student had already undertaken classroom observations using the methods of frequency recording, continuous recording, and sample recording with satisfactory measures of reliability, the student would only produce these measures and reliability indices to complete the unit.

The units for each module are sequenced in what is an apparently appropriate order for the student to complete them. The students' progress through the units is self-paced, and each unit must be mastered before going on to the next (Michaels, 1971).

Experienced elementary and special class teachers begin study in the summer and continue on for two additional academic years. The complete training program is composed of 60 graduate credit hours with 15 of these hours in formal course work, 21 hours in practica involving applications of principles studied, and 24 hours of supervised internship in a Vermont school district.

Individualizing instruction, analysis of behavior, and research modules all form enabling objectives for the achievement of the consulting/training module. During the course of their training to be consulting teachers, students serve 32 handicapped learners, two during the initial summer, 10 during the first academic year, and 20 during the internship year. During the internship year, students conduct a workshop for teachers who have referred children to the interns. A series of practica courses is developed which the intern will begin to teach the year following his internship to teachers in his district who have entered a part-time Master of Education Program preparing master teachers with special education skills. The intern also has a half-time aide provided by his internship district, and during the internship year the aide is trained by the intern to conduct classroom observations, graph measures of students' progress, and develop individualized instructional materials.

Consulting Procedure

To help teachers and parents of referred children learn and apply the principles of individualizing instruction and analysis of behavior, students are taught to follow specified steps which form a procedure for consulting. These steps have been effective in teaching consulting skills and are outlined below:

Step 1: Referral Procedure. When a teacher has identified a child in his class who is not progressing satisfactorily, the teacher contacts his principal and receives a referral packet. In this packet, the teacher specifies behavioral deficits of the child and returns the packet to the principal, who contacts a consulting teacher. The consulting teacher arranges the first meeting with the teacher (typically by telephone) and outlines in general the steps which teacher and consulting teacher will follow.

Step 2: First Meeting of Teacher and Consulting Teacher. The con- consulting teacher helps the teacher define the problem in specific terms so that relevant behaviors are observable by at least two. An instructional objective is defined. The specified time period during which the behavior will be measured is chosen. A measurement procedure is defined as well as when the first data will be taken. The consulting teacher prepares a graph demonstrating how data points will be plotted. An inventory which identifies potential reinforcers for the child is completed. Consulting teacher and teacher agree to meet again when, and only when, the teacher has obtained and graphed measures of the child's behaviors.

Step 3: Second Consulting Teacher and Teacher Meeting. The teacher must bring plotted data to this meeting. The definition of instructional objective and measurement procedures are reviewed. Arrangements for establishing the baseline are discussed: the baseline will include stablized measures of behavior, a preliminary description of the concurrent teaching procedures and materials, as well as reliability measures obtained by the consulting teacher or his aide. A description of the child and a seating chart demonstrating his placement in the classroom is written, and arrangements for the first meeting with the parents of the child are made.

Step 4: First Parent Meeting. Teacher, consulting teacher, and parents go over the graphed data. A joint decision as to what will constitute a baseline is reached. Also discussed are potentially reinforcing objects and activities in the home. Parents sign letters indicating their consent for the use of special procedures to help their child.

Step 5: First Classroom Visit by Consulting Teacher. The consulting teacher observes the child in the classroom and notes the teaching/learning procedures and materials in effect. He attempts to identify modification procedures which will lead to more satisfactory educational growth of the child.

Step 6: Selection of Modification Procedures. One or more meetings are held with the teacher to specify the changes in teaching/learning procedures that will be implemented to improve behaviors of the child.

Step 7: Second Parent Meeting. Present at this meeting are the consulting teacher, principal, parents, and occasionally the child. The procedures which appear to be good candidates for beneficially modifying the child's behaviors are discussed. The consulting teacher clarifies these procedures and insures that all at the meeting understand and agree to the procedures. If the child is present at this meeting, the consulting teacher pays particular attention that the child agrees to the procedures.

Step 8: Implementation of Modification Procedures. The selected procedures are implemented with the teacher continuing to take measures of the child's behaviors, with reliability checks of measures made by the consulting teacher's aide.

Step 9: Evaluation of Procedures. Teacher and consulting teacher begin evaluation of modification procedures immediately upon implementation. If the procedures are reliably changing the referred child's behaviors in a satisfactory way, then consulting teacher and teacher go on to Step 10. If procedures are not satisfactorily effective, they return to Step 6.

Step 10: Maintenance and Follow Through. Once the child's behaviors have reached the levels of the instructional objective, measurements are taken only occasionally, rather than daily. If reinforcement has been used in the modification, the schedule of the reinforcer is gradually thinned: it is made contingent upon the response only occasionally. At this point an exit interview is held for the parents and teachers where data showing the changes in the child's behaviors are reviewed.

EVALUATION OF TRAINING OF CONSULTING TEACHERS

Services to Children

The major evaluative index of the training of consulting teachers is the services they perform for children. During the internship year, students perform services with reduced consultation from faculty, and each intern has as his objective providing services to 20 children as demonstrated by measured changes in children's behaviors. Two case studies, P_1 and P_{60}, are presented below as representative examples of the services the two interns currently in the program have provided for 40 children.

P_1 (Christie, 1971)

P_1 was referred to the consulting teacher intern because of his disruptive behaviors and his inconsistency in completing assigned work. Proceeding through the consulting steps, the focus behavior for P_1 was defined as percentage of written work completed each school day in reading, arithmetic, social studies, language arts, and science. Each day the teacher was to total the number of written responses P_1 had completed, divide these by the total responses assigned, and multiply by 100. In this way, a percentage of work completed each day could be derived and graphed.

Reliability was determined by the intern's aide rechecking P_1's papers and recalculating percentages completed. On several occasions the intern also checked P_1's work. Percentages of work completed, calculated by aide, intern, and teacher were identical.

On the intern's first visit to the class during baseline conditions, she observed the following behaviors during a half-hour period:
1. P_1 sat in the sink, swearing, squirting water at classmates, and pounding his feet on the cabinets.
2. He crawled inside the cabinets, making loud noises, throwing contents on the floor.
3. He went to his desk, as instructed by the teacher, knocked his chair over, pulled the contents of the desk out, and knocked the desk over.
4. He made airplanes out of workpapers and sailed them around the room.

5. He walked by a group of desks, yelled at the children, threw their papers on the floor, and tipped one desk over.

During that half-hour, P_1 was engaged in appropriate behavior 6/10 of a minute or 36 seconds.

Baseline measures (Figure 2) indicated for a 15-day period that P_1 completed on the average 40% of his assigned written responses, with wide day-by-day variability. The second conference was held with P_1's mother. (P_1's mother and father were divorced with P_1 living with his mother.) It was decided that P_1 would earn the new bicycle which the mother had planned to purchase. Each day he might earn 10 points for completing reading, five points for math, and 10 points for "good" behavior. No points were earned for completing written responses in social studies, language arts, and science because written assignments were not made every day in these subjects and P_1 had completed these assignments with better consistency than math and reading. A card signed by the teacher was sent home indicating how many points P_1 had earned for the day. The mother was given a large bar graph with sections marked with pictures of bicycle parts. P_1 could first earn one pedal of the bicycle which cost 50 points. The total price of the bicycle was set at 1,000 points, with different point costs for different parts of the bicycle.

The objective was for P_1 to complete 100% of his work on each school day, and to demonstrate more appropriate social behaviors as judged by his teacher. With the points and their exchange at home for bicycle parts in effect, P_1's percentages complete markedly increased (Home Consequences, Figure 2). During this time, as judged by the teacher, P_1's good behavior also increased. Every 30 minutes the teacher would go to P_1 and discuss his behavior during the preceding 30-minute period and award him a point if behaviors met her requirements. P_1 earned eight to 10 points per day for his good behavior.

Beginning with day 29 (Figure 2), P_1's mother left home for a trip. Although his percentages complete maintained for several days, they soon became variable. During this time he continued to earn points for his work completed and good behavior and had his card signed by the teacher to take home, but as he was staying with a relative, and his bar graph was at his mother's home, no longer was he exchanging earned points for bicycle parts. On day 40 (Figure 2), his mother returned from the trip. Subsequently, P_1's behavior reached the 100% level where it has remained. With the return of his mother, P_1 earned nine to 10 of the 10 points for good behavior each day.

P_{60} (Flood, 1971)

P_{60} was among 12 pupils in a transitional first grade classroom. Each of the 12 pupils had had previous kindergarten experience,

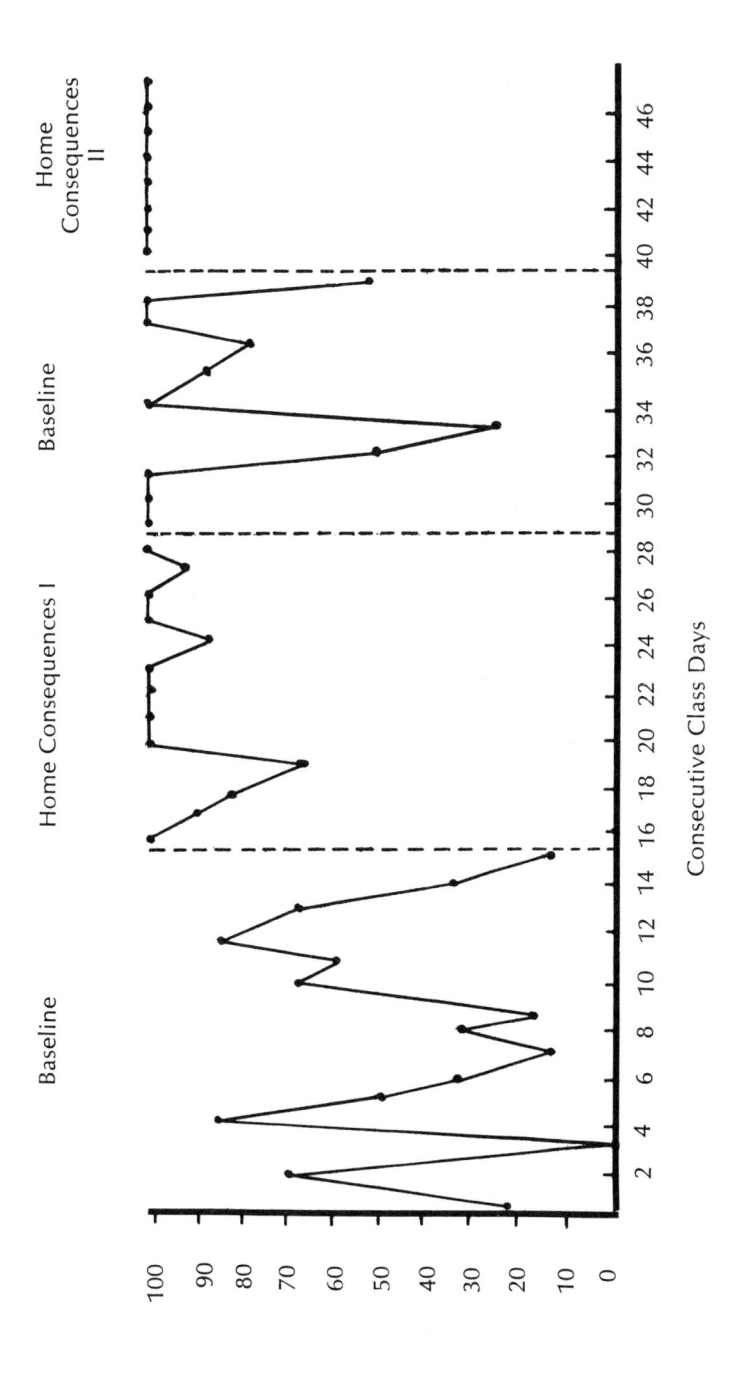

Figure 2. P$_1$'s Percentages of Daily Written Responses Completed.

but were judged to lack appropriate academic and social skills required in a regular first grade classroom.

The teacher had worked with the intern since the beginning of the year. During the first half of the school year, the teacher had modified social behaviors. During the second half of the school year the teacher chose to modify language behaviors. The majority of her pupils did not complete their assignments, made careless errors, and were very easily distracted from their work. The teacher, with the help of the intern, decided to establish a token reinforcement program for the language behaviors of her entire class. Measurements were kept for all 12 children. However, only the data of P_{60} are here presented.

Three language behaviors were defined. The first involved the daily writing lesson in which 10 letters and five words were printed. The words included the name of the day, the month, the child's first and last name, and address. Each of the letters and words written "correctly" would count as one point. To be considered correctly written, letters had to rest on the lines of primary writing paper: the top and bottom of the letter had to touch darker lines and the appropriate middle portion of the letter had to rest on the lighter line, and the lines forming each letter could not meet the lines of any other letter (see Figures 4 and 5). Each child was also given four teacher prepared workpapers daily. Workpapers involved reading readiness skills, such as color and word matching. The third behavior measured was the percentage correct on two reading workbook pages which were taken from the Palo Alto Reading Program. Each child worked on his own level for both workpapers and workbook pages.

Reliability checks were made periodically by the intern and her aide. They scored papers independently of the teacher and the two sets of scores were compared. Independent scores of workpapers and workbook assignments were identical. However, agreement of scores of writing assignments were less than desirable for the first few baseline measures, though agreements soon increased to 100% for the remainder of baseline and continued at 100% for the entire contingency period.

During baseline the teacher corrected each paper and recorded the number of correct letters and words, and percentages correct of the four workpapers and two reading workbook pages.

During contingency, when the child finished his writing lesson he would raise his hand and the teacher would correct it by circling those letters or words which met her criteria. One point was given for each letter and one for each word printed correctly. Points were immediately recorded on an index card marked in 100 squares.

The pupil then went on to complete his workpapers, at which point the teacher corrected these papers. A workpaper which was

100% correct on the first attempt earned 10 points. A corrected workpaper earned five points. One point was also given for each time the child wrote his name on a workpaper.

The child would then go on to complete his two workbook pages. Here, a completely correct page on the first effort was worth 20 points, while a corrected page was worth 10 points. Again, one point was given for a child writing his name on each page.

Pupils worked on their language assignments from 8:30 to 10:00 every morning. From 10:00 to 10:30 points were spent for desired activities, such as use of a workbench, painting materials, books and toys, and erector set. From 10:30 to 11:00 children attended a gym period. From 11:00 to 11:30 the children bid for class helper jobs for the following day. The pupil with the greatest number of unexpended points was able to trade his remaining points for a job first. The one with the next most points traded second, and so on until each child had a job and no remaining points. In this way, all points earned for a given school day were expended and a new point card was begun each school day. As points were spent, the teacher crossed them off the card.

After 14 days of baseline for writing, P_{60} began to earn points for his writing behavior (Figure 3). The number of words and letters written correctly for his writing assignment increased markedly. As P_{60} could earn a maximum of 15 points at this time, the activities for which points were exchanged were priced low. Because reliability of writing behavior is difficult to determine, P_{60}'s writing papers were retained for both baseline and contingency conditions so that additional observers could judge whether his writing behavior had improved. Figure 4 is a photograph of P_{60}'s writing behavior during baseline on day three, and Figure 5 is a picture of his writing behavior during contingency on day 33.

On day 24, P_{60} began earning points for teacher-made workpapers with an associated increase in his percentages correct for these workpapers (Figure 3). On day 34 (Figure 3) P_{60} could earn points for correct responses on his assignments in reading workbook leading to an increase in percentages correct on the workbook pages.

As additional points could be earned for correct responses on workpapers and workbook assignments, prices of purchased activities were increased.

Additional Evaluations

As students training to be consulting teachers complete instructional units, units are evaluated and returned with suggestions for further work and rewriting, if such is necessary. Frequently units are presented by the student both in written and oral forms and both occasions lead to feedback and suggestions for additional work if needed. In addition, each student has a study committee composed

Figure 3

P₆₀'s Writing, Workpaper, and Workbook Percentages Correct.

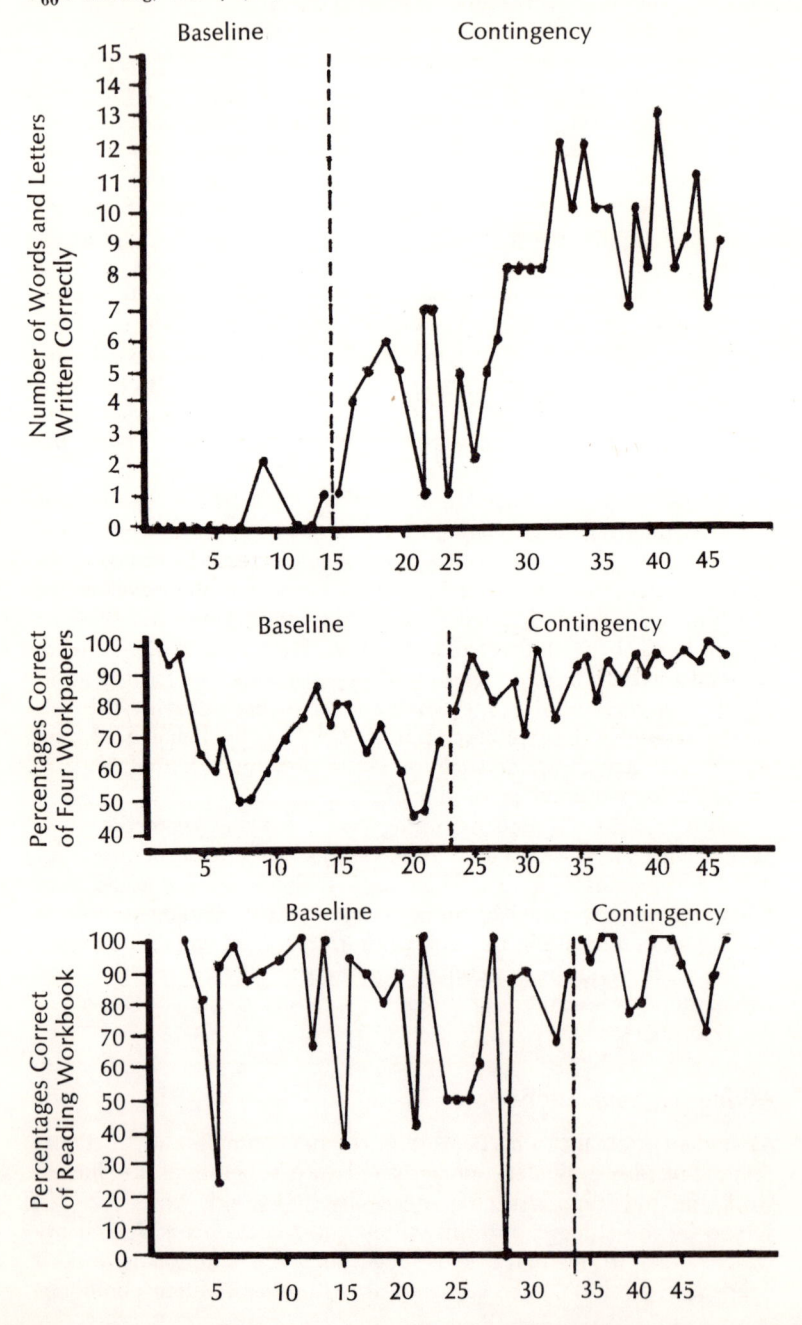

120

Figure 4

Sample of P_{60}'s Writing on Day Three of Baseline Conditions.

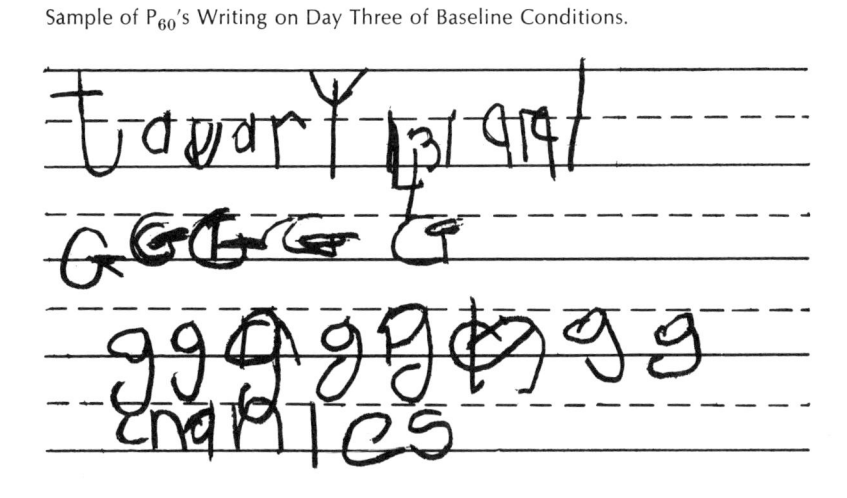

Figure 5

Sample of P_{60}'s Writing Behavior on Day 33 of Contingency Conditions.

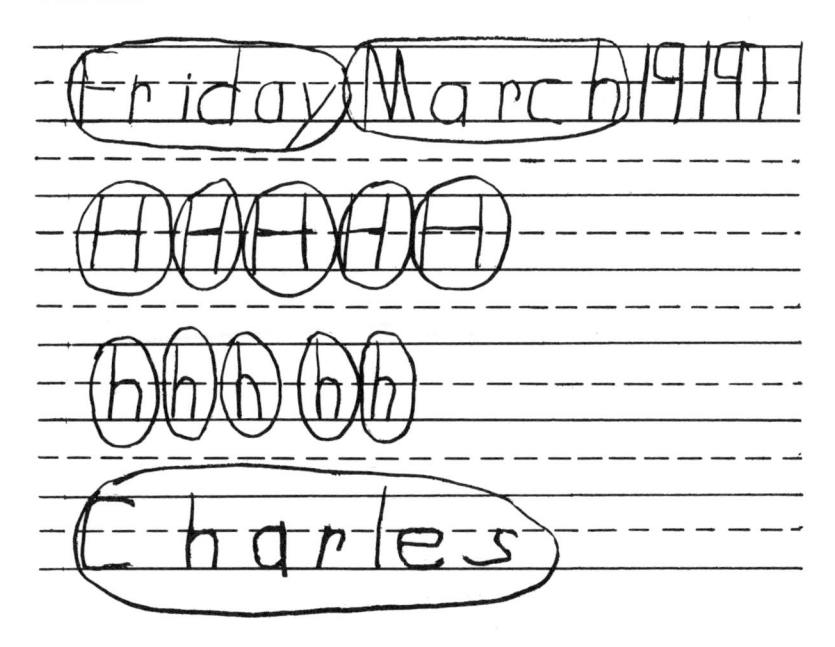

of faculty who conduct periodic reviews of units and case studies completed by students. Feedback and individual instruction is given to the student based on these reviews. Evaluation of units and reviews of student work serve as evaluations of the training program and have led to modifications of the program.

An interesting additional evaluation is provided by the number of teachers, who after working with consulting teachers-in-training on referred children, have gone on to apply the techniques they have learned, including measurement techniques, to non-referred children. For example, during the 1969-1970 school year over 200 children were referred by teachers to consulting teachers-in-training. An additional 200 non-referred children were served through applications of procedures learned with referred children.

It is the goal of the Special Education Program at the University of Vermont to train approximately 200 consulting teachers for Vermont. In this way, it is planned that a comprehensive community mental health program, as described by Patterson (1969), can be put into effect for all schools in Vermont. To date, 24 of Vermont's 52 superintendencies have been contacted in regard to their receiving interns who, following the internship year, would be employed as full-time consulting teachers. All 24 superintendencies have indicated their wish to employ consulting teachers, demonstrating additional positive evaluation of the training program.

Summary

Evaluations indicate that the training of consulting teachers is successful and that these personnel can effectively contribute to the academic and social development of handicapped children, while at the same time training regular classroom teachers in special education skills. Moreover, results indicate that certain handicapped children can be effectively managed and educated within regular classrooms. The consulting teacher approach thus appears to be a viable supplement to other delivery systems for providing special educational services. It should be both interesting and exciting to watch the expansion of consulting teacher services to include the entire state of Vermont.

REFERENCES

Baer, D., Wolf, M., and Risley, T. Some current dimensions of applied behavior analysis. *Journal of Applied Behavior Analysis,* 1968, 1, 91-97.

Bateman, B. D. Visually handicapped children. In Haring, N. G. and Scheifelbusch, R. L. (Eds.), *Methods in special education.* New York: McGraw-Hill, 1967. Pp. 257-302.

Christie, L. Home consequation of academic behaviors in a disruptive second grade boy. Internship report, Special Education Program, University of Vermont, 1971.

Darrah, J. Forum: Diagnostic practices and special classes for the educable mentally retarded — A layman's critical view. *Exceptional Children,* 1967, *33,* 523-528.

Dunn, L. M. Special education for the mildly retarded — Is much of it justifiable? *Exceptional Children,* 1968, *35,* 5-22.

Flood, C. Improving language behaviors in a transitional first grade classroom. Internship report, Special Education Program, University of Vermont, 1971.

Fox, W. L. The Master of Education Program to Prepare Consulting Teachers. Unpublished manuscript, Special Education Program, College of Education, The University of Vermont, 1970.

Hall, R. V., Lund, D., and Jackson, D. Effects of teacher attention on study behavior. *Journal of Applied Behavior Analysis,* 1968, *1,* 1-12.

Hanley, E. M. Review of research involving applied behavior analysis in the classroom. *Review of Educational Research,* 1970, *40,* 597-625.

Lindsley, O. R. Direct measurement and prosthesis of retarded behavior. *Journal of Education,* 1965, *147,* 62-80.

Mager, R. F. *Preparing Instructional Objectives.* Palo Alto, California: Fearon Publishers, 1962.

McKenzie, H. S. *1968-1969 Report of the Consulting Teacher Program, Vol. I.* Burlington, Vermont: Special Education Program, College of Education, The University of Vermont, 1969.

McKenzie, H., Egner, A., Knight, M., Perelman, P., Schneider, B., and Garvin, J. Training consulting teachers to assist elementary teachers in the management and education of handicapped children. *Exceptional Children,* 1970, *37,* 137-143.

McKenzie, H. S. A report on the University of Vermont's Consulting Teacher Program: Some measures of and contingencies for some school behaviors. Paper presented at Kansas Symposium on Behavior Analysis in Education, University of Kansas, Lawrence, Kansas, April, 1970.

Michaels, J. L. Individualized mass education without TV or computers. Paper presented at the Third Banff International Conference on Behavior Modification, University of Calgary, Calgary, Alberta, Canada, April, 1971.

Patterson, G. R. A community mental health program for children. In Hamerlynck, L. A., Davidson, P. O., and Acker, L. E. (Eds.), *Behavior modification and ideal mental health services.* Calgary, Alberta: University of Calgary, 1969. Pp. 131-179.

Skinner, B. F. *The technology of teaching.* New York: Appleton-Century-Crofts, 1968.

Terrace, J. S. Discrimination learning with and without "errors." *Journal of the Experimental Analysis of Behavior,* 1963, 6, 1-27.

The Responsive Teaching Model: A First Step In Shaping School Personnel As Behavior Modification Specialists
R. Vance Hall and Rodney E. Copeland

PIONEERING STUDIES IN SCHOOL SETTINGS

In the early 1960's Patterson (1965) and Zimmerman and Zimmerman (1962) reported on the first applications of systematic reinforcement procedures used to modify behavior of pupils in special laboratory school classrooms.

These studies were followed by a series of experiments carried out in the laboratory preschool at the University of Washington by Baer, Wolf, and their colleagues (e.g., Harris, Wolf, and Baer, 1964) which demonstrated that systematic teacher attention was an effective reinforcer for modifying the behaviors of pupils enrolled in a laboratory preschool. In the latter part of the 60's a number of persons including Wolf, Becker, O'Leary, McKenzie, and Hall carried out studies which demonstrated that teacher attention and token systems backed by various reinforcers could be used to modify both social and academic behaviors of pupils in public school special education classrooms. These were followed by studies carried out in regular elementary school classrooms (Hall, Lund, and Jackson, 1968; Thomas, Becker, and Armstrong, 1968) and later in secondary school classrooms (Hall, Panyan, Rabon, and Broden, 1968). These experiments were largely carried out by skilled researchers who used outside observers to record behavior and who specified when and how experimental procedures would be carried out.

These experiments as well as those by Quay, Wolf, and others were important in that they demonstrated conclusively that teacher attention, classroom privileges, games, and token reinforcement systems were effective in decreasing disruptive behaviors and increasing academic performance in regular classes of so-called normal pupils.

Unfortunately, however, these demonstrations of what could be done, as has been previously pointed out by Patterson (1969) at the first Banff Conference, were merely that, demonstrations. There was some evidence that at least some of the teachers who participated in these experimental studies continued the practices that had resulted in improved pupil behavior and performance after the experiments were over, but there was also evidence that in some cases the teachers involved soon reverted to less effective practices once the experimenters withdrew.

These studies were certainly justified, however. In terms of their contribution to the literature and as research they have provoked a great deal of the interest that is apparent today and which has resulted in conferences and workshops on behavior modification throughout the United States, Canada, Mexico, and countries abroad.

THE RESEARCHER AS TRAINER MODEL

The experimenter-directed research study is not, however, a good model for training individual teachers. For one thing it is prohibitively expensive. Furthermore, even though all the available trained researchers quit writing books and giving presentations at conferences and workshops to devote full time to working with teachers in their classrooms, only a very small fraction could be reached.

Besides, it is no wonder at all that teachers who have been involved in experiments contrived by someone outside the classroom have failed to continue carrying out experimental procedures after the experimenters have left the scene. One reason for this is that often these experiments were dependent on systems requiring equipment and observers not available in normal classroom situations and the system collapsed when the equipment and observer were withdrawn. Another probable reason is that some of the procedures, especially complex token systems, required so much energy and effort that the gains in pupil performance were not enough to maintain the teacher's behavior once the social and whatever other reinforcers that had been provided by the experimenters were no longer available to the teacher.

THE LECTURE MODEL

In the past few years many teachers have been "taught" the learning theory principles which are basic to using behavior modification in the schools. However, there is little evidence that exposure to learning theory principles and the research literature in college classrooms and teacher workshops has generated much more than increased interest in behavior modification. Very few teachers, counselors, principals, and school psychologists translate what they have learned in the usual workshop or lecture type class into actual practice in their roles as educators.

Thus, although experimental studies carried out by skilled researchers have played an important role in generating interest and demonstrating that behavior modification works in the classroom, they have not provided a good model for training teachers, nor have they necessarily provided procedures which teachers can adapt and use in their own classrooms with the resources currently available to them.

By the same token, learning about learning theory principles and behavior modification studies in the usual college lecture class or through school inservice workshop does not seem to be a good model for rapidly changing the role of teachers, principals, and counselors to become specialists in behavior modification.

THE RESPONSIVE TEACHING MODEL[1]

What then might be a more effective approach? An approach which might produce experimental studies demonstrating procedures which can be carried out by teachers given the resources currently available? (This is a necessary condition if procedures are to be put rapidly into practice.)

1. What kind of an approach will not only expose teachers to the basic learning theory principles they need to know, but result in getting them to apply those principles in their own schools and classrooms?
2. What kind of an approach will be more likely to result in a continuing development of the technology of behavior modification and at the same time sustain the enthusiasm it has generated in order that its potential as an approach to learning and education may be fully realized?
3. What kind of an approach will result in the rapid training of an increasingly larger number of the teachers already in the classroom and improve the likelihood that they will continue to use behavior modification techniques after initial training is terminated?

There may be a number of approaches which will achieve the desired results. Our personal knowledge of the Consulting Teacher Program under McKenzie at the University of Vermont and Bushell's Headstart Follow-Through Model at the University of Kansas are promising examples.

The Responsive Teaching Model which a group of graduate students have helped develop at the University of Kansas also seems to show a great deal of promise.[2] We have outlined the program in a special issue of *Educational Technology* on contingency management (Hall, 1971).

Essentially the program involves enrolling teachers, principals, counselors, school psychologists, and any other school-related per-

---

[1]The development of this model was supported in part by the National Institute of Child Health and Human Development and the Public Health Service (HD-03144-03 Bureau of Child Research and Department of Human Development and Family Life.) Reprints may be obtained from R. Vance Hall, Juniper Gardens Children's Project, 2021 North Third Street, Kansas City, Kansas 66101.

[2]The students who helped develop the Responsive Teaching Model include Jasper Harris, Rodney Copeland, Herb Rieth, Dick Fox, Hector Ayala, Marilyn Clark, Lois Cox, Jerry Wyckoff, Johnny Freeman, Ace Cossairt, Jerry Albright, Mike Davis, Jerry Gregerson, and Harriet Barrish.

sons interested (including speech therapists, substitute teachers, school nurses, and parents) in a college or district credit course or workshop. It is preferable to teach such a course in the teacher's home district and when possible to involve the entire staff of a given school, including principals, teacher-aides, and interested parents.

As summarized in Hall (1971) the Responsive Teaching program is designed to:
1. Provide reinforcement through the earning of professional and/or academic credit.
2. Teach practical measurement and recording procedures which can be used in the classroom.
3. Present basic learning theory principles which form the basis for behavior modification.
4. Present information on previous research and applications in school settings.
5. Have participants carry out studies in their own school situation.
6. Provide as much contact with other participants and their studies and with someone skilled and knowledgeable to assist in understanding principles and in carrying out a classroom study.

Professional and/or Academic Credit

Since this model requires active participation and responding on the part of participants, as much reinforcement as possible should be available to those who make the responses. Since college or professional credit is desired and is needed by most school personnel, such credit should be arranged for whenever possible.

Practical Measurement and Recording Procedures

More precise observation and measurement is the backbone of behavior modification training and application. Therefore the first emphasis should be, and is, on ways teachers can observe and measure behavior as they teach. While automatic recording devices and interval recording by a trained observer have been used in many of the research studies which have appeared in the literature, both are generally impractical in most classrooms in terms of availability and expense.

Therefore participants are urged to attempt to scientifically define behaviors of concern to them, and to obtain baseline records of those behaviors using *event recording* procedures, *duration measures, direct measurement of a permanent product* or *time sampling* procedures. All of these procedures can be carried out by school staff members while they are on the job without incurring a great deal of expense.

Figure 1 presents baseline records of behaviors recorded by teachers using these observation techniques.

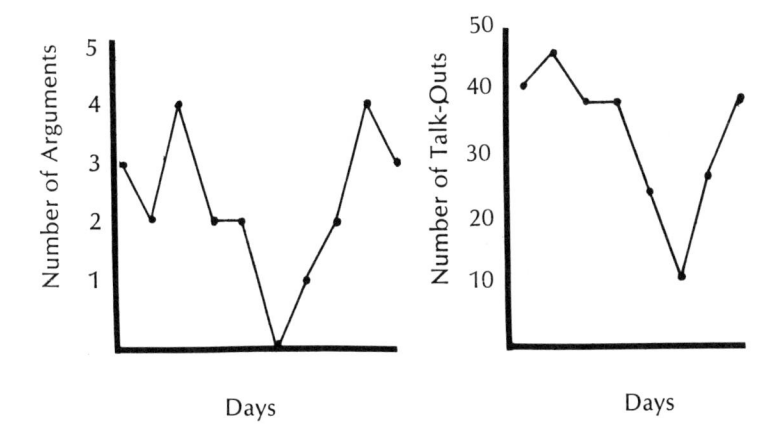

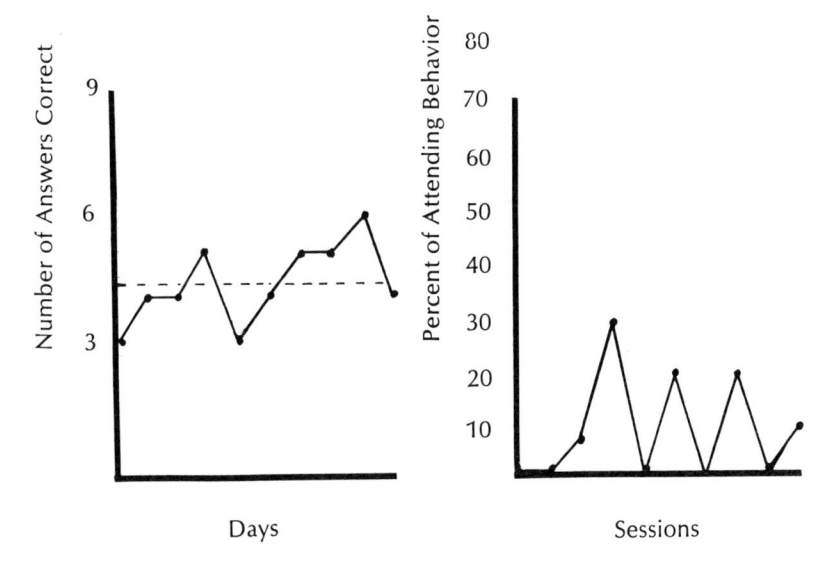

Figure 1

As participants begin to attempt to record behaviors which concern them, they are taught how to graph them as simply and clearly as possible.

Figure 1 presents conventional graphs of baseline records of behaviors recorded by teachers using the four most commonly used observation procedures. The conventional graph has the advantage of being familiar to and easily interpreted by most educated persons and since it can be drawn on regular graph or even plain notebook paper its cost is negligible.

Cumulative records are also introduced and some teachers choose to present data as a cumulative record. In addition, participants are taught about obtaining measures of the reliability of their observations. Usually the second observer who makes reliability checks by making a simultaneous observational record is a fellow teacher, a teacher-aide, the principal, counselor, or very often a responsible pupil. Reliability records are often shown right on the graph presenting the primary observer's data.

Participants are also introduced to applied behavior analysis scientific verification procedures (Baer, Wolf, and Risley, 1968) which allow them the opportunity to turn their project into an applied experimental study.

As will be seen in the studies presented later both reversal and multiple-baseline designs lend themselves to studies of individual and group behaviors in school settings.[3]

Learning Theory Principles

Once participants are well-launched in learning how to measure and record behavior and have begun graphing their baseline data, they are introduced to the principles which are basic to behavior modification through class lectures and reading (e.g., Hall, *Part II: Basic Principles of the Behavior Management Series*) and research reports found in journals such as the *Journal of Applied Behavior Analysis* and *Exceptional Children*.

Previous Applications in School Settings

The presentation of data from several studies carried out by persons who have previously taken the class is of prime importance in providing examples of the application of principles and procedures. For example Figure 2 might be used to illustrate the effects of systematically reinforcing a desired behavior which had a low baseline rate. (See Appendix I for a complete write-up of the data in Figure 2.)

---

[3]For a more complete description of what is taught participants regarding how to record and measure behavior and how to carry out an applied behavioral experiment see *Behavior Management Series Part I. Behavior Modification: The Measurement of Behavior (1970).*

Figure 2. A record of the percent of an arithmetic worksheet completed by a third grader. $Baseline_1$: Prior to experimental conditions. *Surprise at Home:* Parents gave surprise contingent on 60% of the worksheet being completed. $Engineer_1$: Subject earned activity for entire class and led the activity contingent on 100% of the worksheet being completed. $Baseline_2$: Other pupils allowed to be class leader. $Engineer_2$: Earning activity for class and being leader in that activity again contingent on completion of worksheet.

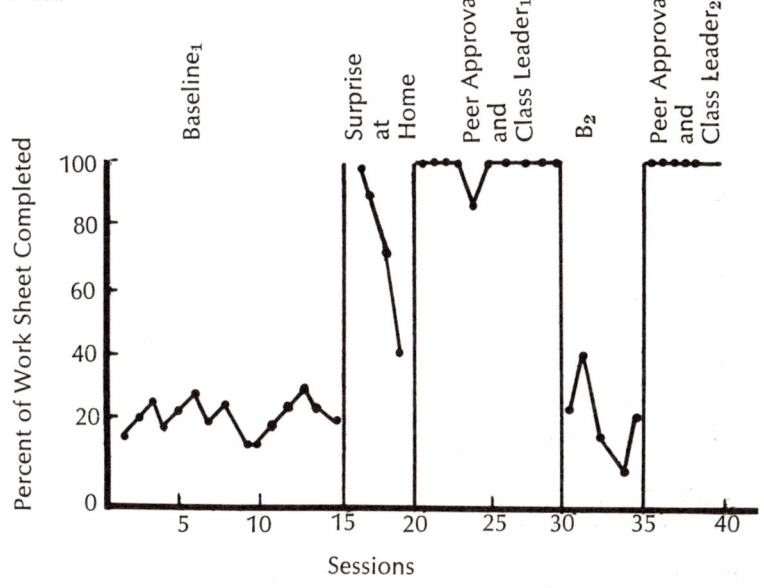

The data from the study in Figure 3 might be used to illustrate escape behavior. (See Appendix II for a complete write-up of the data in Figure 3.) In this case a boy was reinforced for increasing the accuracy of doing math problems by allowing him to escape from the tutoring session as soon as he worked 15 problems correctly.

The application of an extinction procedure might be illustrated by presenting the data in Figure 4. (See Appendix III for a complete write-up of the data in Figure 4.)

Punishment is also presented in terms of examples of studies which previous participants have carried out. Care is taken to emphasize that punishment is a technical term and is defined by its effects on behavior rather than by its topographical characteristics. Cautions and ethical considerations of when punishment is appropriate form the basis for considerable discussion and interchange within class sessions.

Data from an example of a simple punishment procedure are presented in Figure 5. (See Appendix IV for a complete write-up of the data in Figure 5.)

Figure 3. A record of the number of correct answers to fifteen math problems by an eighth grade boy in daily tutoring sessions. *Baseline₁*: Prior to experimental conditions when subject has engaged in daily tutoring session. *Contingent Escape from Tutoring₁*: Escape from tutoring contingent on number of correct math problems. *Baseline₂*: A return to pre-experimental conditions in which length of sessions was not contingent on performance. *Contingent Escape₂*: Escape from the tutoring situation again contingent on number of correct math problems.

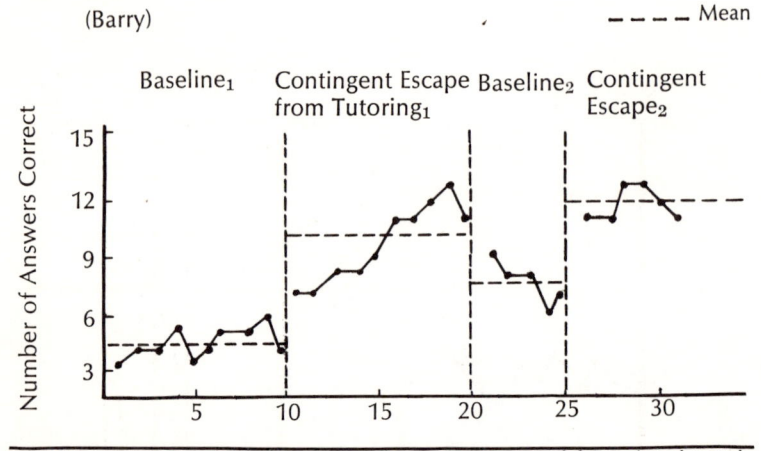

Figure 4. A record of the number of arguments emitted by a fourth grade boy during thirty-minute tutoring sessions. *Baseline₁*: Prior to experimental conditions. *Ignore₁*: The tutor ignored the subject if he disagreed with her directives. *Baseline₂*: A return to pre-experimental conditions. (The tutor attended to arguing behavior.) *Ignore₂*: The tutor once again ignored arguing behavior.

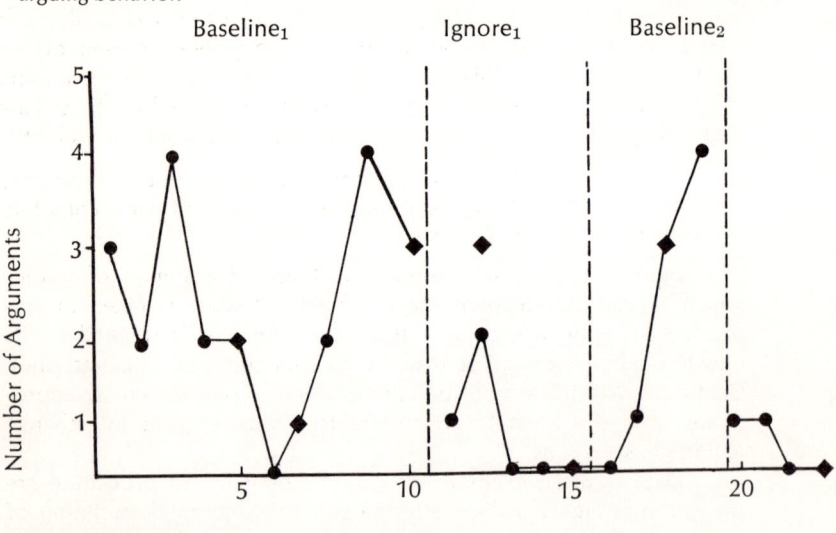

Figure 5. A record of the number of cries, whines, and complaints of a seven-year-old, emotionally disturbed boy during reading and math periods. *Baseline₁*: Prior to experimental procedures. *Slips Taken Away for C., W., or C.*: Slips of paper with his name written on them were taken away contingent on cries, whines, or complaints. *B₂*: (Baseline₂) A return to pre-experimental conditions. *Slips₂*: The taking away of slips was again made contingent on cries, whines, and complaints.

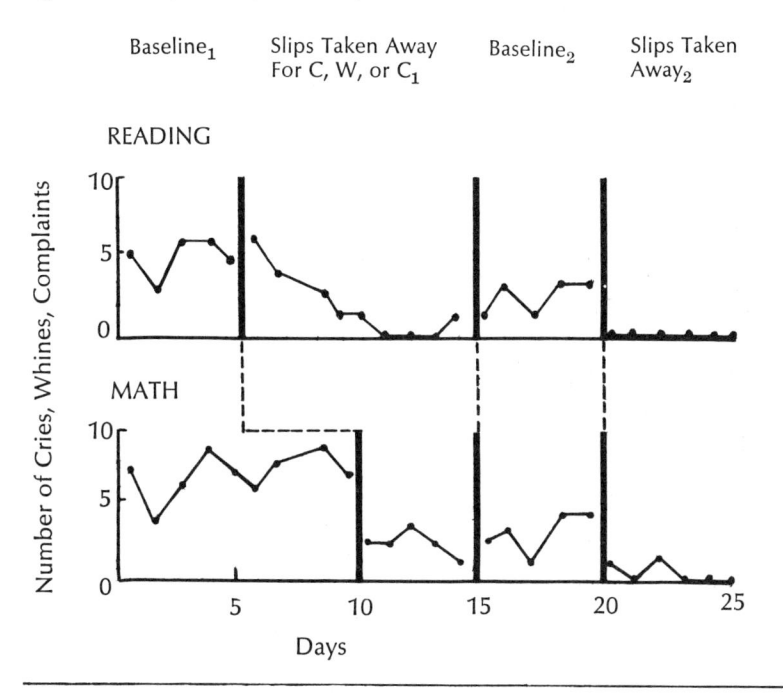

Other studies such as that in Figure 6 are used to illustrate how shifting from a continuous schedule of reinforcement to an intermittent one can be effective in maintaining a behavior once it has been established at desired levels. (See Appendix V for a complete write-up of the data in Figure 6.)

In summary, an attempt is made to relate behavior modification principles and procedures to numerous examples of their application in school settings.[4] Whenever possible studies carried out by previous class members are used.

Studies Carried Out by the Participants

The real backbone of the Responsive Teaching Model, however, and the aspect which probably accounts for the greatest amount of learn-

---

[4] A presentation of the basic principles and number of additional examples of studies are available in Parts II and III of the Behavior Management Series.

133

Figure 6. A record of the percent of daily assignments completed by a fifth grade girl. *Baseline₁*: Prior to experimental procedures. *Reinforcement₁*: Privileges were contingent on completing 100% of the daily assignments *Baseline₂*: A return to pre-experimental conditions *Reinforcement₂*: Privileges were once again contingent on the completion of all daily assignments. *Post Checks*: Privileges were contingently available on an intermittent basis.

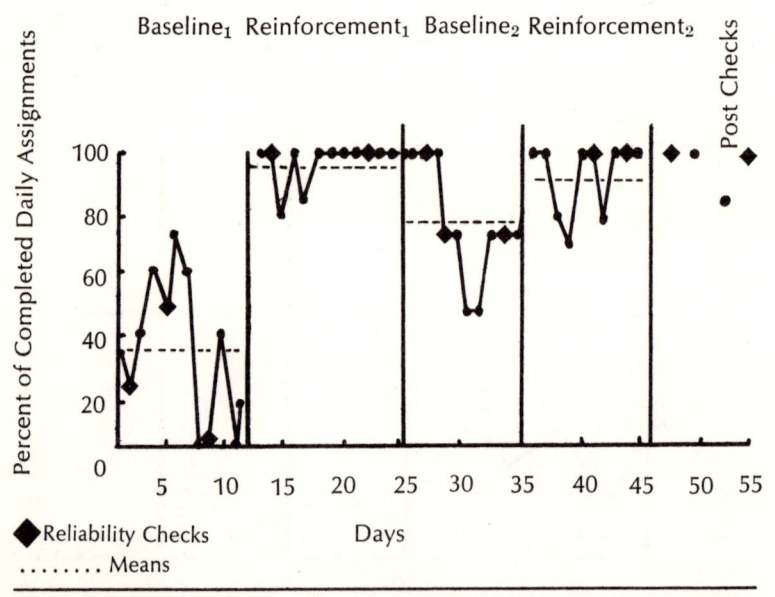

ing is, of course, the study carried out by the participants themselves. In carrying out a study the teachers, counselors, and principals have an opportunity to measure behavior, to obtain reliability checks, to present their data in graphic form, to apply systematic experimental procedures, and to scientifically verify whether their experimental procedures were causally related to the changes in behavior that were observed.

In doing so a great deal of learning seems to take place. Teachers become aware of the importance of observing and measuring behavior more closely than they had previously and learn how to measure and record the behaviors most important to them. They begin to recognize the close relationship between behavior and the current environmental events which shape and maintain it. They discover that by using systematic behavior modification procedures they can teach more effectively. They seem to develop a realistic appreciation of what behavior modification has to offer realizing that these powerful procedures can do a great deal but that they require concerted effort and concentration if they are to be implemented.

At the same time they add to the growing file of practical behavior modification procedures which other educators can look at and use. Since their studies involve behaviors that teachers in the field consider important and since the procedures used for measuring behavior and the stimulus materials and consequences applied were available in actual school settings, the studies and procedures developed are far more likely to be relevant and applicable immediately than the more contrived studies conducted by outside experimenters.

Contact with Other Participants and Someone Skilled in Behavior Modification Techniques

One of the most important aspects of our model is that participants have an opportunity to follow the progress of the studies carried out by other members of the class. When we started out the class was small, that is 10 or less. Since a good portion of time was set aside in each class session for progress reports and discussion of problems encountered, participants learned not only from their own study but from participating in the discussion of all other studies being carried out as well. During recent semesters our classes have increased in size to as many as 70. Since time would prevent everyone from being able to present data each time in so large a class, we have been dividing the class into groups of 10 to 15 participants. These groups meet during the last half of each session. The groups are led by someone that has taken the class previously and who has shown particular interest and an ability to apply behavior modification procedures.

Within the group, members have an opportunity to ask questions and take quizzes over the lecture presentations but primarily they are used for sharing and discussing the data from each member's study. During the last two or three sessions brief presentations of each study are made to the entire class so that all have an opportunity to learn of the many different behaviors measured and the consequences used to modify them.

The experience of being a group leader is of key importance also. Whenever possible it is given to a school principal, counselor, helping teacher, special education consultant, or other school district person who can consult with the teachers during the week and provide support and assistance and/or check on the reliability of measurement when necessary. This results in the further training of the group leader. As a result they often become, in effect, the behavior modification consultants for their schools or districts. Some have subsequently given inservice workshops in their own districts or have led workshops in other areas of the country. More importantly, they have been able to provide expert counsel and reinforcement for the efforts of teachers in their districts who have a desire to continue applying behavior modification procedures in their classrooms and schools.

Excellent examples of this are provided in the program being carried out by Herb Rieth in the Shawnee Heights Unified District in Tecumseh, Kansas. In his role as school psychologist Dr. Rieth has been giving inservice workshops designed after the Responsive Teaching Model presented here. He has then been able to follow up and assist teachers who receive this training through ongoing contacts with them.

Jerry Wyckoff and Marilyn Clark and their colleagues in the Shawnee Mission Unified School District have played a similar role of doing on the job follow-up with teachers who have referred problem pupils to the special education department of their school district. By helping teachers modify problem behaviors of pupils in their own classrooms many pupils who might otherwise have been labeled as emotionally disturbed, learning disabled, or retarded have been maintained successfully in the regular classroom.

Summary

The Responsive Teaching Model as we have outlined it here is not necessarily unique, nor is it necessarily the only good approach. But it does seem to offer several features which make it a promising approach for capitalizing on the current interest in behavior modification and it would seem to have the following advantages:

1. It fits into the current system of inservice training or extension courses which can be offered to school staffs during the school year. (And it can be adapted to a workshop format.)
2. It provides reinforcement for participants in the form of effective techniques which they can actually apply and which make them more effective as educators of children and in the form of professional and/or academic credit.
3. It seems to provide enough of a background in learning theory so that participants have more than a bag of tricks to apply to the behavior and learning problems of their pupils.
4. It seems to promote further interest and disposes the participants toward wanting to learn more and to continue using what they have learned. A surprising number of students have followed the behavior modification or applied behavior analysis approach in pursuing their graduate training.
5. It provides for further training of a certain number who participate as group leaders and who can thus act as resource persons and trainers of others.
6. It provides teachers with measurement and research skills which allow them to become researchers in their own classrooms. This new disposition to observe and measure behavior and then to scientifically verify the efficacy of their teaching procedures will

probably be the greatest long range contribution of behavior modification to education.

7. It has resulted in many studies which have demonstrated procedures that can be carried out by teachers, principals, and counselors within the structure of the school system as it now exists.
8. Thus, it adds to the technology of teaching procedures which increase teaching effectiveness *now*.
9. Since participants have been all but unanimous in their acclaim of behavior modification after participation in the program, since there is evidence they have been able to continue to use what they have learned in teaching practice, since they have "sold" their fellow teachers and school administrators on this approach to learning and behavior, it seems to be an important early step in the process of shaping our educational systems toward fully embracing behavior modification and what it has to offer the children in our schools.

An outline of the current format and schedule of assignments and exams for the course is presented in Appendix VI.

REFERENCES

Baer, D. M., Wolf M. M., and Risley, T. R. Some current dimensions of applied behavior analysis. *Journal of Applied Behavior Analysis,* 1968, *1,* 91-97.

Barrish, H., Saunders, M., and Wolf, M. Good behavior game: Effects of individual contingencies for group consequences on disruptive behavior in a regular classroom, *Journal of Applied Behavior Analysis,* 1969, *2,* 119-124.

Hall, R. V. Training teachers in classroom use of contingency management. *Educational Technology,* 1971, *9,* 33-38.

Hall, R. V. *Behavior management series — Behavior modification: Part I: How to measure behavior; Part II: Basic principles; Part III: Applications in school and home.* Lawrence, Kansas: H & H Enterprises, 1971. (P.O. Box 3342, Lawrence, Ks. 66044.)

Hall, R. V., Panyan, M., Rabon, D., Broden, M. Instructing beginning teachers in reinforcement procedures which improve classroom control. *Journal of Applied Behavior Analysis,* 1968, *1,* 315-322.

Hall, R. V., Lund, D., and Jackson, D. Effects of teacher attention on study behavior. *Journal of Applied Behavior Analysis,* 1968, *1,* 1-12.

Harris, F. R., Wolf, M., and Baer, D. M. Effects of adult social reinforcement on child behavior. *Young Children,* 1964, *20.*

Patterson, G. R. An application of conditioning techniques to the control of a hyperactive child. In L. Ullman and L. Krasner (Eds.), *Case studies in behavior modification,* New York: Holt, Rinehart and Winston, 1965. Pp. 370-375.

Patterson, G. R. A community mental health program for children. In L. A. Hamerlynck, P. O. Davidson, and L. E. Acker (Eds.), *Behavior modification and ideal mental health services.* Calgary, Alberta: University of Calgary, 1969. Pp. 130-172.

Quay, H. C. and Galvin, J. P. *The education of behaviorally disordered children in the public school setting.* Final Report Project No. 482207, U. S. Office of Education, Bureau of Education for the Handicapped, 1970.

Thomas, D. R., Becker, W. C., and Armstrong, M. Production and elimination of disruptive classroom behavior by systematically varying teacher's behavior. *Journal of Applied Behavior Analysis,* 1968, *1,* 22-35.

Zimmerman, E. H. and Zimmerman, J. The alteration of behavior in a special classroom situation. *Journal of The Experimental Analysis of Behavior,* 1962, *5,* 59-60.

APPENDIX I

Author: A. Tribble and R. Vance Hall

Title: Effects of Peer Approval on Completion of Arithmetic Assignments

Source: Education 115, University of Kansas

Population and Setting: John, a third grader in an elementary public school was an active and capable participant in group classroom activities; however, he had poor independent work skills. Individual assignments received very little attention from John, as he engaged in other behavior at those times such as playing with his comb, rolling his pencil up and down his desk, making airplanes, and drawing cars.

Behavior Measured: In arithmetic class the teacher generally explained and discussed with the students the day's work and had different students work example problems at the board. Subsequently she gave the pupils an individual work sheet to complete. A daily measure was taken on the percent of the problems John completed on the work sheet in arithmetic.

Experimental Procedures and Results: Baseline$_1$: The daily mean percent of arithmetic problems completed in the 15 baseline sessions was 18%. *Surprise at Home:* At the beginning of arithmetic class on the 16th day it was explained to John that if he completed 60% of his arithmetic worksheet he could take a card home and exchange it for a surprise his parents had for him. This contingency had previously been arranged with the parents. John responded to the surprise on the first day but by the fourth day of this condition his percent of work completed was back to the baseline level. *Peer Approval and Class Leader$_1$:* On the 20th day of the study the teacher announced a new game to the class. John was designated as engineer, and if he completed his arithmetic worksheet, the whole class with John as leader would get to engage in a special activity. The activities varied, but each day the class would urge John on and clap for him if he got the worksheet done. John's daily percent of assignments completed during this 10-day condition was 100% on all but one of the days on which it was 80%. *Baseline$_2$:* For 5 days the teacher let another child be the engineer and John's mean daily percent of the worksheet completed was 21%. *Peer Approval and Class Leader$_2$:* John was again allowed the opportunity to be the class leader of the special activities if he completed his worksheet. He finished his work sheets at a 100% level for the entire 5-day period. *Intermittent Reinforcement:* In order for the class leader and special activity contingency to affect all members of the class, the teacher began picking the engineer at the close of the study period. If the chosen person had finished his seatwork he received the applause of the class and got to lead them in the teacher designated activity. The teacher reported that John as well as others completed work at higher levels under this contingency.

Discussion: This study reveals that the opportunity to earn an activity for one's peers is a powerful reinforcer for certain individuals. John's rate of completing arithmetic worksheets increased markedly. Also, the study demonstrates the procedure of trying other treatment conditions in those cases where the initially planned treatment program is ineffective.

APPENDIX II

Author: Janet Milleret Van Cleave and R. Vance Hall

Title: Escape from a Tutoring Situation as a Reinforcer for Improvement in Math

Source: Education 118, University of Kansas

Subject and Setting: Barry was an eighth-grade boy whose history of low achievement in math was attributed to careless errors in computation. The author, a graduate student, had been assigned to tutor Barry in math for 30 minutes each school day. She had noticed little improvement in his work over the first few tutoring sessions.

Behavior Measured: Barry was given 15 addition, subtraction, multiplication, or division problems to do at the beginning of each tutoring session. The tutor recorded the number of problems Barry worked correctly each day before handing in the paper. After correcting the paper the teacher gave Barry the answer sheet and let him recheck his paper. This served as a reliability check. Over the course of the experiment Barry found two problems the teacher counted wrong that were right.

Experimental Procedures and Results: Baseline$_1$: During the first two weeks the tutor urged Barry to try harder so that he would do better. Under these conditions his mean of the scores was 4.3 problems correct (see Figure 3). *Escape From Tutoring$_1$:* Following baseline the teacher told Barry that for every problem he solved correctly before handing in his paper to be corrected he would earn a one-minute reduction in the length of his math tutoring session. Under these conditions his arithmetic scores increased rapidly. The mean of the scores for this phase was 10 problems correct per session. *Baseline$_2$:* In the second baseline phase the tutor told Barry he needed more practice and the tutoring sessions would be kept their usual length no matter what his scores were but she urged him to continue trying to do well. Under these conditions his scores decreased during the next week to a mean of 7.4. *Contingent Escape$_2$:* When experimental conditions were instituted once more during the following week, the average of Barry's math scores was 12 per session.

Discussion: This study demonstrated that escape from the tutoring situation was an effective reinforcer which increased Barry's computation accuracy. The modification was scientifically verified by a brief reversal in which baseline conditions were reinstituted. This study presents a good example of escape behavior, that is the behavior of concern *increased* in strength when it resulted in the removal of something punishing. (This is sometimes called negative reinforcement, a much misused term which should not be confused with punishment.)

APPENDIX III

Author: Sharon Jones
Title: Extinction of Arguing Behavior in a 4th Grade Boy
Source: Education 118, University of Kansas
Population and Setting: Mitch was an 11-year-old boy enrolled in a regular 4th grade classroom. He had been labeled brain-damaged and learning disabled and was tutored six hours a week in reading, writing, spelling, and arithmetic. He would often disagree with his tutor over the correctness of his work. For example, the tutor reported that he would do an addition problem, she would tell him the answer was wrong, and Mitch would argue with her. Their dialogue typically went as follows:
Tutor: Mitch, you better check that answer over again.
Mitch: (Without looking at the problem) There's nothing wrong with it!
Tutor: Yes, there is.
Mitch: No, there isn't.
Tutor: Mitch, please look at the problem and think about your answer.
Mitch: It's OK! (He still hadn't looked at it.)
Behavior Measured: The tutor recorded the number of times Mitch argued with her during 30-minute tutoring sessions by making a mark on a note pad with a pencil each time he did so. An argument was defined as any disagreement with the tutor over the correctness of an answer. An observer independently recorded arguments during seven tutoring sessions distributed throughout the study. There was perfect (100%) agreement in six sessions. In one session the second observer recorded one more argument than the tutor (66-2/3 agreement).
Experimental Procedures and Results: Baseline$_1$: The number of arguments per session were recorded while the tutor carried out her usual interactions with Mitch. The number of arguments ranged from 0 to 4 per session with a mean of 2.3. *Ignore$_1$:* In this phase the tutor told Mitch only once if his answer was wrong. If he questioned her statement she pretended to be busy with something else and did not answer. During the five sessions of this phase the mean number of arguments was 0.6 per session with none in the last three sessions. *Baseline$_2$:* The tutor began responding once again whenever Mitch contradicted her when she told him he had made an error. By the fourth session there were four arguments. The mean rate was two per session. *Ignore$_2$:* When the tutor once again began ignoring Mitch's contradictions, arguments again quickly extinguished. The mean rate was 0.5 per session.
Discussion: This study showed that the tutor had been inadvertently reinforcing Mitch's arguing behavior by responding to his con-

tradictions when she told him he had made an error. When she withdrew this reinforcement, arguing quickly extinguished. A reversal procedure verified that withdrawal of attention was responsible for the decrease in arguments. The tutor reported that when she first began ignoring Mitch he went on to the next problem. She thereupon checked the problem wrong after he had finished the page. He soon began rechecking and correcting his answers.

APPENDIX IV

Author: J. Shellman and R. Vance Hall

Title: Reduction of Cries, Whines, and Complaints Through the Use of Punishment

Source: R. Vance Hall, Training Teachers in Classroom Use of Contingency Management, *Educational Technology,* April, 1971

Subject and Setting: The subject of this experiment, Ralph, was a seven-year-old boy who had been labeled emotionally disturbed and who attended a special education class with six other boys who had also been so labeled. The teacher reported that Ralph often disturbed the class by crying, whining, and complaining.

Observation: Ralph was observed for 30 minutes each day during arithmetic period and again for 30 minutes during reading period by a graduate student who was taking a practicum course in special education. Each separate instance in which he uttered a cry, whine, or complaint was tallied with pencil and paper. Periodic reliability checks were made by the teacher. The agreement of their records was always 83% or higher.

Procedures and Results: Reading: Baseline data were recorded for five days during the reading period. As can be seen in Figure 5, the mean number of cries, whines, and complaints was found to be about five per session. At the beginning of the reading period on the sixth day, the teacher gave Ralph five colored slips of paper with Ralph's name written on them. He was told that one slip would be taken from him every time he cried, whined, or complained. No other contingencies were placed on his behavior. Under these conditions his cries, whines, and complaints were reduced to near zero over the next ten days. During a brief return to baseline conditions (Baseline$_2$), cries, whines, and complaints increased in rate, but decreased to zero once Ralph was again given slips which were to be taken away contingent on cries, whines, or complaints. *Math:* Baseline data were recorded for 10 days during math period. When removal of the slips was instituted for cries, whines, and complaints during reading, no reduction was seen during math sessions. In fact, there was a slight increase in these behaviors during the second five days of baseline during math. The mean baseline rate was seven per session. On the eleventh day Ralph was given slips with his name on them for math as well as for reading period. One was taken away whenever he cried, whined, or complained. As can be seen in Figure 5, during a brief reversal in which this procedure was discontinued his rate again began increasing but decreased once again to near zero levels when the procedure was reinstituted.

Discussion: This study illustrated the use of both multiple-baseline and reversal research tactics to explore the effects of a punishment procedure which was effective in controlling cries, whines, and complaints in an emotionally disturbed boy in a special education classroom.

APPENDIX V

Author: Mary Jane Merrill, Ace Cossairt, and R. Vance Hall
Title: The Effects of Contingent Privileges on Increasing the Completion of Daily Assignments
Source: Education 118, University of Kansas
Population and Setting: Van was a fifth grade girl who seldom completed class assignments. Earlier in the year a school counselor had seen Van on a regular basis, regarding her low productivity. However, no change in behavior had occurred in the classroom. The study was carried out during the last four months of school.
Behavior Measured: Each school day the teacher directly measured the number of class assignments completed. A percentage of completed assignments was derived by dividing the amount of finished papers by the number of required papers. A dependable student in the classroom independently counted the finished papers on two or three days within each condition of the experiment. Agreement between the teacher and the student was always 100%.
Experimental Procedures and Results: Baseline$_1$: The mean percentage of assignments completed during the 12 days of baseline was 34%. *Privileges for Completing Assignments:* Beginning in session 13 Van was told she would have certain privileges if she completed 100% of her assignments for the day. The privileges Van choose to engage in were, (1) writing on the chalk board, (2) running errands, and (3) helping the teacher make bulletin boards. For each day that Van completed 100% of her assignments she would put an "X" on a chart which signified she had earned her privileges. During this 12-day experimental condition Van completed 96% of her assignments, while failing to meet the 100% criterion on only two occasions. *Baseline$_2$:* Beginning in session 25 Van was told she no longer needed to keep track of assignments completed. Privileges were given non-contingently. During this 11-day phase the daily mean percent of assignments handed in was 79%. *Privileges for Completing Assignments$_2$:* When privileges were once again made contingent on completing 100% of the assignment, the mean number of daily assignments completed increased to 94%. *Intermittent Reinforcement:* On the 45th day of the study Van was shifted from a continuous schedule of reinforcement to an intermittent schedule. Privileges were available to Van on a variable ratio schedule, in that she was allowed the special privileges contingent on completed assignments every several days. Van's mean percentage of completed papers remained above 90% as evidenced by several post checks.

Discussion: The problem of low daily rate of productivity was remedied by making natural classroom privileges contingent on completion of assignments. A shift to intermittent reinforcement on a variable ratio schedule maintained the high rates of productivity.

APPENDIX VI

Outline of Course Development and Current Format and Schedule

The course was first offered and developed through the extension services of the University of Kansas. Several conditions imposed by Extension Service rules helped to shape the format of the class. These included:
1. The course must meet three hours a week for 16 weeks.
2. There must be a final exam with a grade of 90-100% = A, 80-89% = B, 70-79% = C, 60-69% = D, 59% and below = F.

Other practical considerations that imposed constraints were:
1. It must be held after school hours.
2. It must be held away from the main campus in Lawrence (35 mi.) since most were teachers, counselors, and principals in the Kansas City area.
3. Most teachers did not have ready access to the campus library.

The course has been modified considerably as it has developed over the past four years. Until the present year no suitable text material was available so the content was presented in the form of lectures. During the present year the *Managing Behavior Series* of booklets which cover the content presented in the course lectures have probably made the lectures less essential. Even so, however, most participants have attended class regularly and have rated the lectures highly. This is possibly due to the fact that an integral part of the lectures has been to allow class members to make responses in class in the form of both verbal and written quizzes over the main points covered. Immediate feedback as to the correctness of responses on quizzes is a feature of their use. Quizzes are kept by the student for future reference and no grades are recorded.

The basic requirements of the course are as follows:
1. Read 14 studies, at least 7 of which are found in the literature outside the text. A brief report of the 7 studies must be handed in by mid-term, 7 additional are due at the end of the course. Reports include the following information:
Author:
Title:
Subject and Setting:
Behavior Measured: (Reliability assessed?)
Experimental Procedures:
Results:
Scientific Verification Procedures Used:
Significance:
All 14 reports which are limited to one page or less must be handed in for a passing grade in the course. Reprints are made available on a rotating basis at each class session and include studies such as those by Patterson; Zimmerman and Zimmer-

man; The University of Washington preschool studies; Becker and O'Leary; McKenzie, Wolf, Hall, and their colleagues.
2. A final examination which determines 40% of the final grade. A pre-final exam covering essentially the same material as that on the final is given on week 2. This provides feedback to students and the teacher of the course on how well the lecture and reading material has been learned and is used by the students in preparing for the final.
3. An applied study is carried out. This determines 60% of the grade. The student records behavior, attempts a modification and a scientific verification, and writes up the study in appropriate form which includes:
Title:
Author:
Abstract:
Introduction: (Cite 3 or more studies)
Subjects and Setting:
Behavior Measured:
Observation Procedures: (Reliability)
Experimental Procedures and Results:
Discussion:
Although it is hoped that a successful modification will be carried out, this is not a requirement for a top grade. Honesty in recording data with checks on reliability of observation are stressed. If a procedure is unsuccessful students are encouraged to discover why, to use alternate strategies, and to scientifically verify the effects of their procedures using reversal or multiple-baseline strategies. An interpretation of the results or lack of them in the discussion is given great importance in determining the final grade.

The general format of class sessions has been as follows:
1½ hours — Lecture, demonstrations, films and short in-class verbal quizzes over material presented.
½ hour — Small group discussions *re* the class lecture and written quiz which is self-corrected.
1 hour — Presentation of data, discussion of measurement problems, etc., by class members in small groups.

The course calendar is as follows:
Lectures:
1. Structured lectures, demonstrations, films—*weeks 1-11*.
2. First examination—*week 12*.
3. Review, discussion of issues of ethics, morality, limitations, and further clarification—*week 13-15*.
4. Final examination—*week 16*.
Readings:
1. First 7 due week 8; returned week 9.
2. Second 7 due week 15; returned week 16.

Project:
1. Share data and problems weekly in small group sessions beginning week 2.
2. Hand in first write-up of project at 9th class session; returned week 10.
3. Hand in final write-up week 16; returned.

The duties of the Group Leaders are as follows:
1. Lead discussions *re* class lectures, answering questions, clarifying, etc.
2. Give in-class written quizzes, explain, and clear up errors *re* responses.
3. Monitor data and discussions of studies presented by group members.
4. Refer problems that can't be solved to instructor.
5. Carry out at least one reliability check visit for each study in group if at all feasible.
6. Check reports on readings, help grade exams and reports on projects.
7. Attend weekly seminar.
   a. Get copy of instructor's lecture notes.
   b. Help prepare examinations.
   c. Discuss problems encountered.
8. Give lectures or parts of lectures including the presentation of data.

Direct Intervention in the Classroom: A Set of Procedures for the Aggressive Child

G. R. Patterson, J. A. Cobb, and R. S. Ray[1]

This report outlines a set of procedures designed to be applied in the classroom to improve both social and academic skills of emotionally disturbed, or more appropriately, out-of-control children. The approach, which we have labeled "Direct Intervention," has evolved gradually as a result of our continuing efforts to meet the crises encountered when treating aggressive boys in the classroom setting. Many of the procedures which eventually comprised the approach were based upon the work of other investigators, but together they constitute a set of flexible approaches to problems encountered in the classroom. The procedures will be described in detail, along with reference to "historical" background material where it is relevant. The approach was used for 11 consecutive cases of aggressive-disruptive boys, all from different classrooms. Observation data will be presented from baseline, intervention, and follow-up which summarize the effectiveness of the approach.

Direct Intervention is a technology which is characterized by low response cost on the part of the teacher; it also emphasizes involvement of peers and, to a lesser extent, parents, at all phases of the classroom program. Because most of the teachers with whom we worked had a deep antipathy towards the whole idea of behavior modification, the emphasis has been to develop an approach which requires low response cost from the teacher. Therefore, during the early phases the behavior modifier assumes personal responsibility for bringing about immediate changes, both in the social system and in the behavior of the problem child. In effect, the behavior modification approach is tailored specifically to the setting. The first section which follows summarizes the writers' speculations about the components of this system which are relevant to the production of disruptive behavior in children.

---

[1]The preparation of the manuscript was supported by PHS grant #1330, NIMH grant #15985, and Career Development Award MH 40,518. Many of the ideas expressed here were contributed by our colleagues, Dave Shaw, N. Wiltz, J. Reid, Helen Walter, Vern Devine, and Karl Skindrud. We owe a particular debt to the cadre of professional observers who provided the high quality data used to evaluate the intervention procedures: LaVella Garber, Rachael Condon, Betty Brummett, Jonni Johnson, Irene Troup, Terri Shaw, Shirley Cole, and Jo McDowell. We are also indebted to Steve Johnson for his careful critique and editing of an earlier version of this manuscript.

The Classroom as a Social System

The low rate of reinforcement and the haphazard use of contingencies, serve to indict the classroom as an anachronistic social system. Performance within this system is presumably maintained as a function of two hypothesized internalized abstractions, "a love of learning," on the one hand, and a reciprocal "love of teaching" on the other. The designers of the contemporary classroom have ignored the necessity for providing appropriate contingencies necessary to insure performance. This omission in turn led to the construction of a social system that is destructive to productive functioning in both the teacher and the child.

Traditionally, the child has been viewed as an information processing system which required no particular reinforcers. Hence, in the traditional view, the teacher is not specifically trained to provide high rates of contingent social and non-social reinforcers. In keeping with this tradition, most classroom observation studies show that in the course of an hour, teachers dispense very few reinforcers such as praise, a smile, a touch, or even attention. For example, observation data from Madsen, Becker, and Thomas (1968) indicated that teachers averaged *less* than one social reinforcer per minute for appropriate classroom behavior. Comparable data from Hotchkiss (1966) also showed less than one reinforcer per minute for each of two teachers in a classroom of educationally handicapped children. Assuming a classroom of 30 children, this means that, on the average, a child could expect one teacher-dispensed social reinforcer every 30 minutes! This seems an extraordinarily lean schedule of reinforcers to support the acquisition process in the young child.

It is hypothesized that one outcome of such a lack of attention to social engineering is that the appropriate social or academic behavior of some children cannot be maintained by such reinforcement schedules. Some lack the social and academic skills necessary to produce even the average schedule of two teacher-dispensed reinforcers per hour. Their adaptive behaviors will not be controlled by the teacher-dispensed reinforcing contingencies. Instead, these children are likely to learn that disruptive behaviors will produce high rates of peer reinforcement (Ebner, 1967) and teacher attention (Hotchkiss, 1966; Hall, Lund, and Jackson, 1968; Walker and Buckley, 1971a).

At one level, it is perhaps paradoxical to note that teachers tend to be relatively non-reinforcing for adaptive behaviors but are quick to respond to disruptive or deviant behaviors. The explanation for this paradox lies in the apparent effectiveness of aversive stimuli in controlling social behaviors. The details of this process are outlined in several recent publications (Patterson and Reid, 1970; Patterson and Cobb, 1971). Suffice it to say here that many forms of disruptive behaviors which occur in the home and the classroom represent powerful means of coercing the social environment into providing social reinforcers. In this coercion process, the teacher is placed in the odd position of reinforcing the very behaviors which make her life miserable as a teacher. Several observation studies have shown that the *majority* of teacher "attention" followed *non*-study behavior! (Hall, et al., 1968; Hotchkiss, 1966; Werry and Quay, 1968; Walker and Buckley, 1971a).[2] Observations made in a special classroom showed that a small group of disruptive children monopolized most of the teacher's attention. For these deviant children, the rates of deviant behavior co-varied with the rate of teacher attention (Anderson, 1964). This, of course, is a very inefficient use of teacher time; but, as pointed out by Staats (1968), in many classrooms only the very deviant *or* the academically skilled child can consistently produce high rates of teacher attention and interest. While the middle-class child may have been previously trained to respond with appropriate academic and social behaviors under such lean schedules, the culturally deprived child, the "immature" child, and the emotionally disturbed child may be generally deficient in such skills. The limited supply of social reinforcers available in that setting may not be sufficient for their acquisition. The increasing discrepancy between the environmental demands and the child's repertoire leads to a situation in which the child is probably going to develop either escape and avoidance behaviors or learn some highly coercive methods of forcing the environment to respond.

Most of his time is expended in talking to his neighbor, walking around the room, giggling, clowning, or fooling around in his seat, all of which are presumably reinforced by peers and the attention of the teacher. Presumably, the normal and deviant child differ from each other in the rates with which they emit these and other behaviors. Data presented by Werry and Quay (1968) indicated that the deviant child was out of his seat over twice as much as the normal child; he made noise 25 times as often; he vocalized inappropriately twice as often. While the normal child attended to his task about 77% of the time, the deviant child was on task only 54% of the time. These data are in essential agreement with the figure of 39% provided by Walker, Mattson, and Buckley (1969) for a class of disturbed boys. Similarly, Hamerlynck, Martin, and Rolland (1968) showed that a special class of retarded children spent an average of only 45% of their classroom time "on task."

---

[2]That there may be wide individual differences among teachers in their reinforcing reactions to both deviant and appropriate child behaviors is suggested by an observation study of two elementary teachers (Madsen, Becker, & Thomas, 1968). The baseline classroom data showed that one teacher reinforced appropriate child behavior an average of 19.2 (frequency per 20-minute session), while the comparable contingencies for the other were 1.2. These same teachers reinforced inappropriate behaviors an average of 1.9 and 8.7 during the same time periods.

As shown in the prediction study by Cobb (1970, 1972), the work skills necessary for academic achievement consisted of such observable behaviors as "attend," "talk to peers about academic materials," and "compliance," and that other behaviors competed with work-oriented behaviors. *As demonstrated by Cobb (1970) with two samples of fourth-grade children, these and other observable classroom behaviors provided multiple regression coefficients of .63 and .61 with arithmetic achievement scores.* The results have been replicated with first-graders for both arithmetic and reading skills (Cobb, 1970).

Although no data are available, it is our assumption that the reinforcing contingencies necessary to maintain effective teacher behaviors are usually inadequate as currently provided by the children, parents, or other community agents. The current philosophy of education de-emphasizes the necessity for external reinforcers (Bruner, 1963).

It is hypothesized that not only are classroom contingencies for teachers provided on very lean schedules, but also that teachers receive *high rates of aversive stimuli*. This latter accrues in large part from the high rates of out-of-control child behaviors found in the primary grades. That this "punishment" has an impact upon the teacher is suggested by the study reported by Gotts (1967) which showed that one of the most frequent causes of stress for the teachers lay in their difficulty in managing children's disruptive behaviors. These findings suggest that not only should teachers be trained to make better use of contingent social and non-social reinforcers during the primary grades, but also additional training in the construction and application of programmed materials, contingency contracts, and data collection.

CLASSROOM INTERVENTION

The most efficient approach to the problem of dealing with children who do not adjust to the classroom undoubtedly lies in re-designing the school system. Applications of modern programming methods, and a careful functional analysis of both teacher and student behavior would produce more effective academic performance and a "happier" lot of students and teachers. The Distar Program outlined for the first two primary grades described by Becker, Engelmann, and Thomas (1969) constitutes such a beginning. However, until such systems are fully developed and adopted by the public schools, the problem remains with us.

The last decade of behavior modification research within the classroom setting has produced a variety of techniques which can be grouped, for purposes of this paper, into three alternative approaches to dealing with the disruptive child who may additionally be failing in his academic studies: (1) the child may be removed from the classroom and placed within a special token culture classroom; (2) the teacher may be trained in contingency management techniques and expected to handle the problem herself; (3) the behavior modifier may go into the classroom aand assume responsibility for initiating and insuring the success of the intervention program before turning it over to the teacher and the peer group. Each of these alternatives has particular assets and liabilities associated with its use. Presumably, the well-trained school counselor or psychologist would be familiar with all three.

Token Culture Classrooms

In many respects, the most dramatic application of behavior modification principles was to be found in the reports describing the token culture classroom. Although innovated as recently as 1962-1963, procedures such as those described in the reports by Zimmerman and Zimmerman (1962), Homme, de Baca, Devine, Steinhorst, and Rickert (1963), and Birnbrauer, Bijou, Wolf, and Kidder (1965) led to attempts to extrapolate the procedures and to provide extensive data with which to evaluate their efficiency (Haring and Kunzelmann, 1966; Kounin, Friesen, and Norton, 1966; Valet, 1966; Quay, Werry, McQueen, and Sprague, 1966; Hotchkiss, 1966; Hewett, 1967; O'Leary and Becker, 1967; Walker, et al., 1969; Clark, Lachowicz, and Wolf, 1968). The sum of evidence from these studies supporting the effectiveness of token systems in altering deviant social behavior for groups of children is overwhelming (O'Leary and Drabman, 1971). Although no data have been provided explicitly on this point, most of the authors imply that the procedures were effective for the majority of the children with whom they have been employed. Even for severely disruptive children, problem behaviors have been brought under control within a matter of a *few days* (Walker, et al., 1969).

The problem with this approach lies in the lack of information about what happens when these children are eventually returned to the public schools. Systematic follow-up data were provided by Walker, et al. (1969) for six of their subjects who had successfully participated in a token culture classroom. The children were returned to their regular classrooms in the public schools. *Their teachers received some training in order to continue the program. The follow-up data showed that approximately one-third of the boys were not adjusting to the regular classroom setting.* In a more recent study, Walker and Buckley (1971b) experimented with several procedures designed to maximize transfer of training effects from token classrooms to the public school classrooms. They found several which significantly facilitated transfer from the token classroom to the public school classroom. One of the more effective techniques used to produce this "generalization effect" consisted in large part of the Direct Intervention procedures involving the peer group which are the focus of the present report.

The Walker studies on generalization suggest that it may be possible to retrain children in token culture classrooms and then return them to the public schools by making provision for a brief training program for peers and teachers. However, the writers hypothesize that it might be best to leave all but the most extremely disruptive children in the classroom, and to carry out the modification program there. This would obviate the need for implementing both a token culture and then an intervention program to insure the transfer of the training effects.[3]

Teacher Training

Considering the large numbers of problem children involved, it would seem most efficient *to train teachers such that they could bring the behaviors under control*. The Precision Teaching group (O. Lindsley, Kansas Medical School) have specialized in training teachers in techniques of pinpointing, observing, graphing, and consequating behaviors (Haughton, 1968; Koenig, 1967). *Many studies have demonstrated the impact of teacher-dispensed social reinforcers upon children's behavior in the classroom* (Madsen, et al., 1968; Walker and Buckley, 1971a; Becker, Madsen, Arnold, and Thomas, 1968; Hall, et al., 1968). It has also been shown that teachers can apply contingency contracts (Cantrell, Cantrell, Huddleston, and Woolridge, 1969), natural consequences (Evans, 1967), or tokens (Bushell, Wrobel, and Michels, 1968), and also manipulate children's behavior.

The notion that the teacher can be trained to apply effective social engineering procedures to the problem child has several possible side effects which further enhance its attractiveness. Conceivably, she would apply these procedures to other children in the classroom and thus facilitate the acquisition of both pro-social and academic skills. The fact that she is the change agent should also facilitate both the persistence and the generalization of effects. Attractive as these possibilities might be, there are several considerations which mitigate against the approach constituting the only, or perhaps even a major, treatment alternative. The difficulty lies in

---

[3]It is also hypothesized that most special education classrooms, other than token culture classrooms, are settings in which the peer group is most likely to reinforce its members for deviant behavior (Ebner, 1967). It is our general impression that even normal peer groups seemed programmed to pay off with rather rich schedules for disruptive and ineffective behaviors. Presumably, homogeneous groups of problem children would have even richer schedules of reinforcement for these behaviors.

the "motivation" of the teacher. As noted by Hall, et al. (1968), and Krumboltz and Goodwin (1966), not *all* teachers seemed amenable to the training programs even though they volunteered to participate. In our own experience, some teachers are extremely resistant to learning or trying out such "novel" procedures. Unless the school district would permit us to pay them additional "combat pay" for their participation, it is unlikely that we could obtain their cooperation. Ogden Lindsley (personal communication) described a school district that permitted such reinforcers. He indicated that he had little difficulty in obtaining cooperative behaviors from the teachers.

In the same context, it is essential to have follow-up data on the proportion of teacher "trainees" who actually continue to perform their newly acquired skills. A study by Brown, Montgomery, and Barclay (1969) showed that when the experimenters discontinued reinforcing the teacher, her application of reinforcing contingencies to the problem child in her classroom returned to baseline, and the behavior of the child again went out of control. This is in keeping with our own impression that many teachers who have been trained to use behavior modification techniques cease to perform the skills shortly after the training program terminates. The training of teachers in contingency management skills must provide for teacher-reinforcers (pay increases, social reinforcement from peers and supervisors) if teachers' behaviors are to be maintained. Perhaps simple feedback data at regular intervals on how well the teacher is doing would serve a simple purpose as suggested in the Cooper, Thompson, and Baer study (1970).

At this point the teacher training alternative has several limitations in that some teachers will resist acquiring new skills, an unknown number will not continue to perform them once they are acquired, and appropriate teacher-reinforcers may not be available. There are also findings from the study by Walker and Buckley (1971b) which showed that investing 10 hours of time in training the teacher was not as effective in maintaining control of the problem child as investing a similar amount of professional time in working directly in the classroom with the peer group, teacher, and the problem child.

Direct Intervention

Direct Intervention is a label applied to the set of intervention procedures designed for application in the public school classroom. The procedures have evolved over the past six or seven years as a result of a continuing interest in working with hyperaggressive boys and their families.

The term "direct" refers to the fact that the training program occurred in the classroom setting rather than in an office or a clinic.

If there was a unique characteristic of the approach, it lay in the emphasis upon the experimenter's demonstrating, *in situ,* the effectiveness of his techniques. The teacher observed the procedures being modeled and was able to see the concomitant changes in the child's behavior. All of this occurred with minimal time expenditure by the teacher. By demonstrating the effectiveness of the procedures before turning them over to the teacher and peers, the initial high response cost necessary to bring these behaviors under control was *paid by the behavior modifier.* In this manner, the teacher entered the picture as behavior manager at a point when the least effort was required.

Direct Intervention programs typically took place in three stages. The first components of the direct intervention program included training the problem child in attending and work skills. Then arrangements were negotiated with parents and the school for the control of high amplitude coercive mands, such as fighting or the destruction of property. After several weeks, these programs were turned over to the teacher and other school personnal while the behavior managers arranged for yet a third stage designed to accelerate the acquisition of reading and/or arithmetic skills. In the latter, programmed materials and reinforcing contingencies were arranged such that a peer-teacher or parents assisted the child as he acquired these academic skills. It should be emphasized that not all of the procedures were used for each case. While generally the sequence was the same, it was also the case that it could be altered to fit the needs of a particular child or teacher.

Observation data were collected in the classroom during baseline, intervention, and follow-up.

The Work Box. The first phase of the program generally involved the use of the Work Box. It was hypothesized that this served two functions. First, its application resulted in involving the peer group with a concomitant increase in status for the problem child. Second, it facilitated the acquisition of a necessary set of survival skills.

One might say that the deviant child occupies a special "role" within the classroom. The high rate deviant child, with his multiple sets of disruptive behaviors, is very likely to have lower status among his peers (Moore, 1967). It is hypothesized that the low-status problem child probably finds himself on a different set of contingencies than does the non-deviant child. One might expect, for example, that he receives fewer initiations or invitations to play than do other children, and relatively higher rates of punishment. Observation studies showed that both deviant (Ebner, 1967) and low status children (Hartup, Glazer, and Charlesworth, 1967) received more punishment.

It has been our general experience that it is relatively easy to produce short-term changes in the reinforcement contingencies received by a child from his peers. For example, one can arrange for such a child to be elected "class president," or nominated to pass out the goodies at a party. These are techniques employed by many knowledgeable teachers. Our first contact with the phenomenon occurred when observing a hyperactive child. He received a mean frequency of 36.5 social reinforcers per day during 12 baseline recess periods. Then, for six consecutive days, he was given bags of candy to hand out during recess. The frequency of social reinforcers *received* increased to an average of 68.5 reinforcers per session! Then, during the three-day period when no candy was available, the rate of reinforcers dropped to a mean of 18 per session. When the largesse was resumed, the level returned to a mean of 52 social reinforcers over the two days.

The Work Box procedure was designed to take advantage of the ease with which "status" may be manipulated. At the same time it was designed to provide an occasion for acquisition of academic survival skills.

The apparatus consisted of a small box placed on the child's desk. It was a signaling device activated either by a radio transmitter or by a microswitch operated on the classroom circuit. In addition to a signal light, the device contained an electric counter which was also readily visible to the child. On the occasion of each reinforcement, the light flashed and the counter emitted a barely audible "click" as the event was recorded. Typically, the child was signaled on those occasions in which he attended to the teacher or worked at his desk. Details of the procedure were described by Patterson (1965), Patterson, Shaw, and Ebner (1969), and Ray, Shaw, and Cobb (1970).

After negotiating with the teacher, the following instruction may be given to the class:

> We are interested in learning how children work. This is a "Work Box." Each time the light flashes, it tells you that you have been sitting still and working. The counter in the box tells how much work got done. We are going to let several people try the box. If the person works real hard and gets 50 points, the whole class will get out five minutes early for recess today. If he works pretty hard and gets 30 points, the class gets out two minutes early. Who would like to try?

The contingencies are tailored in such a way that on the first trial the child will obtain the requisite points to earn extra recess time for his peers. Thus, initially, the child is reinforced for performing well within his limits. Gradually the contingencies are altered so that the time interval during which he must consistently work or attend is increased from five to ten seconds to twenty, and eventually to 60 or 100 seconds (see Ray, et al., 1970, for sample schedules). The conditioning sessions generally last from 20 to 60 minutes each day for a series of up to 10 days; they typically occurred during individual work at the desk rather than in group situations. The back-up reinforcers earned by the child were varied every few days and were selected by the peer group.

In a number of instances the parents have taken responsibility for applying the Work Box (Patterson, 1969; Patterson, et al., 1969). Supervising the parent in this setting provides a double pay-off for the expenditure of professional time. The parents learn at first hand about dispensing reinforcers on a contingent basis, and also obtain objective data on their child's inefficient classroom behaviors. The school, on the other hand, can see that the parents are committed to assisting them in altering these behaviors.

In most classrooms one or two children will "peek" at the counter during the trial and either touch the subject or whisper words of encouragement to him. At the end of the session there are almost invariably cheers when his successful performance is announced. In our experience such ovations occur often in the classroom of "normal" children, but seldom in "special" classes for problem children. The latter seem generally less reinforcing of pro-social behaviors.

The series of studies reviewed in the monograph by Patterson, et al. (1969) showed that four hyperactive control subjects showed no change in rates of observed deviant classroom behaviors over a four-week, no-treatment period. Disruptive, non-work-oriented classroom behavior was found to be relatively stable over this time interval. Data were also provided for six hyperactive subjects who participated in the Work Box procedure. The children ranged in age from 9 to 12, and in IQ from normal to retarded. Some of the children were severely brain-damaged and most were in special classrooms. Data on rates of disrupting and non-attending behaviors were collected for baseline and conditioning periods. The latter were obtained on occasions when the apparatus was *not* present, and thus constituted generalization data. Five of the six experimental subjects showed significant generalization effects in that their rates of non-attending behaviors were reduced. The median reduction in rate of 20% from baseline level required from 3 to 10 hours of classroom conditioning. The Friedman analysis of variance produced an X_r of 8.6 ($p < .02$).

These pilot studies encouraged us to attempt the devising of still more powerful procedures. In further studies the Work Box procedures were faded out after a few days, to be replaced by teacher-dispensed point systems. In one case, which represented an "emergency," it was possible to fade the Work Box procedure out and replace it with teacher-dispensed contingencies in a one-day marathon (Patterson, et al., 1969). In a series of three cases, these and other alterations (Patterson, et al., 1969) produced reductions from baseline in non-work-oriented behaviors of 50%, 70%, and 45%. These gains were brought about by expenditures of staff time of 7, 30, and 12 hours, respectively. These extensive decreases in rates of observed deviant behaviors were also accompanied by "clinical reports" of much improved social and academic skills, to the point where these children were no longer considered to be "disturbed." Extensive follow-up observation data collected in the classroom showed that the effects persisted. This series of developments served as a prelude to the procedures described in the present report.

In the present study, the Work Box produced immediate control over the deviant behavior. By the end of the first or second week, the child was usually placed on a point system administered by the teacher. In either case the points earned natural consequences for the peers and the problem child. Over a period of weeks the point system was in turn faded out until the child's behavior was maintained entirely by the usual schedules of social reinforcers supplied in the classroom.

A number of other investigators have used signaling devices of this kind with equal success (Koenig, 1967; Ward and Baker, 1968; Walker, et al., 1969; Bricker, 1967; Craig and Holland, 1970) with individual children. Several investigators have employed signaling devices of this type to work with an entire group (Quay, Sprague, Werry, and McQueen, 1967; Wolf, Hanley, King, Lachowicz, and Giles, 1970). While application of such devices as the Work Box will quickly bring attending and work-oriented behaviors under control, this does not necessarily insure generalization and persistence of such effects. For example, the careful studies by Quay, et al. (1967) and Ward and Baker (1968) showed that the control was quickly lost when the conditioning procedures were not present. It was hypothesized that one of the necessary components for generalization of conditioning effects lay in the involvement of the peer group. In addition, the gradual fading of the control procedures to teacher-dispensed reinforcers should also maximize the continuance of the effects brought about initially by the Work Box.

As a means of familiarizing themselves with the general terms, language, and procedures of behavior modification approaches, the teachers were urged to read *Living with Children* (Patterson and Gullion, 1968). More recently, other investigators have prepared programmed materials which may be more suitable for the classroom teacher (Buckley and Walker, 1970; Homme, Csanyi, Gonzales, and Rechs, 1970). To date, no control studies have been carried out to determine the unique contribution of either this or the Work Box procedure.

Walker and Buckley (1971b) provided data which bear on the importance of involving peers in the classroom intervention procedures. Forty-four children were trained in a token culture classroom and then at the end of two months of training were randomly assigned to one of four follow-up procedures. For one group, the public school teachers were given intensive training and supervision, as well as academic credit for the extra work involved. Teachers in the second group were given the same programmed materials and contingency programs used in the token culture classroom. After observing the special classroom, they attempted to apply the same principles in their own classrooms. Children in the third group were transferred to the public school with no particular training for the teacher other than a conference in which the program was explained. Teachers in the fourth group were given no particular training, but were instructed to keep daily records of the pupil's disruptive outbursts. Twice a week, if a child had "behaved," the behavior manager came to the classroom with the Work Box and made it possible for the child to earn a wide range of reinforcers for his peers.

The most direct test of the hypothesis about the importance of peer involvement was provided in the study by Wolf, et al. (1970). A signaling device was used to control classroom behaviors. Points earned for "self" were not as effective in controlling behavior as were points earned for "self plus peers."

The cost in professional time for the employment of the Work Box was only an average of five hours per child, in contrast to costs of eight to ten hours for other procedures. Observations of child behavior showed that children in the "Peer Involvement Group" displayed a mean of 77% work-oriented behaviors. The group in which the teachers used the same program and materials but received no intensive training displayed 75% work-oriented behaviors. The group in which the teacher was trained as a behavior modifier produced only 69%, and the untreated control group, 65%. The differences between these groups were significant and suggested that application of the Work Box in conjunction with peer involvement was the most efficient means of maximizing transfer of training.

The analysis by Cobb, Ray, and Patterson (1971) showed that the combination of Work Box, peer involvement, and fading the contingency controls to the teacher was very effective.[4] There were

---

[4]All of the children in that sample *also* participated in programs in which the parents received intensive training in child management skills. The details of the training program were outlined in the monograph by Patterson, Cobb, and Ray (1971). It was our hypothesis that the results of successful parent training would not generalize to the school. The studies by Wahler (1969) and Skindrud (1971a) showed, for small samples of children, that even though the parents were successful in bringing behavior under control in the home, no commensurate changes were observed in the school. Behavior seems to be under the control of specific settings. Each major setting such as the home and the school apparently requires its own intervention program.

instances in which additional innovations were necessary. Some children were so out-of-control that it was necessary to construct contracts integrating the efforts of the school and the parents. In addition, the fact that one-third to one-half of these children were failing in academic skills dictated the necessity for additional programs. These additional programs are described in the sections which follow.

Time Out, contingency contracts, and other addenda. Data from several individual case studies suggested that simply teaching a child to attend in the classroom will produce dramatic reductions in rates of high amplitude, disruptive behaviors (Bricker, 1967; Patterson, et al., 1968, see the case of Keith, Staats, and Butterfield, 1962). However, such beneficial side effects were not inevitable; and occasionally it became necessary to intervene directly to prevent severely disruptive behavior such as aggression and destructiveness. The procedures described here are ordered from least to most expensive. Generally, an attempt was made to apply the least costly procedure first and, if this was not effective, more "expensive" procedures were tried.

Time Out. Anderson (1964), Ebner (1967), and Walker and Buckley (1971a) demonstrated that, in both special and ordinary public school classrooms, the disruptive child captured a disproportionate share of the teacher's time. For example, Walker and Buckley found that 77% of the teacher's attention was contingent upon the behavior of the problem children. When a teacher responded to problem children, 89% of her attention was for inappropriate behavior, while only 11% was for appropriate behavior. The comparable percentages for non-deviant children were 24% and 76%. Ebner's (1967) data suggested that the reinforcement schedules provided for disruptive behavior by peers might be even richer. These findings raised problems for classroom intervention procedures. Even though the Work Box procedures provided massive reinforcement for attending and other classroom survival skills, the coercive behaviors were *also* receiving teacher- and peer-dispensed social reinforcement (e.g., attention, giggling). For this reason it was often necessary to employ a special procedure to "weaken" the disruptive behavior. Time Out served such a function.

Time Out was a mildly aversive consequence which could be arranged to follow disruptive classroom behavior. In such an arrangement, the child was removed from interaction for a period of one to ten minutes, and placed in a non-reinforcing setting. As shown in the research by White, Nielson, and Johnson (1972), the time interval may be relatively short. In that study one minute was as effective as 30 minutes for many of the children studied. As shown in several reviews (Leitenberg, 1965; Patterson and White, 1969), such arrangements, when applied *consistently,* produce reliable effects on most out-of-control children.

The use of TO must, of course, be negotiated with the principal, teacher, parents, and school counselor. In fact, the difficulties involved in such negotiations seem to constitute the chief factors mitigating against its use. A screened-off corner of the classroom served as an adequate TO place; for more extreme cases, it was necessary to send the child home.

TO was used *each* time the disruptive behavior occurred. For some subjects, TO was applied only for "hitting." For others it was applied to a wider range of behaviors, including "pushing" and "out of chair."

In many cases, by the end of the first week the teacher had observed a substantial number of applications of TO. All of them were carried out by the behavior modifier. Typically, TO produces an immediate reduction in the amount of disruptive behavior and serves to reassure the teacher that there is indeed some "hope." At this point many of the teachers were encouraged to read the programmed textbook which explains principles of contingency management (Patterson and Gullion, 1968; Buckley and Walker, 1970; Homme, et al., (1970).

Walker, et al. (1969) made a careful analysis of the effects of Time Out in the token culture. The classroom was first carefully programmed, using a combination of social reinforcers, token point contingencies, and Time Out. Once the class displayed very high rates of attending behaviors, Time Out procedures were discontinued. This resulted in a *loss* of control for four of the five deviant children. A similar withdrawal of token points resulted in no loss in attending behaviors. This analysis suggested that for some high rate deviant children, the use of Time Out might be a necessary component for the early phases of intervention. A more recent study by Walker (in preparation) suggested that a response cost contingency would serve a similar function.

Contingency contracts. It was our growing conviction that when *both* the parent and the school personnel participated in planning interlocking programs, the process of intervention was accelerated. The negotiations were centered around the construction of a "Contract."[5] Typically, the process began with the teacher, counselor, and principal pinpointing the child behaviors which they considered to be the most important prerequisites to the child's continuation at school. Frequently, school personnel will call for the reduction of "fighting," "throwing things in classroom," "stealing," and "fighting with the

---

[5]The adaptations of contingency contracting described here were introduced to us by J. Atkinson. We are particularly grateful for his contributions to our technology.

teacher or classmates," and an increase in "attendance," "completing work assignments," "doing work neatly," and "participating in class discussions." Even if these behaviors did not occur at home, the parents could provide back-up contingencies which would facilitate their control in the classroom.

Because this first stage in building the contract might be construed by some parents as another in a long series of attacks, each item was discussed in as neutral a fashion as possible. Although primary emphasis was placed upon those behaviors which were of most concern to the school officials, the parents also added to this list. All of the parents in the present study were extensively exposed to the language and literature of behavior modification. It seemed wise to require, at a bare minimum, that *both* parents respond to programmed materials on social learning theory *before* the school personnel committed themselves to an intervention program.

Natural consequences were specified for behaviors. For example, in order to leave the house in the afternoon or evening, the child was required to earn a certain number of classroom points. He might also earn the right to watch TV, to use his bicycle, or to stay up later at night.

The parents also agreed to provide negative consequences for the high amplitude behaviors of greatest concern to the school. For example, a fight could lead to a telephone call by the child to his mother, describing the fight. The mother would then take him home, put him to work for several hours, and then return him to school. In this way the parent reacted to crises which occurred in the school. By so doing, the school and the parent became allies in working together for behavioral control. Both parties to this contract participated in daily exchanges of data, and the communication was about *specific behaviors* rather than vague abstractions or innuendos about "sick parents" or "inept teachers."

The contractual arrangement was particularly useful in handling those difficult "transitional settings" as the school bus, lunch room, time between classes, and the walk to school. Similar applications of contingency contracts have been made by Phillips (1968) in working with pre-delinquent boys and by Cohen, Filipczak, Bis, and Cohen (1969) in work with delinquents. Many of the specific procedures in the application of contingency contracting are based on the prior work of Homme (1966, 1970).

As an example, Figure 1 provides the contract designed for Sam, a 10-year-old boy, who had placed some children under a physician's care because of physical attacks and who had stolen bicycles and destroyed school property. The Work Box procedure had decreased several of Sam's objectionable behaviors, but he still was creating problems not only in the classroom, but also in the lunchroom and recess yard. The parents met with the teacher, counselor, principal, and interventionist. A contract was drawn up as shown in Figure 1. The purpose of the contract was to delineate the role played by each person and to specify their behaviors following each crisis. In the past, the lack of communication between the home and school compounded the problems for effective intervention. The father would often complain that the school was unfair and the school complained that the parents were disinterested. By having the principal call the father each time Sam was sent home and specifying what had occurred, the father began to realize the justification for the school's concern. The principal, in turn, stated that the father was making great strides in caring about his son. Such agreements were modified regularly to fit changing conditions and were, of course, negotiated with all concerned parties.

Figure 1

Sam's Contract

The following is a contract between Sam and his teacher, his principal, and his counselor, in order for Sam to learn ways to behave during school. Sam will earn points during the school hours so that he can do some of the things he enjoys at home. The total number of points which can be earned each day is 50. The behaviors are the following:
- Talking in a normal tone of voice, e.g., not yelling.
- Cooperating with his teacher, e.g., not arguing and doing what is asked on the playground and in the halls.
- Minding other teachers.
- Remaining in chair unless school work requires moving in the classroom, e.g., not roaming around the room.
- Talking to other children at proper times, e.g., not disturbing other children when they work.
- Following his teacher's directions for work, e.g., doing the work assigned.

Sam will start with a total of 50 points each day and will lose a point for each time he does not follow the above rules. Each time he loses a point, he is to be placed in Time Out for five minutes. At the end of each school day his teacher will call his mother to give her a total of points earned for that day. Sam will be allowed five minutes of TV for each point.

Training for academic skills. In our earlier studies, intervention was terminated when the disruptive behaviors were brought under control. At that time arrangements were made for remedial programs for those children with severe academic deficiencies. To our dismay, the follow-up studies showed that the good intentions of the schools did not result in their initiating *effective* remediation programs. While some of the schools arranged for bi-weekly visits with the regular remedial teacher, in every case their efforts were *unsuccessful*. Typically, out-of-control children have been excluded from remedial programs *because of* their behavior.

Recent behavioral approaches to rehabilitating juvenile delinquents have emphasized the importance of increasing their academic skills in order to increase their chances of survival in society (Cohen,

---

For the following behaviors Sam is to be sent home from school for the day:
1. Destroying property.
2. Fighting with other children to the point of hurting them.
3. Taking property belonging to someone else.
4. Swearing.
5. Refusing to go into Time Out.

When Sam is sent home his principal will call his father to tell him what Sam has done. His principal will then call his mother so she will know that Sam is being set home. When Sam arrives home, he is to do some task around the house or yard until school is out, at which time he can follow the normal routine of the household except watching TV that night.

When Sam does not follow the rules of the lunchroom he is to be sent from the lunchroom to the principal's office without finishing his meal.

His mother will keep the number of points earned each day in order to assess Sam's progress. His mother will also continue to teach Sam reading skills until such time as he is able to handle reading material in the classroom. The therapist will continue to supervise Sam's mother until the reading program is completed. (To be signed by all parties.)

Date *Feb. 3, 1971*   Sam *Sam*
                          Mother *Mom*
                          Father *Dad*
                          Teacher *Mrs. Hansen*
                          Principal *Mr. Dean*

et al., 1968). The work of Staats (1968, 1962) probably served as the impetus for many of these developments. His emphasis on the use of programmed materials and carefully arranged reinforcement schedules served as a model for much of the work that followed. In one experiment (Staats, Minke, Goodwin, and Landeen, 1967), 36 adolescents who read poorly were selected and randomly assigned to an experimental group. This group relied upon adult volunteers and high school students to implement the training program. Tokens which could be traded in for money were used as reinforcers for performance. While an average of 38.2 hours of training was given to each child, standardized achievement tests showed no significant differences between groups. At present, it remains to be established that these more systematic, contingency-oriented remediation programs are more effective than those in traditional use.[6]

In addition to the pioneering efforts of Staats, other investigators have made use of peers as behavior managers in such programmatic approaches to remediation (Koenig, 1967; Patterson, et al., 1968; Hauck and Haring, 1968). In the present project, the parents of two boys (Sam and Mac) were selected as behavior managers to supervise the use of programmed remediation materials in the home. The parents were trained in a series of about six sessions to use a phonics approach and programmed reading materials to teach reading and spelling skills. The teaching skills were first modeled by the experimenter and then the parents practiced under supervision in the laboratory. After several supervisory sessions, the parents were contacted regularly by telephone to obtain the data on the child's reading progress.

For a more complete description of the application of these intervention procedures developed by Skindrud (1971), the interested reader is referred to Appendix I. There, the case of "Mac" is described in detail.

---

[6]Comparisons with control groups treated by regular classroom procedures also produced equivocal results for the evaluation study carried out by Hewett, Taylor, and Arturo (1967). In a partially confounded design, six teachers were first trained, then randomly assigned, to experimental and control group conditions in which the teachers in the "experimental groups" used reinforcing contingencies, including token points, but the teachers in the "control group" were instructed not to use tokens. The children, ages eight to twelve, in the experimental group, received four hours of class instruction per day for an entire year. Reading achievement tests showed no significant differences between groups; there was, however, a gain of 1.2 years in arithmetic achievement for the experimental group as compared to 0.4 years for the control group.

Several investigators have demonstrated significant increases in reading achievement test scores but in failing to include control groups, it is difficult to evaluate their results. For example, Barclay, Montgomery, and Barclay (1969) trained teachers and psychologists to work with a group of aca-

Sample

The eleven out-of-control boys for whom the school programs were designed were also participants in family intervention programs that have been described in several reports (Patterson, et al., 1968; Patterson, Cobb, and Ray, 1972).

Table I summarizes the data describing the sample of boys participating in the present study. The classification of fathers' occupational status was based upon the system provided by Hollingshead and Redlich (1958) with Class 1 denoting higher executive or major professional occupations, Class 4 as clerical, and Class 7 as unskilled laborer.

The median age of these boys was 8.5 years. They represented some of the more extreme out-of-control problems found in the community. The referral problems included aggression, temper tantrums, destruction of property, stealing, lying, hyperactivity, general disruptiveness, failure in school, and underachievement. In each case, the school was extremely concerned about the child's behavior, and in seven of the eleven cases, the child had either been previously expelled, restricted to half-day attendance, or was currently under the threat of expulsion. In short, these boys were regarded by the school personnel as major behavior problems.

While the data for fathers' occupations might seem to suggest that lower socio-economic status families were over-represented, the distribution is probably not different from that which obtains for the community at large.

Observation in the Classroom

Children were observed in the school setting by professionally trained observers. The classroom settings sampled included group and individual academic work situations as well as physical education classes and recess periods. The determination of the observation setting was a function of the teacher's concern. For example, if the

---

demically retarded children during a summer training session. Reading achievement tests showed an increase of .24, while arithmetic scores showed a gain of .36, and spelling, .25. Achievement tests scores also showed significant increases for the children in the special classroom engineered by Walker, et al. (1969; 1971b). Similar findings were obtained for underachievers, ages 12 to 16 years, in the special class designed by Nolan, Kunzelmann, and Haring (1967).

Thus far, the only adequately controlled study which demonstrates unequivocally that the "new look" in remediation was effective is found in the study by Clark, Lachowicz, and Wolf (1967). Subjects in a neighborhood youth center earned money for participating in a programmed learning situation which produced mean increases of 1.3 years for members of the experimental class and 0.2 years for members of a control group.

Table I

Demographic Data for Cases

Subject	Case Number	Age	Grade	Referral School Problems	Expulsion	Referral Source	Occupational Level
Ron	01	6	First	Underachieving, assaultive, temper tantrums, distrusting, disruptive, yelling, out of seat	√	School	1
Harold	08	8	Third	Aggressive, disruptive, failing, little peer interaction	√	School	6
Kim	12	10	Fourth	Underachieving, hyperactive, poor work habits, poor sport	√	School	1
Carl	15	13	Seventh	Hits other children, disruptive, short attention span, failing, disliked by other children, delinquent	√	Juvenile Court	4
Zeke	16	10	Fifth	Disruptive in school, violent temper, not getting along with peers	√	Psychiatrist	5
Will	17	9	Fourth	Steals, lies, disruptive in school, disliked by peers, runaway		Juvenile Court	4
Mark	22	8	Second	Hitting children 4 times per hour, disruptive, failing, out-of-control	√	Clinic and School	6
Sam	24	8	Second	Fighting, lying, stealing, disruptive, failing, out-of-control, destroying property	√	Clinic	5
Steve	26	10	Fourth	Fighting and disruptive, troublemaker		School	2
Jack	27	8	Second	Defiant, cries		School	3
Cory	31	9	Fourth	Out of seat, yelling, aggressive, destroying property, won't do assignments		School	1

subject had major difficulty during arithmetic periods, the observational data were collected during these periods. All teachers complained about classroom behavior, and consequently, all children were observed during academic periods. Since only a few subjects were observed during recess, these data are not included in the present report.

Two related observational schedules were used to collect data. The schedule used in observing the first nine cases was described in an earlier report (Patterson, et al., 1969). More recently, several modifications have produced significant improvements. The modified schedule was used for the last two cases, and is reproduced in Appendix I. Both schedules use a time-sampling approach and sample both the child's behavior and the reactions to the behavior by teachers and peers. When the first schedule was used, the subject was observed at 15-second intervals for 12 minutes, then a peer was observed in the same manner for six minutes. For the second schedule, the subject and peers were observed alternately at six-second intervals. The first schedule contained 14 child behaviors and 7 codable reactions to his behavior by others. The second schedule contained 19 behaviors and 19 reactions. For the present report only subject behaviors were analyzed.

In order to analyze all subject behaviors, they were dichotomously classified separately for each schedule as appropriate or inappropriate, depending upon their presumed acceptability in an academic setting. In addition to their obvious face validity, several of the specific categories have been demonstrated to correlate in the predicted direction, i.e., appropriate behaviors correlated positively and inappropriate behaviors, negatively, with academic achievement for elementary school children (Cobb, 1970; 1972). Since there existed discrepancies in definitions between the code categories for the two schedules, only those specific behavioral categories that were similarly defined on both schedules were analyzed; the categories were Noisy, Physical Negative, Not Attending, Self-Stimulation, Attending, Volunteering, and Initiation to Teacher.

Video-tapes of classroom interaction were used to train observers. After reaching a specified criterion on the television tape, the observers practiced in the classroom situation with reliable observers. Observer training with the use of video-tapes required a minimum of four hours and resulted in reliability during the final training hour of 85% (Cobb, 1972). The *in situ* reliability of observers for the present report was based upon the sum of their agreements divided by the total number of events recorded. The data collected in 21 sessions for the 11 subjects and peers produced 84.5% agreement for coding subject behavior.

Reliability of observers was one major consideration in determining the adequacy of data collection procedures; behavioral stability was considered equally important. Using the modified coding system, Cobb (1972) observed 120 fourth-graders during arithmetic classes. Each child in the classroom was sampled sequentially for a 10-second period; the series was replicated for an average of 14 minutes per child over a 10-day period. The range of event sampling per child was from 12 to 24 minutes. Comparing rates of behaviors on alternate days, the median correlation across all code categories was .56. The magnitude of individual correlations varied as a function of the rate of occurrence of each behavior; as might be expected, the low-rate behaviors showed lower event sampling coefficients. The correlation between rates of occurrence and magnitude of the stability coefficient was .64 ($p < .01$).

Considerably more data were collected for the present report. An average of 159 minutes per subject was obtained during each phase of the school programs, with 210 minutes during baseline, 311 minutes during intervention, and 147 minutes during follow-up.

One major problem in analysis of the data was the lack of homogeneity of variance between groups, and also over time within groups, for several of the observation categories. Due to the lack of homogeneity of variance, non-parametric statistics were applied to all data, even though some of the data could have been treated parametrically.

Dependent variables. There were two kinds of dependent variables involved in the tests of hypotheses about changes in classroom behavior. One consisted of increases or decreases from baseline levels for specific code categories. The other was a summary score for Appropriate Behavior. The specific behaviors, Noisy, Physical Negative, Not Attend, Self-Stimulation, Attending, Volunteering, and Initiation to Teacher were common to both coding systems. Comparisons were made between groups, and across trials, for each of these categories.

The omnibus category, Appropriate Behavior, was formed by including the code categories Attend, Volunteer, and Initiation to Teacher, which were synonymous across coding systems. In addition, Recite and Appropriate Talk were added from the earlier system; and Compliance, Approval, Appropriate Talk with Teacher, and Appropriate Talk with Peer were added for cases observed under the revised system.

RESULTS

The Deviancy Label

The first hypothesis was that the aggressive child would exhibit higher rates of inappropriate behaviors than the "normal" peers in his classroom. To correct for possible differences in interaction rates, the frequency for each code was divided by the total number of interactions for that session. The mean proportion for each of the measures for the identified problem child and for the normal peers is summarized in the first column of figures in Table II. Column two gives the results for the Wilcoxon matched pairs signed ranks test (Siegel, 1956, p. 75).

Table II
Comparisons of Aggressive Boys and Normal Peers on Classroom Behaviors

Behaviors	Group	Baseline	Wilcoxon[a] T	Intervention	Follow-up	Friedman[b] X^2_r
Appropriate Behaviors	Deviant	.573	4**	.749	.757	13.64**
	Normal	.748		.775	.781	1.63
Noisy	Deviant	.028	0**	.008	.004	7.14*
	Normal	.005		.002	.003	2.23
Physical Negative	Deviant	.010	0**	.005	.005	3.82
	Normal	.002		.001	.001	1.40
Not Attending	Deviant	.160	10*	.092	.116	6.55*
	Normal	.100		.098	.102	.14
Self-Stimulaton	Deviant	.039	38	.025	.028	.86
	Normal	.030		.022	.022	3.45
Attending	Deviant	.440	0**	.608	.625	10.09**
	Normal	.625		.668	.720	4.55
Volunteering	Deviant	.012	17	.009	.004	4.23
	Normal	.012		.008	.007	.95
Initiations to Teacher	Deviant	.054	10	.047	.078	2.59
	Normal	.044		.026	.021	4.41

[a] All significance levels are for one-tailed test
[b] All significance levels are for two-tailed test

*$p < .05$
**$p < .01$

Based on 11 subjects for all variables except IT and PN, which had complete data for only 9 subjects.

The data for the summary score an Appropriate Behavior showed clear differences between the identified problem child and his peers. Fifty-seven percent of the behavior of the problem child was appropriate, while the comparable figure for his peers was 75%. The latter figure is comparable to the 77% reported for normal children by Hamerlynck (1968) and Quay and Galvin (1970) and the 82% figure reported by Cobb (1970) for first-graders. An analysis of 105 fourth-graders' data by Cobb (1972) showed a mean of 76% for Appropriate Behaviors.

The figure of 57% for the aggressive child matched the 54% reported by Quay and Galvin (1970) for conduct problem children and was somewhat higher than the 39% appropriate behavior reported by Walker, et al. (1969). The lower figure obtained by the latter investigators seemed to be a function of methodology rather than a real difference in populations. Walker, et al. (1969) calculated percentages by including a category for "neutral behaviors" which would increase the denominator used to calculate percent appropriate behavior. The current investigation did not include such a category. By recalculating the Walker, et al. data to correspond to the method used in the present report, the figure of 53% was obtained for their sample. Identified problem children spent significantly less of their time engaged in appropriate behaviors. Examination of the data for individual subjects (Table III) showed that 10 of the 11 identified problem children performed at a lower level than did their normal peers. In this restricted sense, their behavior warranted the label "deviant."

The comparisons between the two groups by specific categories also revealed a number of significant differences. In keeping with the previous findings by Werry and Quay (1968), the identified problem child was observed to be significantly "noisier" and to spend less of his time "attending." The data from the present study also showed the deviant boys to hit, push, and shove significantly more than their peers.

It is instructive to note the differences among *classrooms* in terms of the average rate of appropriate behavior generated by peers. The range in proportion of appropriate behaviors for peers runs from 59% to 89%! Clearly, some social systems were programmed more effectively than others for the production of work-oriented behaviors.

Intervention

It was hypothesized that the intervention procedures would be associated with marked increases in the observed rates of appropriate classroom behavior for the identified problem child. Presumably these changes would persist during the follow-up period.

The observers noted that some teachers applied contingencies to children other than the identified child, and in some cases, completely reprogrammed their entire approach to working with the children. This led to the hypothesis that there would be significant generalization to the classroom peers as reflected by increases in the proportion of their appropriate behaviors. The study by Reppucci and Reiss (1970) had obtained significant decreases in the disruptive behavior of "normal peers" as a function of training four teachers to work effectively with problem children in their classes.

Table III

Mean Proportion of "Appropriate" Behaviors During Baseline, Intervention, and Follow-up

			Follow-up Months			
Subjects	Baseline	Intervention	1-3	4-6	7-24	Mean

Problem child

Ron	.465	.698		.882		.882
Harold	.424	.687	.765	.844	.812	.810
Kim	.485	.676		.576	.764	.722
Carl	.796	.875	.824	.918		.907
Zeke	.455	.706	.602			.602
Will	.543	.731		.755		.755
Mark	.705	.717	.623			.623
Sam	.486	.645	.831		.783	.801
Steve	.615	.854		.751		.751
Jack	.663	.754	.741	.676		.711
Cory	.665	.896	.722	.732	—	.727
Mean	.573	.749	.730	.767		.754

Peers

Ron	.592	.633		.733		.733
Harold	.823	.530	.790	.720	.651	.736
Kim	.841	.853		.795	.651	.685
Carl	.888	.866	.917	.820		.830
Zeke	.664	.761	.874			.874
Will	.879	.887		.821		.821
Mark	.763	.872	.798			.798
Sam	.741	.705	.767		.700	.726
Steve	.613	.880		.821		.821
Jack	.719	.744	.719	.660		.691
Cory	.701	.796	.868	.803	—	.836
Mean	.748	.775	.819	.772		.777

The data for individual subjects in Table III showed substantial changes in appropriate behavior during intervention for all but one subject (Mark). These changes in 91% of the subjects were produced at an average cost of 27.5 hours of professional time. The changes were maintained through follow-up, as shown by a comparison of the mean of .573 for baseline, .749 at termination, and .754 for total follow-up. The Friedman two-way analysis of variance for the deviant child group (Siegel, 1956, pp. 166-172) showed that these changes were significant. The X^2_r was 13.64 ($p < .01$). The comparable analysis for the normal peer groups showed the increase was not significant; the X^2_r was 1.63 (n.s.).

Findings from previous studies showed that the procedures were effective in altering behaviors such as Noisy and Not Attending, but relatively ineffective for behaviors such as Self-Stimulation (Patterson, et al., 1969). The analysis of changes in behavior by specific sub-categories summarized in Table II and detailed by subjects in Appendix II replicate the previous findings for these categories.

A review of observation data from earlier studies showed that over time intervals of four weeks or less, four non-treated "hyperactive" boys did not improve if treatment manipulations were not introduced (Patterson, et al., 1969). A similar finding for a control group of hyperactive boys was obtained by Nixon (1966). These findings were in close agreement with those obtained in clinical studies reviewed by Werry (1968), which showed that non-treated hyperactive children exhibited no significant changes in behavior.

The changes in behavior were produced at an average cost of 27.5 hours of professional time. The intervention intervals ranged from four to 24 months. Records were kept of time expended during intake, telephone calls, staff conferences, classroom intervention, school conferences, and transportation to and from the school. The estimate does not include time required for the collection of observations. As observation data constituted an integral part of the intervention procedure, the figure reported above should be corrected to include roughly 20 hours for five baseline, intervention, and follow-up sessions. The additional five hours should cover transportation time. Setting the cost per hour for professional time at $10.00 and for observers at $3.00 would give an average cost per case of $355.00 per child.

Follow-up

Baseline, intervention, and follow-up data were collected routinely in the classroom in which the intervention had taken place. Typically, the follow-up in the original classroom lasted for a three-month period. However, in four cases (Ron, Kim, Will, Steve), the termination of intervention corresponded with the beginning of the sum-

Figure 2

Mean Proportion of Appropriate Behaviors

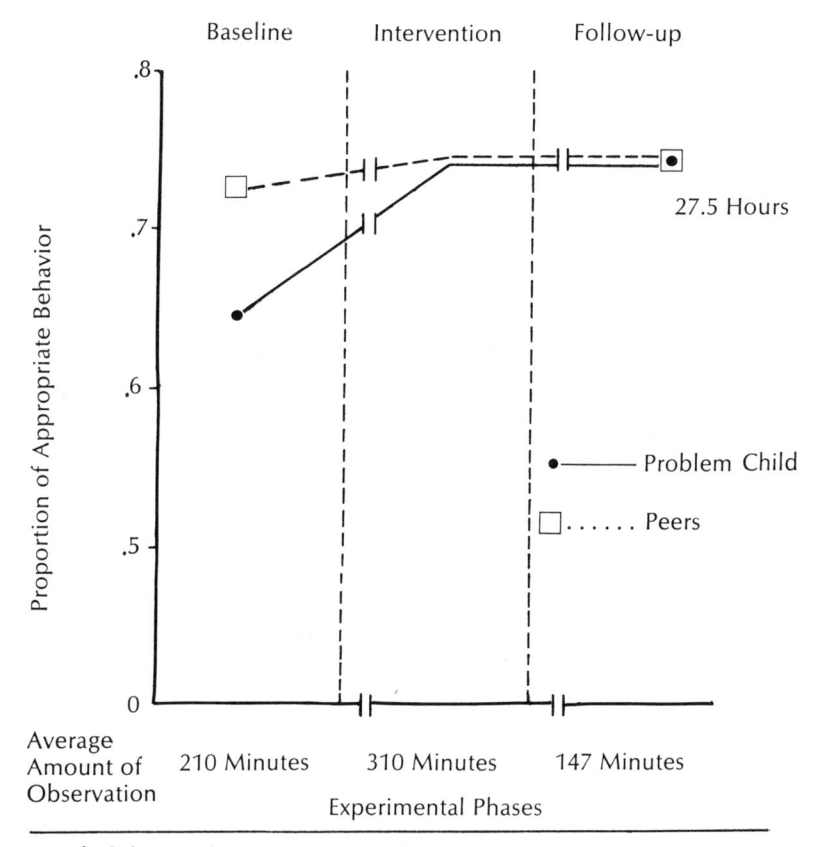

```
                          Baseline    Intervention    Follow-up
                      .8 ┐
                         │
                         │                                    ┌─•┐
                         │       ┌─┐    ─┤├──═════╪═══════├──┘  │
                         │   ┌─┘─┘ └─    ─┤├─                    
                         │  ─┘           ┤├                      27.5 Hours
                      .7 │                ├┘
                         │              ┘ │
                         │            ┘   │
                         │          •     │
                         │                │
                         │                │
                      .6 │                │
                         │                │              •────── Problem Child
                         │                │
                         │                │              □ ······ Peers
                         │                │
                      .5 │                │
                         │                │
                         │                │
                         │                │
                       0 └────────────────┴────────────────────
Average
Amount of          210 Minutes      310 Minutes       147 Minutes
Observation
                              Experimental Phases
```

mer holiday, and it was not possible to obtain follow-up data until the beginning of the next academic year. In effect, termination data were not collected for these four cases, but data were collected which demonstrated whether the training effects would generalize to a new classroom. Generalization data of this kind were available for all subjects except Mark and Zeke.

Figure 2 summarizes the changes in behavior for the identified problem child and his peers during baseline, intervention, and follow-up. The figure in the box in the upper right-hand quadrant is the average number of hours of professional time required to produce the changes. Only the data from those subjects for whom follow-up data were available during the four- through six-month period were used to construct the graph. The baseline, intervention, and follow-up points exclude the data for the three subjects.

As shown in Figure 2, the intervention effects were maintained during the three- to six-month follow-up period. This maintenance of effects replicates the follow-up findings for the classroom intervention (Patterson, et al., 1969). In view of the fact that during follow-up many of the boys had been enrolled in new classrooms, the persistence of the effects is rather surprising. It is of interest to note that the follow-up data for the classroom intervention held up somewhat better than did the follow-up data for the family intervention procedures (Patterson, et al., 1970). While the differences in maintenance are not large, they suggest that the effects of alterations in the peer group may be easier to maintain than alterations in family interactions.

As shown by the data in Table III, six of the eleven subjects had actually improved in appropriate behaviors over their performance during intervention. Only one subject (Mark) did not reflect substantial increases over baseline values when compared to the mean follow-up level. In fact, almost half of the problem children were now functioning at a level equal to, or greater than, their normal peers.

Achievement Testing

It was only after the first few years of intervention that it became clear that it would be necessary to assume responsibility for teaching academic skills as well as classroom survival skills. For this reason, the parents-as-tutor programs were initiated for two of the last subjects in this sample (Skindrud, 1971b).

The pretest achievement levels for Mark on the WRAT were 1.4 in arithmetic and 2.4 in reading. The comparable values for the posttest seven months later were 2.4 and 3.0, reflecting only modest increases. The pretest scores for Sam were 1.4 for reading and 1.3 for arithmetic. Six months later, the posttest scores were 3.8 and 2.6, respectively. The substantial gains probably reflect the greater investment of time given by Sam's mother, who was determined to bring her child up to grade level.

Currently, achievement tests are being used routinely with all children involved in tutorial programs. It is hypothesized that the parents of these children will be able to bring them up to grade level.

DISCUSSION

These findings showed that seven years of pilot testing with individual cases, with constant feedback from large quantities of observation data, have produced a technology for the classroom setting which is of at least modest utility. The fact that the procedures were effective for approximately 90% of these consecutive cases suggests that the procedures warrant replication by other investigators. Twenty to thirty hours of professional time seem sufficient to produce dramatic changes in the classroom adjustment of extremely "disturbed" boys.

It might be noted that there are several levels of analysis which now seem called for in order to properly understand these procedures. Studies are badly needed which analyze the individual components of the procedures such as the Work Box, TO, the use of contracts, the academic programs, and the contribution of the parents, the peer group, and the teacher. The multiple baseline design would seem to be ideally suited to such a task. Such studies are currently under way (Cobb, in preparation).

On the basis of existing knowledge, it would seem feasible to attempt demonstration projects consisting of teams of a trained behavior modifier (sub-doctoral level) and three technician-observers. Such a team could serve grades one through five for a substantial number of schools. The technician-observers would not need to have training other than that provided in their apprenticeship on the job. In our own case, we have trained housewives to high levels of competence as professional observers and are so impressed with their contribution that we are currently expanding their role to include the technical aspects of intervention. In the school setting, such inexpensive staff would not only collect the baseline observations in the classroom (which serve as the primary data for planning intervention), but also would assist in carrying out some of the routine operations involved in the classroom procedures. Observation data collected after termination would provide a sound basis for evaluating the outcome. The cost of treatment could be easily expressed in terms of dollars and cents required to bring about specified levels of change in a specified number of children. Such practical data describing the meaningful process of helping children should be of great value in "selling" the programs at the community level.

While studies of the kind described here might well describe a technology which has practical utility, they leave undisclosed the process which produces and maintains the changes observed. One of the basic assumptions underlying the present approach is that the most effective approach to altering behavior and maintaining these changes is to alter the social system in which the child interacts. However, no data are as yet forthcoming from our work that show that the peers, and/or teachers, actually alter their behavior. Is the "social system" itself changed in any significant way by these procedures? It could well be that such analysis of process and systems will result in considerable improvements in the efficiency of technologies such as the ones described here.

As the techniques now stand, there is a considerable amount of artistry involved in their application. The procedures themselves are well understood by the staff, but the difficulties lie in the ambiguities involved in negotiating with the school personnel, the child, and his family. Each teacher, each child, and each parent must be approached differently. There is little doubt, for example, that a considerable amount of the total professional time expended in the program is used for such negotiations. It is interesting in this regard that even though there seem to be individual differences among the staff in these negotiation skills, the treatment outcomes seem comparable.

Dynamic theories of personality emphasize the correlation between deviant child behavior and the "sick parent." This point of view contributes to the impasse which frequently occurs in the dialogue between the community agencies and the parents of the deviant child. School personnel may, after making strenuous efforts to help a child and failing, create the myth of the "sick parent" to serve as an explanation for the failure. In this process, parents may invariably be seen as "evil," "malevolent," or "dangerous." Fragments of parent behavior which may be complete distortions, or have occurred years ago, get passed from babysitter to counselor to nurse to teacher and principal. With each retelling, some further distortions are added. Interestingly enough, the deviant child becomes one of the main contributors. Perhaps he senses the excitement which his reports occasion and gleefully contributes to the denouement of all adults involved in his case by distorting some new feature of his family's interactions. For example, Sam, noting her intense interest, described to his counselor numerous incidents of gross parental mistreatment, including being locked in a dark room for long periods of time as punishment. While no such special room existed, this spectre of parent brutality passed from one rumor monger to the next, and the room assumed all the proportions of the Black Hole of Calcutta.

Shortly thereafter, the mother missed her next appointment at the school; her car had broken down. She called in to explain the situation, but the episode was "interpreted," from the standpoint of the myth, to mean that the parents were "uninvolved" and that the case was impossible.

As similar myths are built up around the family, the parents find out that they are confronted with sly innuendos or open interpretations to the effect that the child's acting out in school is their own fault, and *they* must "do something" about it. While the parent may try to cooperate, the behavior of the child remains out-of-control, which proves to the school how "sick" the parents really are. Eventually, the cooperative efforts of both parents and school are extinguished, and they describe each other in mutually negative terms.

The parents now construct their "myth" of what it is that the school is "really" doing to their child. In some instances, the parent becomes so incensed that he may make the unfortunate mistake of threatening physical violence (Mac). From the viewpoint of the school, this, of course, pushes the family beyond the pale and, in the case of Mac, was one of the things that led the school to believe that the child should be institutionalized.

The carefully pinpointed behaviors and the daily exchanges of frequency counts between the parent and the school personnel seem very effective in altering such myths. It might be noted in passing that it is our impression that such faulty and hostile communications between parents and the school were not the *cause* of the child's deviant behavior, but rather were one of the concomitants of it. In our opinion, the causes seemed to lie more in the lack of defined contingencies provided by the classroom teachers and the parents. Altering either one, or both, of these seemed necessary to produce reduced rates of deviant behavior in that setting.

REFERENCES

Anderson, D. E. Application of a behavior modification technique to the control of a hyperactive child. Unpublished master's thesis, University of Oregon, 1964.

Barclay, J. R., Montgomery, R., and Barclay, L. K. Effectiveness of teacher training in social learning and behavior modification techniques. *Measurement and Evaluation in Guidance*, 1971, *4*, 79-89.

Becker, W. C., Engelmann, S., and Thomas, D. R. *Teaching: A course in applied psychology.* Palo Alto, Calif.: Science Research Associates, 1971.

Becker, W. C., Madsen, C. H., Jr., Arnold, C. R., and Thomas, D. R. The contingent use of teacher attention and praise in reducing classroom behavior problems. *Journal of Special Education*, 1967, *1*, 287-309.

Birnbrauer, J. S., Bijou, S. W., Wolf, M. M., and Kidder, J. D. Programmed instruction in the classroom. In L. Ullmann and L. Krasner (Eds.), *Case studies in behavior modification.* New York: Holt, Rinehart & Winston, 1965. Pp. 358-363.

Bricker, D. D. Tennessee Re-Ed Center Interim Report. Cumberland housing studies in behavior modification. Tennessee Re-Ed Center, 3409 Belmont Blvd., Nashville, Tenn., 1967.

Brown, J., Montgomery, R., and Barclay, J. An example of psychologist management of teacher reinforcement procedures in the elementary classroom. *Psychology in the Schools*, 1969, *6*, 336-340.

Bruner, J. S. *On knowing.* Cambridge, Mass.: Belknap Press, Harvard University Press, 1963.

Buckley, N. K. and Walker, H. *Modifying classroom behavior: A manual of procedures for classroom teachers.* Champaign, Ill.: Research Press, 1970.

Bushell, D., Wrobel, P., and Michels, M. Applying group contingencies to the classroom study behavior of preschool children. *Journal of Applied Behavior Analysis*, 1968, *1*, 55-63.

Cantrell, R. P., Cantrell, M. L., Huddleston, C., and Woolridge, R. Contingency contracting with school problems. *Journal of Applied Behavior Analysis*, 1969, *2*, 215-220.

Clark, M., Lachowicz, J., and Wolf, M. M. A pilot basic educational program for school dropouts incorporating a token reinforcement system. *Behavior Research and Therapy*, 1968, *6*, 183-188.

Cobb, J. A. Survival skills and first grade academic achievement. Report #1, University of Oregon Center for Research and Demonstration in the Early Education of Handicapped Children. Office of Education, 1970.

Cobb, J. A. The relationship of discrete classroom behaviors to fourth-grade achievement. *Journal of Educational Psychology*, 1972, in press.

Cobb, J. A., Ray, R. S., and Patterson, G. R. Increasing and maintaining appropriate classroom behavior of aggressive elementary school boys. Paper presented at the meeting of the Second Annual Symposium on Behavior Modification, Lawrence, Kansas, May 1971.

Cohen, H., Filipczak, J. A., Bis, J. S., and Cohen, J. E. Contingencies applicable to special education of delinquents. In R. Burgess and D. Bushell, Jr. (Eds.), *The experimental analysis of social process*. New York: Columbia University Press, 1970.

Cooper, M., Thomson, C. L., and Baer, D. M. The experimental modification of teacher attending behavior. *Journal of Applied Behavior Analysis*, 1970, *3*, 153-157.

Craig, H. B., and Holland, A. L. Reinforcement of visual attending in classrooms for deaf children. *Journal of Applied Behavior Analysis*, 1970, *3*, 97-109.

Ebner, M. An investigation of the role of the social environment in the generalization and persistence of the effect of a behavior modification program. Unpublished doctoral dissertation, University of Oregon, 1967.

Evans, G. W., and Oswalt, G. L. Acceleration of academic progress through the manipulation of peer influence. *Parsons Research Center Working Paper*, No. 155, 1967.

Gotts, R. E. Factors related to teacher's irritability in response to pupil classroom behavior. Paper presented at the meeting of the American Psychological Association, 1967.

Hall, R. V., Lund, D., and Jackson, D. Effects of teacher attention on study behavior. *Journal of Applied Behavior Analysis*, 1968, *1*, 1-12.

Hamerlynck, L. A. Direct observation of student behavior to validate teacher reports. Paper read at the Conference of the Canadian Psychological Association, Calgary, Alberta, June 1968.

Hamerlynck, L. A., Martin, J., Rolland, J. Systematic observation of behavior: A primary teacher skill. *Education and Training of the Mentally Retarded,* Spring, 1968, *3,* No. 1, 39-42.

Haring, N. G., and Kunzelmann, H. The finer focus of therapeutic behavioral management. *Educational Therapy.* Vol. 1. Seattle, Wash.: Special Child Publications, 1966.

Hartup, W. W., Glazer, J. A., and Charlesworth, R. Peer reinforcement and sociometric status. *Child Development,* 1967, *38,* 1017-1024.

Hauck, M. A. and Haring, N. G. Individualized reading program with continuous evaluation of progress. Paper presented at the Conference of the Washington Organization for Reading Development, Lynwood, Washington, April 1968.

Haughton, E. Training counselors as advisors of precision teaching. Paper presented at the meeting of the Early Childhood Education Convention, New York, April 1968.

Hewett, F. M. Educational engineering with emotionally disturbed children. *Exceptional Children,* 1967, *33,* 459-467.

Hewett, F. M., Taylor, F. D., and Arturo, A. A. The Santa Monica Project. Demonstration and evaluation of an engineered classroom design for emotionally disturbed children in the public schools. Project #62893, OEG 4-7-062893-0377. Office of Education, Bureau of Research, U. S. Department of Health, Education, and Welfare, 1967.

Hollingshead, A. B. and Redlich, F. C. *Social class and mental illness.* New York: Wiley, 1958.

Homme, L. D. Contingency theory and contingency management. *Psychological Record,* 1966, *16,* 233-241.

Homme, L., Csanyi, A., Gonzales, M. A., and Rechs, J. *How to use contingency contracting in the classroom.* Champaign, Ill.: Research Press, 1970.

Homme, L. D., de Baca, P. C., Devine, J. V., Steinhorst, R., and Rickert, E. J. The use of the Premack principle in controlling the behavior of nursery school children. *Journal of the Experimental Analysis of Behavior,* 1963, *6,* 544.

Hotchkiss, J. M. The modification of maladaptive behavior of a class of educationally handicapped children by operant conditioning techniques. Unpublished doctoral dissertation, University of Southern California, 1966.

Koenig, C. H. Precision teaching with emotionally disturbed pupils. Research Training Paper, No. 17, Special Education Research, Children's Rehabilitation Unit, University of Kansas Medical Center, 1967.

Kounin, J. S., Friesen, W. V., and Norton, E. A. Managing emotionally disturbed children in regular classrooms. *Journal of Educational Psychology,* 1966, *57,* 1-13.

Krumboltz, J. D. and Goodwin, D. L. Increasing task oriented behavior: An experimental evaluation of training teachers in reinforcement techniques. School of Education, Stanford University, Final Report, Office of Education, Grant 5-85-95, 1966.

Leitenberg, H. Is Time Out from positive reinforcement an aversive event? *Psychological Bulletin,* 1965, *64,* 428-441.

Madsen, C. H., Jr., Becker, W. C., and Thomas, D. R. Rules, praise, and ignoring: Elements of elementary classroom control. *Journal of Applied Behavior Analysis,* 1968, *1,* 139-150.

Moore, S. Correlates of peer acceptance in nursery school children. *Young Children,* 1967, *22,* 281-297.

Nixon, S. B. Ways by which overly active students can be taught to concentrate on study activity. Cooperative Research Project No. 5-379, U. S. Office of Education, 1966.

Nolan, P., Kunzelmann, H., and Haring, N. Behavioral modification in a junior high learning disability classroom. *Exceptional Children,* 1967, *34,* 163-168.

O'Leary, K. D. and Becker, W. C. Behavior modification of an adjustment class: A token reinforcement program. *Exceptional Children,* 1967, *33,* 637-642.

O'Leary, K. D. and Drabman, R. Token reinforcement programs in the classroom: A review. *Psychological Bulletin,* 1971, *75,* 379-398.

Patterson, G. R. An application of conditioning techniques to the control of a hyperactive child. In L. P. Ullmann and L. Krasner (Eds.), *Case studies in behavior modification.* New York: Holt, Rinehart, & Winston, 1965. Pp. 370-375.

Patterson, G. R. The parent as a behavior modifier in the classroom. In J. D. Krumboltz and C. E. Thoresen (Eds.), *Behavioral counseling: Cases and techniques.* New York: Holt, Rinehart & Winston, 1969. Pp. 155-161.

Patterson, G. R. and Cobb, J. A. A dyadic analysis of "aggressive" behaviors. In J. P. Hill (Ed.), *Minnesota Symposia on Child Psychology.* Vol. V. Minneapolis: University of Minnesota, 1971. Pp. 72-129.

Patterson, G. R., Cobb, J. A., and Ray, R. S. A social engineering technology for retraining the families of aggressive boys. In H. Adams and L. Unikel (Eds.), *Georgia Symposium in Experimental Clinical Psychology.* Vol. II. Springfield, Ill.: Thomas, 1972, in press.

Patterson, G. R. and Gullion, M. E. *Living with children: New methods for parents and teachers.* Champaign, Ill.: Research Press, 1968.

Patterson, G. R., Ray, R. S., and Shaw, D. A. Direct intervention in families of deviant children. *Oregon Research Institute Research Bulletin,* 1968, *8,* No. 9.

Patterson, G. R. and Reid, J. B. Reciprocity and coercion: Two facets of social systems. In C. Neuringer and J. L. Michael (Eds.), *Behavior modification in clinical psychology*. New York: Appleton-Century-Crofts, 1970. Pp. 133-177.

Patterson, G. R., Shaw, D. A., and Ebner, M. J. Teachers, peers, and parents as agents of change in the classroom. In F. A. M. Benson (Ed.), *Modifying deviant social behaviors in various classroom settings*. Eugene, Ore.: University of Oregon, 1969, No. 1. Pp. 13-47.

Patterson, G. R. and White, G. D. It's a small world: The application of "Time-out from positive reinforcement." *Oregon Psychological Association Newsletter*, 1969, *15*, No. 2, Supplement.

Phillips, E. Achievement Place: Token reinforcement procedures in a home style rehabilitation setting for pre-delinquent boys. *Journal of Applied Behavior Analysis*, 1968, *1*, 213-223.

Quay, H. C. and Galvin, J. Remediation of the conduct problem child in the school setting. Final Report, Division of Research, Bureau for Educationally Handicapped, USOE, 1970.

Quay, H. C., Sprague, R. L., Werry, J. S., and McQueen, M. M. Conditioning visual orientation of conduct problem children in the classroom. *Journal of Experimental Child Psychology*, 1967, *5*, 512-517.

Quay, H. C., Werry, J. S., McQueen, M. M., and Sprague, R. L. Remediation of the conduct problem child in the special class setting. *Exceptional Children*, 1966, *32*, 509-515.

Ray, R. S., Shaw, D. A., and Cobb, J. A. The Work Box: An innovation in teaching attentional behavior. *The School Counselor*, 1970, *18*, 15-35.

Reppucci, D. N. and Reiss, S. Effects of operant treatment with disruptive and normal elementary school children. Paper presented at the meeting of the American Psychological Association, Miami, September 1970.

Siegel, S. *Nonparametric statistics for the behavioral sciences*. New York: McGraw-Hill, 1956.

Skindrud, K. Generalization of intervention effects from the home to the school classroom. Oregon Research Institute, Eugene, 1971, in preparation. (a)

Skindrud, K. Training mothers of disruptive nonreaders in remedial skills: A preliminary study of a home tutoring program. Unpublished manuscript, Oregon Research Institute, Eugene, 1971. (b)

Staats, A. W. *Learning, language and cognition*. New York: Holt, Rinehart, & Winston, 1968.

Staats, A. W. and Butterfield, W. H. Treatment of nonreading in a culturally deprived juvenile delinquent: An application of reinforcement principles. *Child Development*, 1962, *4*, 925-942.

Staats, A. W., Minke, K. A., Goodwin, W., and Landeen, J. Cognitive behavior modification: "Motivated learning" reading treatment with sub-professional therapy-technicians. *Behavior Research and Therapy,* 1967, *5,* 293-299.

Valett, R. E. A social reinforcement technique for the classroom management of behavior disorders. *Exceptional Children,* 1966, *33,* 185-189.

Wahler, R. G. Setting generality, some specific and general effects of child behavior therapy. *Journal of Applied Behavior Analysis,* 1969, *2,* 239-246.

Walker, H. and Buckley, N. K. Investigation of some classroom control parameters as a function of teacher dispensed social reinforcers. *Journal of Applied Behavior Analysis,* 1971, in press. (a)

Walker, H. M. and Buckley, N. K. Programming generalization and maintenance of treatment effects across time and settings. University of Oregon, 1971, in preparation. (b)

Walker, H. M., Mattson, R. H., and Buckley, N. K. Special class placement as a treatment alternative for deviant behavior in children. In F. A. M. Benson (Ed.), *Modifying deviant social behaviors in various classroom settings.* Eugene, Oregon: University of Oregon, 1969, No. 1. Pp. 49-80.

Ward, M. H. and Baker, B. L. Reinforcement therapy in the classroom. *Journal of Applied Behavior Analysis,* 1968, *1,* 323-328.

Werry, J. S. The diagnosis, etiology and treatment of hyperactivity in children. In J. Hellmuth (Ed.), *Learning disorders.* Vol. 3. Seattle, Wash.: Special Child Publications, 1968.

Werry, J. S. and Quay, H. Observing the classroom behavior of elementary school children. Paper presented at the meeting of the Council on Exceptional Children, New York, April 1968.

White, G., Nielsen, G., and Johnson, S. M. Time out duration and the suppression of deviant behavior in children. *Journal of Applied Behavior Analysis,* 1972, in press.

Wolf, M., Hanley, E., King, L., Lachowicz, J., and Giles, D. The timer-game: A variable interval contingency for the management of out-of-seat behavior. *Exceptional Children,* 1970, *37,* 113-118.

Zifferblatt, S. M. *You can help your child improve study and homework behaviors.* Champaign, Ill.: Research Press, 1970.

Zimmerman, E. H. and Zimmerman, J. The alteration of behavior in a special classroom situation. *Journal of the Experimental Analysis of Behavior,* 1962, *5,* 59-60.

APPENDIX I

Manual for Coding Discrete Behaviors in the School Setting

Joseph A. Cobb and Roberta S. Ray

This manual is a guide to be used in connection with the observation of classroom behaviors. The code has been developed to provide a precise record of behavioral rates in the classroom. Many behaviors have been defined previously by Ray, Shaw, and Patterson (1968).

The observer will look at the subject and each male peer in alternating six-second intervals, i.e., subject, peer; subject, peer; subject, peer; etc. The observer will code the appropriate behavior by placing a circle around the category on the coding sheet. If there is a response to the behavior by another person which can be discerned by the subject, the response is to be coded. A vertical line (|) is to be placed through the symbol of the response on the coding sheet if the response is by the teacher; if the response is by a peer, a horizontal line (—) is used.

An auditory device (clipboard with built-in interval timer and auditory jack) is provided to produce a signal every six seconds so the observer will know when to code a child's behavior. An efficient procedure for coding is to observe the child for a few seconds after the auditory signal occurs and check to see if there is a response from the environment; then code the behavior observed as well as the response; if there is no immediate response, but a response occurs before the end of the six-second interval, code that response, wait for the next auditory signal and repeat the procedure for the next person. Once all male peers have been coded in the classroom, the observer will begin coding in the same order of peers on the same coding sheet as in the original sequence. Sometimes the original order will be difficult to maintain due to movement in the classroom; in these cases the observer should attempt to sample all peers, regardless of order, before returning to coding the same peer twice. If a peer leaves the room or is unobservable for other reasons, do not leave the space blank, just continue and code the next peer.

Space is provided on the sheet for the academic activity, the structure provided by the teacher, and the kind of work (group, individual, and transitional) that was occurring at the time of coding. The observer is to fill in the academic activity, e.g., reading, arithmetic, social studies, etc., the type of structure, and the kind of work. When changes occur in the latter two areas while the sheet is being coded, a symbol is to be placed at the beginning of the subject or peer line in which the change occurred. The symbol should be the first letter of the five categories used to characterize the situation. For instance, if the teacher is lecturing to the class and then begins to have them work on individual work assignments at a point where only part of the class has been coded, an "I" is placed in front of the child's number at which point group work changed to individual work.

The definitions for the five categories are as follows:

Structured. The teacher has provided clear guidelines for the children to follow in carrying out tasks.

Unstructured. The guidelines for the child's behavior are vague or unclear to the observer, i.e., the students can determine what they want to do in terms of academic activity and/or non-intellectual behaviors.

Group. The class is involved as one unit in academic activity, e.g., teacher lecturing, student reciting while entire class listens. Also, "group" is to be coded when there are small groups in the class, as often occurs in reading.

Individual. The majority of the students are doing work by themselves at desks, e.g., social study projects are being done by each student. "Individual" can be checked even though the student asks for and receives help from other peers and/or teachers.

Transitional. This category should be checked when the class is between activities, e.g., waiting for recess, lining up for lunch, class returning from recess, teacher has indicated reading period is finished but has provided no directions for the next activity. As soon as teacher provides directions for the next activity, the "transitional" category is to be omitted and either the "group" or the "individual" category checked.

It is essential that only one behavior be coded for each subject. Although there will be instances in which more than one behavior code is applicable, the observer should code only one. To facilitate a consistent choice of categories among observers, the codes are ordered in the manual as well as on the code sheets in a hierarchical fashion for appropriate and inappropriate behaviors. The observer is to go from left to right until the first applicable code category is reached; that category is to be marked and no other.

The same procedure is to be followed for picking a peer and/or teacher response. The rule to keep uppermost in mind regarding the choice of response is that the response is *specifically* directed at the subject. For example, if the student is attending to his work and a peer drops a book with a loud noise, the student's behavior is coded but not the peer's behavior as the behavior was not directed at the subject; however, if the peer dropped the book on the student's desk, then that response would be coded.

In the following list the code definitions are applicable to both behavior of the subject and to responses from teachers and peers unless noted otherwise:

AP   Approval.   Used whenever a person gives clear gestural, verbal, or physical approval to another individual. "Approval" is more than attention, in that it must include some clear indication of positive interest or involvement. Examples of "approval" are smiles, head nods, hugs, pats on the back, and phrases such as, "That's a good boy," "Thank you," and "That's right," "That's a good job."

CO   Complies.   This category can be checked each time the person does what another person has requested, e.g., the teacher asks class to take out notebooks and pupil does; she asks for paper to be turned in and pupil obeys; pupil asks for pencil and teacher or peer gives him one; teacher tells class to be quiet and pupil is quiet.

TT+   Appropriate talking with teacher.   This category can be checked when the pupil talks with the teacher, whether in private as in indeendent work situations or answers questions in other situations. If the teacher is *interacting* with the child when the child is talking appropriately, the *response* is coded TT+. The reason for coding the subject's behavior and the response in the same category is the difficulty of differentiating other responses in quick verbal interchanges; of course, if other responses are appropriate, e.g., AP, DI, or AT, and can be clearly differentiated, they preclude coding the response at TT+.

IP+   Appropriate interaction with peer.   Coded when the pupil is interacting with peer and is not violating classroom rules. Interaction includes verbal and non-verbal communication, e.g., talking, handing materials, working on project with peer. The response for the peer is IP+ if the peer is *interacting* with the subject. The main element to remember in applying this code is that *an interaction is occurring* or one of the persons is attempting to interact. If two students are working on a social studies project, the code is *IP+* if they are talking to each other or organizing a notebook *together,* but if the subject is simply writing a report, then the appropriate code is *AT*.

VO   Volunteers.   Coded when person indicates that he wants to make an academic contribution, e.g., teacher asks a question and he raises his hand.

IT   Initiation to or by teacher.   Pupil or teacher initiates or attempts to initiate interaction with each other, but not in conjunction with volunteering. Pupil may go to teacher's desk during independent study or raise his hand and seek assistance in solving an arithmetic problem; as a response, teacher may initiate interaction with pupil, e.g., teacher may ask pupil for answer to an arithmetic problem; teacher may *ask* pupil to pick up class papers; pupil asks permission to sharpen pencil; pupil asks what is for lunch, etc.

AT   Attending.   This category is used whenever a person indicates by his behavior that he is doing what is appropriate in a school situation, e.g., he is looking at the teacher when she is presenting material to the class; he is looking at visual aids as the teacher tells about them; he has his eyes focused on his book as he does the reading assignment; he writes answers to arithmetic problems; the teacher or peer looks at the child reciting. "Attending" is to be coded as a *response* when there is an indication that the subject is aware that a teacher or peer is attending to him; thus, when a child is working, and the teacher looks at him, the child must make some recognition of the attending on the teacher's part, e.g., he looks at the teacher.

PN Physical negative. Use of this category is restricted to times when a person attacks or attempts to attack another person with the possibility of inflicting pain. Examples include slapping, spanking, kicking, biting, throwing objects at someone, etc.

DS Destructiveness. Use of this category is applicable when a person destroys or attempts to destroy some object, e.g., breaking a pencil in half, tearing a page from a book, carving name on desk, etc. This category is not to be used when the person is writing an answer or working out a problem on a desk with a pen or pencil.

DI Disapproval. Use this category whenever the person gives verbal or gestural disapproval of another person's behavior or characteristics. Shaking the head or finger are examples of gestural disapproval. "I do not like that tone of voice," "You didn't pass in your homework on time," "Your work is sloppy," "I don't like you" are examples of "disapproval." In verbal statements it is essential that the content of the statement *explicitly* states disapproval of the subject's behaviors or attributes, e.g., looks, clothes, attitudes, academic skills, etc.

NY Noisy. This category is to be used when the person talks loudly, yells, bangs books, scrapes chairs, or makes any sounds that are likely to be actually or potentially disruptive to others.

NC Noncompliance. To be coded whenever the person does not do what is requested. This includes teacher giving instructions to entire class and the subject does not comply.

PL Play. Coded whenever person is playing alone or with another person, e.g., playing tic-tac-toe in class, playing softball at recess, throwing a ball in classroom, etc.

TT— Inappropriate talk with teacher. Use whenever content of conversation is negative toward teacher by pupil or when classroom rules do not allow interaction with teacher. Examples are, "I don't want to finish this lesson," "I won't go to the principal's office," etc. This category should not be used if DI is appropriate.

IP— Inappropriate interaction with peer. Coded whenever peer or pupil interacts with or attempts to interact with each other and classroom rules are being violated. Examples include behaviors and/or responses such as touching a peer to get his attention, calling peer by name, talking to peer, looking at peer *when the student should be working.*

IL Inappropriate locale. This category is not to be used if rules allow for pupils to leave seats without permission and what the pupil is doing is not an infraction of other rules, e.g., a pupil goes to sharpen pencil would not be classified IL, unless he stopped and visited with neighbors on the way; or, unless this activity takes permission from teacher, etc.

SS Self-stimulation. A narrow class of events in which the person attempts to stimulate himself in such ways as swinging his feet, rubbing his nose, ears, forehead, tapping his fingers, scratching, etc., to such an extent that attention to other activities is precluded.

LO Look around. Coded when person is looking around the room, looking out the window, or staring into space when an academic activity is occurring.

NA Not attending. This category is to be used when person is not attending to work in individual work situations or not attending to discussion when teacher is presenting material. This category is applicable to those situations in which the subject is working but he is working on the wrong assignment. Care should be taken in using this category. Be sure that *no other category* is appropriate before checking it.

Following is a description of a hypothetical situation in a school setting. The coding of each sequence is also shown on a sample coding sheet.

The observer has entered the classroom and will be coding the first sheet of the observation. The teacher is presenting a lesson in arithmetic to the whole class.

The subject is looking out the window and the teacher says, "Jimmy, don't you ever pay attention to what's going on?"

The first male peer is looking at the teacher.

The subject looks at the teacher.

The second male peer is scratching and looking at his arm.

The subject talks to a peer while the teacher is still presenting the lesson. The peer talks with the subject.

The third male peer answers a question from the teacher. The teacher smiles and says, "Fine." Some of the children look at the interaction between the peer and teacher.

The subject drops a book on the floor. Several peers giggle. The teacher says, "That's enough of that, Jimmy."

The fourth male peer is rolling a ball down the aisle to his buddy. The buddy rolls the ball back.

The subject raises his hand in response to a question asked of the class by the teacher.

The fifth male peer picks up a piece of paper at the teacher's request. The teacher says, "Thank you."

The subject rummages through his desk while the teacher is presenting the lesson.

The sixth male peer is walking around the room. Several of his classmates look at him.

The subject looks at the teacher.

The seventh male peer hits the child next to him. The child hits him back.

The subject raises his hand as the teacher is talking. She does not look at him.

The eighth male peer looks at the teacher.

The subject still has his hand raised. The teacher asks him what he wants.

The first male peer looks at the teacher.

Subject stomps his foot on the floor. Several peers look at him.

With the teacher's permission, the second male peer explains the lesson to a neighbor, who responds with questions.

Subject stares at the child sitting next to him. The child does not respond.

The third male peer talks to the teacher about the lesson. She answers.

Subject talks to child sitting next to him. The child responds. Teacher says, "Stop that talking."

The fourth male peer looks around the room.

The subject is reading a comic book.

The teacher has told the fifth male peer to sit up straight in his chair. He still slouches in chair.

The subject is still reading a comic book. The teacher takes the book away from him.

The sixth male peer says to the teacher, "That's a nice dress you're wearing." The teacher looks at the child and smiles.

The subject yells, "I want to go to recess!" The teacher says, "Speak in a lower tone of voice, Jimmy."

The seventh male peer rubs an eraser back and forth on the desk.

The subject looks at the clock while the teacher is giving the lesson.

The eighth male peer looks at the teacher.

Subject passes a note to peer. Peer accepts note.

The first male peer tears a page out of his book.

The subject sits quietly in chair, looking at teacher.

Observer _____ Sheet # __1__ Subject _Jimmy_
Date __2-26-71__
Academic Activity __✓__ _arithmetic_

Structured __✓__ Unstructured _____ Group _____ Individual _____ Transitional _____

Pupil

S	AP CO TT+ IP+ VO IT AT PN DS DI	1	NY NC PL TT— IP— IL SS LO NA	S
P	AP CO TT+ IP+ VO IT AT PN DS DI	2	NY NC PL TT— IP— IL SS LO NA	P
S	AP CO TT+ IP+ VO IT AT PN DS DI	3	NY NC PL TT— IP— IL SS LO NA	S
P	AP CO TT+ IP+ VO IT AT PN DS DI	4	NY NC PL TT— IP— IL SS LO NA	P
S	AP CO TT+ IP+ VO IT AT PN DS DI	5	NY NC PL TT— IP— IL SS LO NA	S
P	AP CO TT+ IP+ VO IT AT PN DS DI	6	NY NC PL TT— IP— IL SS LO NA	P
S	AP CO TT+ IP+ VO IT AT PN DS DI	7	NY NC PL TT— IP— IL SS LO NA	S
S	AP CO TT+ IP+ VO IT AT PN DS DI	8	NY NC PL TT— IP— IL SS LO NA	S
P	AP CO TT+ IP+ VO IT AT PN DS DI	9	NY NC PL TT— IP— IL SS LO NA	P
S	AP CO TT+ IP+ VO IT AT PN DS DI	10	NY NC PL TT— IP— IL SS LO NA	S
P	AP CO TT+ IP+ VO IT AT PN DS DI	11	NY NC PL TT— IP— IL SS LO NA	P
S	AP CO TT+ IP+ VO IT AT PN DS DI	12	NY NC PL TT— IP— IL SS LO NA	S
P	AP CO TT+ IP+ VO IT AT PN DS DI	13	NY NC PL TT— IP— IL SS LO NA	P
S	AP CO TT+ IP+ VO IT AT PN DS DI	14	NY NC PL TT— IP— IL SS LO NA	S
P	AP CO TT+ IP+ VO IT AT PN DS DI	15	NY NC PL TT— IP— IL SS LO NA	P
S	AP CO TT+ IP+ VO IT AT PN DS DI	16	NY NC PL TT— IP— IL SS LO NA	S
P	AP CO TT+ IP+ VO IT AT PN DS DI	17	NY NC PL TT— IP— IL SS LO NA	P
S	AP CO TT+ IP+ VO IT AT PN DS DI	18	NY NC PL TT— IP— IL SS LO NA	S
P	AP CO TT+ IP+ VO IT AT PN DS DI	19	NY NC PL TT— IP— IL SS LO NA	P
P	AP CO TT+ IP+ VO IT AT PN DS DI	20	NY NC PL TT— IP— IL SS LO NA	P
S	AP CO TT+ IP+ VO IT AT PN DS DI	21	NY NC PL TT— IP— IL SS LO NA	S

Appendix II

Table A

Proportion of "Noisy" Behaviors During Baseline, Intervention, and Follow-up

			\multicolumn{3}{c}{Follow-up Months}	
Subjects	Baseline	Intervention	1-3	4-6	7-24	Mean

Problem child

Ron	.071	.016		.000		.000
Harold	.120	.016	.000	.000	.000	.000
Kim	.013	.004		.004	.004	.005
Carl	.001	.004	.000	.000		.000
Zeke	.013	.012	.008			.008
Will	.040	.005		.000		.000
Mark	.021	.009	.007			.007
Sam	.006	.009	.000		.008	.005
Steve	.004	.010		.010		.010
Jack	.012	.000	.004	.000		.002
Cory	.010	.000	.017	.003		.010
Mean	.028	.008	.005	.002		.004

Normal peers

Ron	.007	.002		.000		.000
Harold	.000	.000	.000	.000	.019	.003
Kim	.000	.000		.009	.004	.005
Carl	.000	.003	.000	.002		.002
Zeke	.005	.000	.000			.000
Will	.007	.002		.000		.000
Mark	.020	.000	.010			.010
Sam	.004	.008	.000		.026	.016
Steve	.005	.000		.003		.003
Jack	.001	.004	.000	.000		.000
Cory	.006	.002	.000	.010		.005
Mean	.005	.002	.001	.003		.004

Table B

Proportion of "Physical Negative" Behaviors During Baseline, Intervention, and Follow-up

			Follow-up Months			
Subjects	Baseline	Intervention	1-3	4-6	7-24	Mean
Problem child						
Ron	.030	.004		.000		.000
Harold	.016	.003	.000	.000	.000	.000
Kim	.002	.000		.000	.001	.001
Carl	.000	.000	.000	.000		.000
Zeke	.003	.009	.005			.005
Will	.011	.002		.000		.000
Mark	.010	.007	.044			.044
Sam	.002	.015	.000		.000	.000
Steve	.026	.009		.000		.000
Jack	.006	.002	.000	.000		.000
Cory	.002	.000	.003	.003	—	.003
Mean	.010	.005	.007	.000		.005
Normal peers						
Ron	.009	.000		.000		.000
Harold	.000	.000	.000	.000	.009	.002
Kim	.000	.000		.000	.004	.003
Carl	.000	.000	.000	.000		.000
Zeke	.000	.000	.000			.000
Will	.000	.000		.000		.000
Mark	.003	.000	.000			.000
Sam	.000	.009	.000		.005	.003
Steve	.005	.000		.000		.000
Jack	.003	.002	.000	.000		.000
Cory	.002	.000	.002	.002	—	.002
Mean	.002	.001	.000	.000		.001

Table C

Proportion of "Non-Attend" Behaviors During Baseline, Intervention, and Follow-up

				Follow-up Months		
Subjects	Baseline	Intervention	1-3	4-6	7-24	Mean
		Problem child				
Ron	.067	.062		.000		.000
Harold	.269	.114	.159	.097	.128	.125
Kim	.068	.066		.351	.114	.167
Carl	.089	.044	.053	.031		.034
Zeke	.208	.106	.245			.245
Will	.112	.083		.028		.028
Mark	.135	.174	.260			.260
Sam	.337	.161	.062		.129	.104
Steve	.057	.026		.033		.033
Jack	.173	.100	.141	.239		.187
Cory	.243	.078	.138	.119		.129
Mean	.160	.092	.151	.112	.124	.119
		Normal peers				
Ron	.111	.091		.000		.000
Harold	.031	.200	.101	.220	.198	.169
Kim	.065	.062		.118	.194	.177
Carl	.032	.083	.021	.135		.123
Zeke	.140	.099	.099			.099
Will	.030	.036		.000		.000
Mark	.120	.084	.126			.126
Sam	.145	.147	.108		.026	.058
Steve	.122	.050		.080		.080
Jack	.160	.078	.185	.151		.170
Cory	.144	.148	.060	.089		.074
Mean	.100	.098	.100	.099	.139	.098

Table D

Proportion of "Self-Stimulation" Behaviors During Baseline, Intervention, and Follow-up

Subjects	Baseline	Intervention	1-3	Follow-up Months 4-6	7-24	Mean
Problem child						
Ron	.038	.051		.036		.036
Harold	.018	.054	.019	.007	.012	.012
Kim	.089	.022		.046	.037	.039
Carl	.034	.006	.008	.002		.003
Zeke	.080	.025	.027			.027
Will	.058	.031		.077		.077
Mark	.005	.027	.016			.016
Sam	.040	.016	.004		.008	.007
Steve	.043	.021		.062		.061
Jack	.008	.018	.015	.017		.016
Cory	.012	.004	.011	.013		.012
Mean	.039	.025	.014	.033		.028
Normal peers						
Ron	.015	.037		.050		.050
Harold	.044	.076	.052	.010	.047	.036
Kim	.018	.005		.045	.040	.041
Carl	.014	.003	.000	.000		.000
Zeke	.095	.009	.012			.012
Will	.015	.006		.041		.041
Mark	.009	.008	.005			.005
Sam	.038	.019	.000		.016	.010
Steve	.044	.017		.040		.040
Jack	.012	.057	.004	.000		.002
Cory	.021	.003	.019	.002		.010
Mean	.030	.022	.013	.024	.034	.022

Table E

Proportion of "Attending" Behaviors During Baseline, Intervention, and Follow-up

Subjects	Baseline	Intervention	1-3	Follow-up Months 4-6	7-24	Mean
			Problem child			
Ron	.412	.615		.735		.735
Harold	.401	.563	.659	.742	.768	.717
Kim	.321	.548		.500	.616	.590
Carl	.700	.695	.763	.600		.626
Zeke	.391	.603	.488			.488
Will	.408	.549		.653		.653
Mark	.546	.591	.600			.600
Sam	.385	.499	.724		.725	.725
Steve	.463	.569		.484		.484
Jack	.257	.666	.663	.630		.648
Cory	.551	.790	.571	.640	—	.606
Mean	.440	.608	.638	.623		.625
			Normal peers			
Ron	.570	.610		.708		.708
Harold	.814	.454	.762	.706	.623	.714
Kim	.769	.798		.668	.617	.633
Carl	.796	.759	.833	.759		.767
Zeke	.571	.681	.838			.838
Will	.730	.699		.780		.780
Mark	.585	.755	.763			.763
Sam	.561	.601	.717		.584	.636
Steve	.510	.687		.671		.671
Jack	.418	.603	.600	.580		.590
Cory	.579	.700	.735	.744	—	.739
Mean	.628	.668	.750	.702		.713

Table F

Proportion of "Volunteering" Behaviors During Baseline, Intervention, and Follow-up

			Follow-up Months			
Subjects	Baseline	Intervention	1-3	4-6	7-24	Mean

Problem child

Ron	.000	.000		.000		.000
Harold	.009	.000	.000	.005	.000	.002
Kim	.043	.021		.000	.017	.013
Carl	.005	.018	.000	.002		.002
Zeke	.005	.000	.005			.005
Will	.007	.011		.000		.000
Mark	.000	.006	.000			.000
Sam	.032	.005	.000		.000	.000
Steve	.010	.034		.010		.010
Jack	.000	.000	.000	.000		.000
Cory	.016	.008	.013	.000	—	.006
Mean	.012	.009	.003	.002		.003

Normal peers

Ron	.000	.000		.000		.000
Harold	.000	.000	.012	.003	.028	.011
Kim	.013	.023		.014	.008	.010
Carl	.005	.024	.083	.002		.011
Zeke	.022	.000	.028			.028
Will	.008	.008		.000		.000
Mark	.003	.010	.000			.000
Sam	.076	.009	.000		.016	.010
Steve	.000	.008		.010		.010
Jack	.000	.000	.000	.000		.000
Cory	.005	.006	.008	.003	—	.006
Mean	.012	.008	.019	.004		.008

Table G

Proportion of "Initiation to Teacher" Behaviors During Baseline, Intervention, and Follow-up

				Follow-up Months		
Subjects	Baseline	Intervention	1-3	4-6	7-24	Mean

Problem child

Ron	.046	.043		.134		.134
Harold	.007	.063	.076	.090	.024	.072
Kim	.078	.029		.076	.118	.109
Carl	.060	.020	.046	.190		.173
Zeke	.046	.045	.102			.102
Will	.055	.112		.043		.043
Mark	.082	.082	.019			.019
Sam	.026	.037	.058		.033	.042
Steve	.096	.053		.117		.117
Jack	.070	.000	.041	.004		.024
Cory	.027	.034	.010	.005	—	.007
Mean	.054	.047	.050	.082		.077

Normal peers

Ron	.022	.005		.025		.025
Harold	.009	.000	.016	.010	.000	.011
Kim	.034	.005		.014	.013	.013
Carl	.046	.003	.000	.052		.046
Zeke	.046	.000	.004			.004
Will	.080	.087		.024		.024
Mark	.082	.032	.000			.000
Sam	.017	.042	.008		.026	.019
Steve	.054	.049		.070		.070
Jack	.069	.045	.048	.000		.026
Cory	.026	.012	.010	.005	—	.007
Mean	.044	.026	.012	.025		.022